ALLON GAL

DAVID BEN-GURION AND THE AMERICAN ALIGNMENT FOR A JEWISH STATE

The Modern Jewish Experience

Paula Hyman and Deborah Dash Moore, editors

Translated from the Hebrew: David S. Segal

ALLON GAL

DAVID BEN-GURION

AND THE AMERICAN ALIGNMENT
FOR A JEWISH STATE

WITHDRAWN

INDIANA UNIVERSITY PRESS, BLOOMINGTON AND INDIANAPOLIS
THE MAGNES PRESS, THE HEBREW UNIVERSITY, JERUSALEM

Published in association with
The Ben-Gurion Research Center
Ben-Gurion University of the Negev

First published in Hebrew, 1985
by The Ben-Gurion University of the Negev and
The Ben-Gurion Research Center

Published in the United States and Canada by Indiana
University Press, Bloomington, Indiana 47405

Library of Congress Cataloging-in-Publication Data

Gal, Allon.
    [Dàvid Ben-Guryon — li-ḳerat medinah Yehudit. English]
    David Ben-Gurion and the American alignment for a Jewish state /
    Allon Gal.
    p.   cm.
    Translation of: David Ben-Guryon — li-ḳarat medinah Yehudit.
    Includes bibliographical references and index.
    ISBN 0-253-32534-X (cloth)
    1. Ben-Gurion, David, 1886-1973 — Relations with American Jews.
    2. Jews—United States—Politics and government. 3. Zionism—United States.
    4. Palestine—Politics and government—1929-1948.
    5. Prime ministers—Israel — Biography. 6. Zionist — Palestine — Biography.
I. Title.
DS125.3.B32G3513 1991
956.94'05'092 — 91-18446 dc20

1 2 3 4 5 95 94 93 92 91

Printed in Israel
at 'Daf Noy' Press, Jerusalem

To Leonard Kaplan and Lewis H. Weinstein
dedicated Zionists
and committed social humanists

ACKNOWLEDGMENTS

I wish to extend my gratitude to the Ben-Gurion Research Center of the Ben-Gurion University of the Negev, under whose auspices this study was undertaken. There are several advantages to conducting research in a young, small academic center situated in the desert, but there are difficulties as well. The director of the center at the time, Ilan Troen, was of great help to me. Responsibility for the work's form and content, of course, rests entirely with me.

This book is a reedited and chronologically expanded version of my *David Ben-Gurion — Preparing for a Jewish State ... 1938–1941* (in Hebrew). I am grateful to David Simḥa Segal of Ben-Gurion University, who has rendered my work into precise, yet fluent, English. I am thankful to the Lucius N. Littauer Foundation, New York, and the Rabb Center for Holocaust and Redemption Studies, Ben-Gurion University, for their support. My friend Michael J. Bohnen of Nutter, McClennen & Fish, Boston, has been of great assistance in the publication of the English version.

I extend my sincerest thanks to the various readers who examined the draft of the Hebrew book. The late Ben Halpern of Brandeis University sensitively improved the manuscript. Meir Avizohar, the present director of the center, contributed valuable comments. Hebrew University Yehuda Bauer's overall assessment did much to bring the manuscript to its present state. I am grateful to my colleague Isaiah Jellinek, and to Ya'akov Shavit of Tel Aviv University for their help in clarifying several problems.

I am indebted to Ben Halpern, of blessed memory, Zvi Ganin of Beit Berl College, and Jehuda Reinharz of Brandeis University for their valuable contribution to the development of the English version.

Sylvia Landres and the entire staff of the Zionist Archives and Library in New York were of immense help. Mamie Gamoran, Joyce Katie,

Selma Zak, and Lawrence Geller of the Hadassah Archives in New York saved me precious time through their generous service. My efforts profited greatly from the good services of staffers at the American Jewish Committee Archives in New York; the American Jewish Historical Society Archives in Waltham, Massachusetts; The Temple Archive in Cleveland; and the National Archives of the United States in Washington, D.C.

Staff members of the Israel Goldstein Archives and the Central Zionist Archives in Jerusalem — Michael Heymann, Israel Philipp, Yoram Mayorek, and Adina Eshel — were most helpful and understanding. My work at the Weizmann Archives was as pleasant as it was profitable, thanks to Neḥama Chalom and her staff. I am much obliged to Barukh Tor-Raz of the Israel Labor Party Archives at Beit Berl, who was especially forthcoming in meeting my needs. Moshe Tzemach, Sarah Erez, and the entire staff of the United Kibbutz Movement Archives at the Tabenkin Institute in Ramat Efa'al were ever effective and cordial co-workers. I render special acknowledgment to Shimon Rubinstein of the Yad Ben-Zvi Archives in Jerusalem for his resourcefulness. My thanks go as well to the employees of the Labor Archives, the Histadrut Executive Committee Archives, and the Haganah History Archives in Tel Aviv. To Neḥamah Milo, Gad Kochba, Tuvia Friling, and all the employees of the Ben-Gurion Institute Archives at the Sede Boqer Campus, who provided me with help and counsel under difficult conditions, my warm appreciation.

The late Assia Neuberg, together with Abraham Levy, Shlomo Goldberg and the other staff members of the Jewish National and University Library in Jerusalem, took into account the great distance between the Sede Boqer Campus and Jerusalem for my convenience and for the work's profit. Thanks also go to the staff members of the libraries of Ben-Gurion University on both the Be'er Sheva and the Sede Boqer campuses for their friendly aid.

My wife, Snunit, and our children Shaḥaf, Peleg, and Keren constantly reminded me, through their support and warm interest, that a historian worth his salt must be objective yet not neutral and no stranger to anything human.

Allon Gal
Sede Boqer Campus
Spring 1991

CONTENTS

INTRODUCTION

The years 1938 to 1940 were a turning point in Zionist history. At that juncture Britain, the mandatory power in Palestine, retreated from the Peel Commission's recommendation to establish a Jewish state within the country and embarked on a course that threatened to strangle the Zionist endeavor. The background of this volte-face is well known: the "Arab Rebellion," a nationalist wave in Palestine characterized by both boldness and savagery; the growing threat from the Axis powers; and a British policy of appeasement in Europe and the Middle East.[1] Following the St. James Conference — negotiations between Jewish and Arab representatives under British sponsorship, with a scarcely hidden anti-Zionist agenda — Britain issued the White Paper of May 1939, and in the following year it became clear that Britain intended to implement that document's draconian decrees.[2]

A period of horror for world Jewry paralleled this Zionist history. November 1938 witnessed the infamous *Kristallnacht*, a brutal SS attack on Germany's and Austria's synagogues and Jewish communities, heralding the destruction of European Jewry by the Nazis. Fewer than ten months later Hitler launched a war that brought ever-greater sectors

---

1   Michael J. Cohen, *Palestine: Retreat from the Mandate — The Making of British Policy, 1936–1945* (London, 1978), pp. 1–124 ff.

2   Cohen's book (see n. 1) as well as Nathaniel Katzburg, *From Partition to the White Paper: British Policy in Palestine, 1936–1940* [MeHalukah laSefer haLavan: Mediniut Britaniah beEretz Yisrael, 1940–1945] (Jerusalem, 1974); idem, *The Palestine Problem in British Policy, 1940–1945* [Mediniyut beMavokh: Mediniyut Britaniah beEretz Yisrael, 1940–1945] (Jerusalem, 1977) and Ronald W. Zweig, *Britain and Palestine during the Second World War* (London, 1986), serve as a background to this study as far as Britain's Palestine policy is concerned. See also nn. 5, 25 in chap. 3, below.

11

of world Jewry under his barbaric rule. In September 1939 Poland capitulated, and by the last weeks of 1940 all of Europe and its Jewish communities — with the exception of those in Britain and Russia — had either joined the fascist axis or fallen under its sway. During 1938–1940 the Jews of continental Europe had become a captive people. The ensuing period, beginning with Germany's invasion of Russia (June 1941), saw the start of their mass extermination.[3]

The outbreak of World War II raised the dilemma of an appropriate Zionist strategy. The United States, home of the largest Jewish community in the free world, had been neutral for about two years. This neutrality ended, practically speaking, in the spring and summer of 1941 and, officially, in December of that year.[4] Britain was fighting for its survival against Nazism and desperately required the life breath of foreign aid. This raised the possibility and the problem of mobilizing American Jewry to expose the Mandatary's policies, thereby advancing the Zionist cause.

This study focuses on the political response and consequent policies advanced by David Ben-Gurion in the face of these new circumstances. In order to achieve a full appreciation of Ben-Gurion's course, however, the research delves back as far as 1915, when he came to the United States for the first time.

In 1935 David Ben-Gurion served as chairman of the Jewish Agency Executive, a role he filled until the proclamation of the State of Israel. From 1938 to 1942 Ben-Gurion's influence on the Zionist and Jewish world was much less than that of Chaim Weizmann, president of the World Zionist Organization. Ben-Gurion's power base was the Zionist labor movement, particularly its Palestinian component, and the Jewish community of Palestine; but while he was the Yishuv's acknowledged leader, he was little known in the political corridors of the world's capitals. However, the transformations in the political and demographic map of the Jewish people in the period 1938–1940 laid the groundwork

3   Paul Hilberg, *The Destruction of the European Jews* (New York, 1973), pp. 1–242. On the refugee problem, see also Henry Feingold, *The Politics of Rescue: The Roosevelt Administration and the Holocaust, 1938–1945* (New Brunswick, N.J., 1970), chaps. 1–6.

4   William L. Langer and S. Everett Gleason, *The Undeclared War, 1940–1941* (New York, 1953), pp. 252–289, 419–463ff.

for a change of leadership in the Zionist movement. Ben-Gurion was the prominent representative of a Jewish community of growing significance, whereas Chaim Weizmann headed a world movement whose claim to be such had been cruelly undermined by Nazi hegemony over the bulk of continental Europe.

This book sets out to explain David Ben-Gurion's rise to world Zionist leadership on further grounds — the crystallization, in the years 1938–1942, of a Zionist political program designed to meet the challenge of the aforementioned historic events.

The Biltmore Conference of the entire American Zionist movement in May 1942 reflected the realignment suggested by Ben-Gurion during those dark years. This book aspires to shed light on that realignment and its varied origins as well as on the diplomatic road from Biltmore to the creation of the State of Israel in May 1948.

A subtle and shrouded conflict developed during 1938–1942 between Ben-Gurion and Weizmann. After the Biltmore Conference, from June 1942 on, this clash of heroes became conspicuous.[5] To what degree is it historically correct to explain Ben-Gurion's rise to leadership in the Zionist movement by his aggressiveness and proclivity to strong-arm tactics, as opposed to Weizmann's gentility and moderation?[6] This study examines the question while at the same time considering the singularity and potency of Ben-Gurion's political approach. Thus it carefully compares Ben-Gurion with Weizmann — at times his colleague, at times his opponent.[7]

The book examines Ben-Gurion as a statesman in a wide context. His political path differed from that of many of his colleagues in the leadership of Mapai, the Palestine Workers' Party. Special significance attaches to his divergence from a very influential and chiefly kibbutz-based group, of a peculiar leftist leaning, called Faction B, destined to head a separate party, (HaTenu'ah leAḥdut haAvodah, the Movement for Labor Unity).

---

5   Yehuda Bauer, *From Diplomacy to Resistance: A History of Jewish Palestine, 1939–1945* (Philadelphia, 1970), chap. 6; Yosef Gorni, *Partnership and Conflict: Chaim Weizmann and the Palestine Labor Movement* [Shutafut uMa'avak: Chaim Weizmann uTenuat haPoalim be'Eretz Yisrael] (Tel Aviv, 1976), chap. 4.

6   See, for example, Bauer, *From Diplomacy to Resistance* pp. 47–51, 73ff.

7   Ibid., pp. 47ff.; Gorni, *Partnership and Conflict*, esp. pp. 112–206.

Previous studies of Ze'ev (Vladimir) Jabotinsky, president of the rightist New Zionist Organization (the Revisionist Zionist movement), have simplistically associated him with groups within the movement (such as Betar and Irgun Zvai Leumi) prone to use force as the major means for attaining Jewish sovereignty. More recent studies, however, have shown that the matter is more complex. It is Jabotinsky's singular desire to secure international support for Jewish aspirations in Palestine that should be considered in this context. The book tries then to clarify the Revisionist positions while comparing them with Ben-Gurion's policy.

In a word, this study seeks to illuminate David Ben-Gurion's political outlook and overall diplomatic leadership and by these means, to examine the effectiveness of his course for a small, democratic nation seeking political independence against heavy odds.

CHAPTER ONE

AMERICAN JEWRY AS A POLITICAL FACTOR

Compared with the other leaders of his party, Mapai, and with Chaim Weizmann, president of the World Zionist Organization, David Ben-Gurion was intimately acquainted with the United States and its Jewish community, having spent three years (May 1915–May 1918) in America that were crucial to his life and political development. Prior to that sojourn he had prepared meticulously for it.

> He spent his last days in Alexandria teaching himself English. "When I reach America," he observed, "I want to be able to read a newspaper."...
> He saw a resemblance between himself and the American pioneers: he had been expelled from Palestine, they from England. "We, who seek to build a new land amid ruins and desolation, must see how the persecuted exiles from England founded a rich and mighty country singular in its resources and creative powers." He was taken with the "bustling, industrious, materialistic, and pulsing modern life of the most developed and democratic of nations."[1]

In the United States, Ben-Gurion met and married Paula Monbaz, who remained his wife until her death, when he was past eighty. It was in the United States, paradoxically, that Ben-Gurion became the leader of the Palestinian Poalei Zion, a forerunner of Mapai.

> [In the United States] a process began whereby Ben-Gurion

---

1 Shabtai Teveth, *David's Zeal: the Life of David Ben-Gurion* [Kina'at David: Ḥayyei David Ben-Gurion], vol. 1 (Jerusalem and Tel Aviv, 1976), pp. 298–299. For background, see idem, *Ben-Gurion; The Burning Ground, 1886–1948* (Boston, 1987), chap. 6.

shucked his status of second-in-command [to Yizhak Ben Zvi] to assume the role of chief. American and Palestinian societies were markedly dissimilar. Comradeship, concern, likeability and an instinct for justice — all so esteemed in Palestine and, likewise, by members of the branches [of Poalei Zion] in the United States — were not the sole or primary endowments required for high position in America. The United States put greater value on hard work, efficiency, ambition and resourcefulness — all traits that Ben-Gurion had.[2]

The growth and achievements of the American Jewish Congress, in which Ben-Gurion played an active role, taught the Palestinian leader the power of public opinion and mass organization. After the outbreak of World War I, a Zionist-initiated movement sought the convening of a democratic Jewish congress in the United States; that congress was established by and ultimately represented American Jewry at the Paris Peace Conference. After restructuring in 1920, the organization went on to become a motivating force in American Jewry.

When free of the pressures of political activity and writing, Ben-Gurion would read up on American democracy and, in particular, on methods of molding policy in "that most developed and democratic of nations." We know of his reading material in the New York Public Library — "histories of American political parties, practical guides to swaying the masses, books on management and the like."[3] Ben-Gurion's faith in American democracy and in the influence of public opinion was to become central to his political thought.

As yet, no one has studied in depth the period in which Ben-Gurion headed the Histadrut, General Federation of Jewish Labor in Palestine (1920–1935); but there are many indications that it was he who then forged the policy of close relations with the Jewish and general labor movements in the United States.

Ben-Gurion's interest in America was reflected in the frequency of his

2   Teveth, *David's Zeal,* vol. 1, p. 257. For background, see Teveth, *Ben-Gurion,* chaps. 7–9.

3   The eyewitness report is that of Leo Deutsch/Lev Grigoryevich, frequenter of the New York Public Library (Shlomo Grodzensky, "From Reflections on the Personality of D. Ben-Gurion" ["Mitokh Hirhurim ba Ishiyut shel D. Ben-Gurion"], *Davar,* August 27, 1965).

trips to that country. His second visit extended from November 1930 to January 1931; and in the period spanning his service in the Jewish Agency Executive (1933) to the outbreak of World War II, he visited the United States every other year.

Prior to the autumn of 1938, Ben-Gurion's modest activity on the American scene did not have international ramifications, but a new set of circumstances was to change all that.

On August 15, 1938, David Ben-Gurion embarked from Haifa, reaching London, and Chaim Weizmann, within a week. The two men shared grave misgivings that Britain was planning to scuttle the recommendations of the Peel Commission, and during September it became evident to both Ben-Gurion and Weizmann that Britain was indeed beating a retreat, with plans afoot to halt and suppress the Zionist enterprise in Palestine.[4] The two leaders' reactions to the Mandatary's reversal were most dissimilar and led to the emergence in 1939 of two clear blocs in the Zionist movement's leadership in confronting British policy — activists and moderates, Ben-Gurion being prominent among the former.[5] Another difference, however, manifested itself in 1938 in the two men's attitudes toward America and its Jews.

In mid-September 1938 Ben-Gurion, then in London, had several talks with Ben Cohen, a member of Franklin D. Roosevelt's inner circle and a presidential confidant often called upon for a variety of missions or for straightforward advice. At that time (following the Anglo-American Act of 1924), the United States held to an official stance of nonintervention in the affairs of Palestine.[6] Hence Cohen, replying to questions raised by Ben-Gurion, ruled out the possibility of American support for the Yishuv if the latter adopted a militant posture. These contacts with Cohen contributed to Ben-Gurion's marked caution in his letter to Moshe Sharett (Shertok), head of the Political Department of the Jewish Agency, setting out the American role in the Zionist enterprise: "If we have any strong Jewish centers, they are Palestine's and America's, even if America is an unknown quantity. It is hardly

4   Cohen, *Palestine*, pp. 38–49, 66–70.
5   Ibid., pp. 70–71; Bauer, *From Diplomacy to Resistance*, pp. 43–67.
6   Frank E. Manuel, *The Realities of American-Palestine Relations* (Westport, Conn., 1949), pp. 267–307.

likely that America would lift a finger on our behalf officially or that American Jewry at this point would man the barricades. However, if we exhaust all our options here, we must mobilize support as best we can in America. Our real strength lies in Palestine."[7]

In the face of an ongoing policy of appeasement in London and the deterioration of the Zionist position there, Ben-Gurion initiated a second meeting with Cohen, this time in Paris. Asserting that October would be a critical month, Ben-Gurion demanded that "he [Cohen], L.D.B. [Louis D. Brandeis], [Stephen] Wise and their colleagues make a concerted effort to win R's [Roosevelt's] friendly intervention. The question is not one of partition or not, but of Jewish immigration to Palestine." In his diary, Ben-Gurion noted: "B.C. [Ben Cohen] is unsure... . The situation can change from day to day; they will do all that they can."[8]

Ben-Gurion's October 3 report to the Jewish Agency Executive showed the impact of his talks with Cohen:

> Shall we wed ourselves to American support — that is, to official, non-Jewish America, that America that ventured a gesture "for the benefit" of the refugees [the Evian Conference], but paid no attention to Palestine, not even mentioning the country by name? To my mind, this America is being pushed into isolationism by British policy, is distancing itself from all Zionist "entanglements." This America did not stand up for the Czechs. Will she do so for us, will she argue with Britain for our sake? As far as I know, Roosevelt does not believe in Palestine as a haven for Jewish *aliyah*.
>
> I spoke at length on this theme with Ben Cohen, one "close to the throne," before the European drama had yet ended. He was quite skeptical about the possibility of American help. The sellout of the Czechs and the rapprochement of England and Hitler have done nothing to improve our situation; quite the reverse.[9]

The preceding notwithstanding, America continued to rivet Ben-

---

7   Ben-Gurion to Moshe Sharett, *Diary*, September 20, 1938, BGIA #25.

8   *Diary*, October 3, 1938, BGIA #26.

9   Ibid., for the United States position at the Evian Conference, see Feingold, *The Politics of Rescue*, pp. 22–44.

Gurion's attention. Besides advocating self-reliance — "We have only 'Our Father in Heaven' — the Jewish people itself" — he urged a concerted effort to influence public opinion in England, America, and Geneva.[10]

While Ben-Gurion was reporting to his colleagues in Jerusalem, Weizmann, who had weighed action in the United States as early as August, sent a letter to Rabbi Solomon Goldman, president of the Zionist Organization of America (ZOA), asking that he initiate a diplomatic effort and lay the groundwork for the possible involvement of American Zionists. Weizmann intended to dispatch Berl Locker, political adviser of the London Zionist leadership, to the United States to confer with colleagues on ways of dealing with the situation.[11] Weizmann himself chose to go to Turkey rather than to America. From the outset of the crisis with England, the world Zionist leader leaned heavily toward the Turkish option, in his view perhaps the only one open to Zionism. His calculation was that a large Jewish loan to Turkey would block German penetration of that country, thereby bolstering English influence and obligating England to support the Zionist cause. This effort, tailored to the realities of the British Empire, was carried out *sub rosa* through diplomatic channels.[12]

Sharett favored the initiative but criticized its implementation: "Weizmann still labors under the 'heroic,' Feisalian concept [secret contacts with rulers]," he informed his Mapai colleagues.[13] Other Mapai leaders then in London were highly skeptical that Turkey could serve as a political lever. Ben-Gurion viewed the scheme as "a wild goose-chase," and Berl Katznelson noted wryly in his diary, "Chaim's... face lit up. He has discovered a new involvement — Turkey. With the help of a [fifty?] million dollar loan, to wrest it from Germany." The next day Katznelson wrote: "With Ben-Gurion, Dov [Hos] and Locker. Bitter

10 *Diary*, October 3, 1938, BGIA #26.
11 Ibid. and Weizmann's letter to Solomon Goldman, October 3, 1938, in Chaim Weizmann, *The Letters and Papers of Chaim Weizmann*, ed. Aaron Klieman, vol. 18. (Jerusalem, 1979), p. 466.
12 Blanche Dugdale, *Baffy: the Diaries of Blanche Dugdale 1936–1947*, ed. N. A. Rose (London, 1973), pp. 94–118: entries for September 6 to December 12, 1938.
13 Minutes of the meeting of the Mapai Political Committee, October 26, 1938, BGIA.

thoughts on Chaim's plan."[14] Very gradually, voices rose in criticism of Weizmann's diplomacy, such as his Turkish scheme, so patently proving his confinement to the world of imperial British interests. Indeed, Weizmann had become suspect in Ben-Gurion's eyes during the 1930s for his soft position on Jewish immigration and his reluctance to stand up to the British.[15]

By early October Ben-Gurion concluded that "readying public opinion for delivering Palestine to the Mufti has openly begun." On October 6 he observed that "all the morning papers are full of the 'Iraqi suggestions' — the termination of *aliyah* and the formation of an independent [Arab] government in Palestine, with equal rights for all citizens." Against this background Ben-Gurion prepared an emergency cable to America, decrying the attempt to convert the Yishuv into an "Assyrian minority," a group exterminated by the Iraqi Arabs.[16] Dispatched to American Zionist leaders that same day, the cable was tightened and toned down by Chaim Weizmann, but the kernel of Ben-Gurion's proposal remained.[17]

Among other things, the cable asked that its recipients "immediately mobilize all our friends [to] make American voice heard through

---

14   Dugdale, *Baffy*, p. 114, entry for October 21, 1938; p. 115, entry for November 1, 1938. Dugdale cites various initiatives of Pinḥas Rutenberg and Ben-Gurion, just when Weizmann was busy with his Turkish plan, and concludes by noting, "The times are getting ahead of Chaim's present methods" (pp. 63–64, entry for November 22, 1938). See also entries for October 14 and 15, 1938, in Berl Katznelson's notebook, Berl Katznelson Collection, ILPA.

15   Gorni, *Partnership and Conflict*, pp. 103–199.

16   *Diary*, October 5 and 6, 1938, BGIA #26; and cf. n. 17, below.

17   "I suggested a statement on the part of the Executive, an SOS telegram to America. I set down the following cable: 'Seriously apprehensive radical reversal Pa[lestine] policy Crystalisation [*sic*] N[ational] H[ome] stoppage imm[igration] even establishment Arab State. Grave danger must immediately mobilise [*sic*] all our friends make American voice heard through Administration and press. Skipper [Roosevelt] should intervene Br[itish] Ambassador London take immediate action. Most urgent American Jewry issue statement Jews will not submit fate Assyrians. Any [*sic*] give up Jewish Pa[lestine].' Chaim [Weizmann] agreed and we sent this telegram to Goldman, Wise, Lipsky, Jacobs, Hayim Greenberg" (*Diary*, October 6, 1938, BGIA #26).

Administration and press."[18] At the same time Ben-Gurion cabled the Poalei Zion movement in America, urging it to go beyond diplomatic efforts: "Situation grave. Activate press, Justice [Brandeis]. [American Federation of Labor president] Green's help with White House and cable workers' movement here vital urgent, also Geverkshaften (American Histadrut fund) leaders' demand [for] opening Palestine to large immigration. Activate Abe Cahan [editor of the widely read daily *Forverts*]."[19]

Later that same day Weizmann again tried to rein in Ben-Gurion, whose diary reads: "Chaim called me this afternoon, after dining with Jimmy [Rothschild]. Jimmy is opposed to protest meetings in America. In light of governmental criticism over Czechoslovakia such meetings could prove damaging. And Chaim suggests sending a telegram to America to this effect. I told him to remember what G. L. [George Lloyd] had said about Jimmy — that he was the biggest funk the Jews had and that I would not send any telegram until we could confer."[20]

A letter Ben-Gurion sent to Palestine the next day shows how highly he regarded America's potential contribution to the Zionist struggle:

> I have every confidence that this scheme will not materialize. Sooner or later an independent Jewish state will arise. We will found it by ourselves and England will be forced to recognize it. So long as England is not controlled by a fascistic, anti-Semitic regime (a very remote possibility) and so long as America remains a free country, I cannot imagine that the English would dare, or would wish to, subject us to Arab rule. Public opinion in England and America would rebel against any attempt to deliver us to the Arabs by force of arms.[21]

18 The text as sent, Chaim Weizmann to S. Goldman, L. Lipsky, and S. Wise, October 6, 1938, in Weizmann, *Letters and Papers*, vol. 18, p. 468. Interestingly, Weizmann did not send this cable to the Hadassah leadership.

19 *Diary*, October 6, 1938, BGIA #26.

20 Ibid. Of the English branch of the Rothschild family, it was James to whom Weizmann regularly turned on Zionist matters. Dugdale's notes echo Ben-Gurion's assessment of James's pallid personality (Dugdale, *Baffy*, p. 92, entry for November 7, 1938; p. 138, entry for May 16, 1939; and pp. 183–184, entry for May 2, 1941).

21 *Diary*, October 7, 1938, BGIA #26.

Because of Ben-Gurion's opposition, Weizmann did not send a restraining message to the American Jewish community. At the prodding of Solomon Goldman, American Jewry openly and in huge numbers protested Britain's intention.[22]

For all their differences, in the autumn of 1938 Weizmann and Ben-Gurion both sought the convening of a world Jewish conference in America. Again, however, Ben-Gurion's concept was by far the bolder and more sweeping of the two. Starting in the spring of 1938, Mapai explored this issue, largely at the urging of Ben-Gurion, and in September the party passed a resolution calling for "the convening of a large Jewish conference in America (and if that prove impossible, then in London) to exert political pressure on the English government." In light of these events, it is by no means surprising that ZOA president Solomon Goldman developed a very close working relationship with the chairman of the Jewish Agency Executive, rather than with the president of the World Zionist Organization, in all that pertained to activating American Jewry. Reporting (in Hebrew) to Ben-Gurion on action taken in America, Goldman wrote:

> As soon as we got Dr. Weizmann's cable I left Chicago, came to New York and plunged into action. We have managed to unite American Jewry. Even the non-Zionists are on our side, ready and waiting. We have set up an emergency committee....
> We have succeeded in influencing Christian public opinion and the general press. Many of the major daily papers have run first-page, lead stories on us. Over seventy thousand telegrams have reached Washington already.
> You know by now of the delegation sent to the British ambassador and to Cordell Hull. We arranged the Justice's [Brandeis's] visit to the White House in such a way that he was invited by the President: he [Brandeis] spoke to him like a prophet. And B. B.

22   David H. Shpiro, "The Political Reaction of American Zionists to the White Paper during the Years 1938–1939" [HaTeguvah haMedinit shel Tzionei Artzot haBrit al haSefer haLavan baShanim 1938–1939], in Yehudah Bauer, Moshe Davis, and Israel Kolatt, eds., *Studies in the History of Zionism* [Pirkei Meḥkar beToldot haTzionut]. (Jerusalem, 1976), pp. 106–114.

[Bernard Baruch], one of the old-line assimilationists, phoned Winston Churchill. Right now, public opinion in America is on our side.

At present we are busy organizing mass meetings for the next two weeks.... Zionists and non-Zionists are going ahead full guns. This is actually the first time that the Jews of America see themselves as manning the front lines. I hope this burst of energy stays with us.[23]

In his diary and in letters to family and to Zionist leaders in Palestine and abroad, Ben-Gurion noted the impact of American Jewry's response: "For the moment two dangers have passed: (A) the halting of *aliyah*...; (B) the establishment of an Arab state.... This minor improvement can be attributed to a number of factors," he suggested, including "the American response. This time our colleagues in America answered our SOS with enthusiasm, effectiveness and success. It is difficult to overpraise their loyalty and activism and the political value of what they have accomplished."[24]

The success of the American campaign encouraged Ben-Gurion to ask Solomon Goldman to increase American pressure, maintaining that Neville Chamberlain, the key figure in the English government, understood only that kind of language: "England is now negotiating a commercial treaty [with the United States]. If we can make them feel that keeping faith with the Jews and permitting large-scale *aliyah* would facilitate negotiation and improve their relations with America — that would be a great achievement."[25]

A few days later, following a meeting with the colonial secretary, Ben-Gurion sent another letter to Goldman, raising the specter of a British scheme to truncate Jewish territory and drastically delimit the number of Jewish immigrants: "I am afraid that the real crisis might come in February or March [1939]. ... Despite these heavy fears, I remain deeply convinced that the Yishuv can stand firm; and if American Jewry supports us with the same courage and dedication evidenced during the present crisis — we shall never be crushed."[26]

23 S. Goldman to Ben-Gurion, October 23, 1938, BGIA #66.
24 Ben-Gurion to Jewish Agency Executive, October 20, 1938, BGIA #65.
25 Ben-Gurion to S. Goldman, October 21, 1938, BGIA #66.
26 Ben-Gurion to S. Goldman, October 27, 1938, BGIA #66.

Immediately following *Kristallnacht*, the Zionist General Council convened in London (November 11–16, 1938). Weizmann was much shaken by the terrors that had just taken place and by premonitions of the horrors that lay ahead. But for all the passion of his opening remarks, in which he thanked the political leaders of the United States for their help during the preceding autumn, his sole call to action in his closing speech was that American Jewry establish a world Jewish fund for the upbuilding of Palestine.

Taking a different tack, Ben-Gurion emphasized the political weight of the American Jewish community. He claimed that the gains to Zionism from World War I, including the Balfour Declaration, had accrued, because of the focal position held by America's Jews. Pointing to the growing weakness and persecution of world Jewry, he maintained that the Jews of America were sufficiently vibrant and strong to influence British policy once again.

On the course of Palestinian development, too, Ben-Gurion differed from Weizmann. Whereas the president of the World Zionist Organization merely called for continued upbuilding of the country, Ben-Gurion emphasized three further points: *aliyah* as the sine qua non of any serious settlement effort; the conversion of Haifa to a Jewish area and the development of its port; and the purchase of ships to establish a Hebrew navy.[27]

In November 1938 Ben-Gurion returned from London for a short stay in Palestine. In his report to the Jewish Agency Executive in early December, he tempered his enthusiasm for the Jewish awakening and Jewish influence on American public opinion with his observation on Roosevelt's non-Zionist stance; one week later, however, he described America as a suitable base for the Zionist struggle. Eventually he conceived a response both to Colonial Secretary Malcolm MacDonald's policies[28] and to the pogroms of *Kristallnacht* and growing German aggression. At the December 11 meeting of the Jewish Agency Executive he proposed an *aliyah* revolt:

---

27   Minutes of the meeting of the Zionist General Council, London, November 11–16, 1938, CZA S 5/2708.

28   Cohen, *Palestine*, pp. 71–74.

Let us convene a world Jewish conference in America and declare that we are entering upon an *aliyah* war: let us organize, by ourselves, immigration to Palestine and confront England with the need to combat *aliyah* with force.... In this effort we will ring ourselves round with the entire Jewish people, the entire Yishuv, public opinion in America, public opinion in all the countries of Europe and in England as well.... Only the pressure of an *aliyah* revolt can counterbalance Arab pressure. To this end we must convene world Jewry in America.[29]

No opposition was forthcoming to Ben-Gurion's proposal "to convene a conference in the United States, through the Zionist leadership, to save the people and the homeland"; the Jewish Agency Executive in Jerusalem decided to pass this suggestion on to the London Executive, requesting that it begin to contact Jewish federations around the world.

The Zionist General Council, meeting in London, also recommended (without making a public statement) a Jewish conference in the United States. On at least two counts, however, the London resolution differed in tone from that passed in Jerusalem. It emphasized the rescue effort rather than the enlistment of public opinion, and it focused on the transfer and settlement of Jewish refugees, sidestepping the issue of requisite independent political activity in the United States.

At that time Nahum Goldmann presented the London decision to the Zionist General Council's members in Weizmann's name. The militant Berl Katznelson was delighted at the Ben-Gurion American initiative. A staunch supporter of his colleague's American orientation, he had defended Ben-Gurion's departure at the Zionist Executive meeting of

29 Minutes of the meeting of the Jewish Agency Executive, December 11, 1938, BGIA. At the meeting Ben-Gurion had this to say of *Kristallnacht*: "The Jewish question now is no longer what it has been to date. What is being done to the Jews in Germany is not an end but a beginning... millions of Jews are confronted now with physical extinction." At the meeting of the National Council of the Yishuv on the following day he declared, "November 1938 marks a new chapter, perhaps a unique chapter, in the annals of the torments of our people. This is more than an organized extermination, more than an organized physical extermination of a Jewry 600,000 strong, accompanied with sadistic attacks; this is the signal for the extermination of the Jewish people worldwide; and may I be proven wrong." (Minutes of the meeting of the National Council of the Yishuv, December 12, 1938, BGIA.)

December 20, 1938, in Palestine, observing that "even though Ben-Gurion is not here [in this difficult hour], I am glad that he went to America, because Zionist activity is influenced thereby." Having himself spent time in London, from September to November, Katznelson explained, "I can tell you, as an eyewitness, that if New York [i.e., Solomon Goldman] had not called London, all that effort in America [the mass protest of 1938] would not have taken place."[30]

More than any other participant, Katznelson set the tone of the aforementioned Zionist Executive meeting. Two decisions were reached, the second being a clear echo of Ben-Gurion's call to the Jewish Agency Executive on the eve of his departure to America: (1) to reassess participation in the London negotiations; (2) "to convene soon in America a conference of representatives of world Jewry to defend Zionist political objectives and to fight for Zionism's right to undertake concrete steps to solve the problem of the Jewish refugees." At the meeting of the Mapai Central Committee on December 7, Katznelson, further identifying with the viewpoint of Ben-Gurion, noted: "To the degree that we are talking about our foreign policy... we must state frankly that we had only one card: Chaim Weizmann. ... Our foreign policy rested on him for many years. This is no longer possible. It will not do for this turbulent era; at such a time Chaim Weizmann, too, must shift to another track." He continued baldly, "I would have preferred to have seen him in New York or Washington rather than in negotiations during the London Conference... . I think that in these last few weeks we have neglected America again; and that is a grave matter."[31]

At the meeting of the Mapai Central Committee a few days after Katznelson's critique of Weizmann, Ben-Gurion forcefully raised the

30   Minutes of the meeting of the Zionist General Council, November 11–16, 1938, CZA S/52708, and of the Zionist Executive, December 20, 1938, CZA S 5/312. As early as September 27, 1938, Berl Katznelson set down in his diary statements that could as readily have appeared in Ben-Gurion's: "We assembled. I made a suggestion: drafting Palestinians and sending them to America and the other countries, settling the Negev, asking for a speedy advance" (see n. 14, above). On Katznelson's acquaintance with America, see Anita Shapira, *Berl: The Biography of a Socialist Zionist — Berl Katznelson, 1887–1944* (Cambridge, 1984), pp. 117–124, 270–271.

31   Minutes of the meeting of the Zionist Executive, December 20, 1938, CZA S 5/312 and of Mapai Central Committee, December 7, 1938, BGIA.

two proposals that would be the bedrock of his policy during the period that lay ahead — the *"aliyah* war" and a massive Jewish conference in America to give that war public and political backing. Two days later, after he had written to Solomon Goldman, Ben-Gurion left Palestine for the United States.

The chairman of the Jewish Agency Executive met with no significant opposition to his trip to America either from the Mapai Central Committee or from the Jewish Agency Executive, and this was primarily for two reasons: his *"aliyah* war" hinged on the success of the American conference, and the visit did not imply a break with the movement's traditional pro-British orientation. The latter point Ben-Gurion took pains to emphasize: "All this [the *aliyah* war and the American conference] I propose on the assumption that we will, in the end, move the English government toward the relationship of a close ally; I make my proposal not from an anti-British stance, but from a patently pro-British one."[32]

The preceding notwithstanding, Ben-Gurion was becoming increasingly convinced of the great potential of pro-Zionist sentiment among Americans, Jewish and non-Jewish alike. Indeed, his essential rationale for participating in the futile tripartite St. James Conference was not to cede American public opinion. In a letter to the members of the Jewish Agency Executive, sent before his departure from Palestine, he wrote: "All American Zionists insist upon [the Zionist movement's] taking part; and, needless to say, so do the non-Zionists. We would put ourselves in a most difficult situation internally if at this point we should rule out our participation." He warned: "Not only will we create great difficulties for ourselves with American Zionists and American Jews: non-Jewish public opinion... will not understand us and we might, Heaven forbid, undercut the American support that we will yet require."[33]

In a letter sent home from London before he embarked for the United States, Ben-Gurion again opposed boycotting the talks — herein diverging with Berl Katznelson — even though no good could come of them: "Everyone in America is against the boycott, including Brandeis.

32   Minutes of the meeting of the Jewish Agency Executive, December 11, 1938, BGIA.
33   Ben-Gurion to Jewish Agency Executive members in Jerusalem, December 17, 1938; minutes of the meeting of the Jewish Agency Executive, December 18, 1938, BGIA.

Liberal public opinion in America will not understand it and we will lose American sympathy."[34] More than any other leader of his party, Ben-Gurion was sensitive to the international ramifications of Zionist policy.

Even as Ben-Gurion was en route to the United States with his program for an *aliyah* war and a Jewish conference, a year-long effort of "illegal" immigration had already been under way, organized largely by the Irgun Zvai Leumi and the Revisionists. These organizations, working outside the orbit of the World Zionist Organization, professed a brand of nationalistically radical Zionism.[35] Generally speaking, however, their *aliyah* effort lacked a political character. Jabotinsky viewed illegal immigration, which he had defended as early as 1932, primarily as a vehicle to save Jews. To the degree that he viewed *aliyah* as an instrument of political pressure, his focus was Great Britain.[36] England was the only great power that he, like Weizmann, saw as the object of Zionist policy. In advocating an *aliyah* war, Ben-Gurion was differently motivated: he viewed immigration to Palestine primarily as a political lever to open the way to a massive influx of Jewish refugees, and he meant to wage the struggle in such a way as to win maximum international support.

In a sense, Ben-Gurion's trip to America involved an adroit juggling act. On the one hand, in contrast to the Revisionist course, he made his *aliyah* war contingent on the diplomatic support he could muster in the United States; on the other hand, in variance with Weizmann's stance, his purpose in the trip was to create a new political fulcrum rather than to conduct traditional quiet negotiations.

'conference'... (2) security and boats. ..."[37] The following day Ben-Gurion, aboard the *Franconia*, set down in his diary the ten "items I must attend to in America." The first two reflected his view of the immigration issue and the confrontation with England: "(1) pursuit of the 'conference' ... (2) security and boats. ..."[37] The following day Ben-Gurion met in a New York hotel with the leaders of American Zionism

34   Ben-Gurion to Eliezer Kaplan, December 21, 1938, *Diary*, BGIA #26.
35   Bauer, *From Diplomacy to Resistance*, pp. 61–63.
36   Joseph Schechtman, *The Vladimir Jabotinsky Story*, vol. 2 (New York, 1961), pp. 421–433; Yaakov Shavit, "Fire and Water: Ze'ev Jabotinsky and the Revisionist Movement," *Studies in Zionism* 4 (Autumn 1981), pp. 231–235.
37   *Diary*, January 1, 1939, BGIA #26.

and emissaries of Mapai. His quintessential position was that "to strengthen our hand at the bargaining table we must let the [British] government know that a Jewish world conference is slated to take place in America upon the conclusion of the talks — to help implement the agreement"; and in the event that no agreement was reached, "to pressure the British government as it sets out to determine policy unilaterally."[38]

38   Ibid., January 2, 1939.

CHAPTER TWO

"DON'T YIELD!": MEETING AMERICA'S ZIONISTS

Starting with Hitler's rise to power in 1933, the Zionist movement in America expanded steadily. Membership in the ZOA stood at 9,000 in 1933 and at 43,000 in 1939; Hadassah showed memberships of 24,000 and 66,000, respectively, for those two years.[1] Still, considering the size of the American Jewish community, almost 5 million strong, the movement was small indeed.

Looking to an enlarged and vital Zionist movement in America, David Ben-Gurion hoped to channel the wave of protest of the autumn of 1938. Consequently, he invested energy in strengthening his ties with the man who headed that protest — Solomon Goldman, president of the ZOA. Only one other person, it seems, was more important to Ben-Gurion — Louis D. Brandeis, still serving on the Supreme Court. Ben-Gurion lost no time in meeting the Zionist elder statesman, whose circle included Goldman, and the two men soon discovered a great identity of outlook.

He questioned me outright about the illegal *aliyah* effort and I told him what I knew. He was interested in every detail, especially the behavior of the [British] authorities. I realized that my work had been done for me already: I said that I had come to see him primarily about that. ... When I had finished, he launched into a speech. ... He spoke of the burning issue of the refugees, that there could be no solution outside of Palestine. He was aware that people were being killed in Palestine, that this year some two hundred and sixty Jews had fallen. "Regrettable. But many more are killed in wartime. In Germany alone twelve thousand Jews have been killed. One must not panic at losses: they are casualties

---

1   Samuel Halperin, *The Political World of American Zionism* (Detroit, 1961), p. 327.

of war." ... Neither the English nor the Arabs will turn the tide. Everything depends upon us. We must be resolute, that is what counts; we must not give in. Let the [British] government do what it will — we shall stand firm. This is war. We have support here. At this juncture England needs America. If we do not muddle things, if we do not give in, we shall win. What counts most is *aliyah*: we must not yield on the question of *aliyah*.

I told him that I was happy to note that this time we saw eye to eye. I am completely in agreement with his position. ... As I was leaving he warned me once again, "Don't yield!"[2]

In a letter that he sent his wife the next day, Ben-Gurion was profuse in his praise of the Justice. He was delighted to have come to so total a meeting of minds with the doyen of American Zionists.

Ben-Gurion's American campaign and his accord with Brandeis followed by nearly a decade the apparent denouement of the bitter and drawn-out dispute (1919–1930) between the Brandeis circle and the Chaim Weizmann–Louis Lipsky camp. The conciliation between the two groups in the summer of 1930 was, however, purely formal. Mutual trust between Brandeis and Weizmann, if there ever had been such, was not renewed. Ostensibly, Weizmann and Brandeis clashed over internal Zionist issues — appropriate stratagems for building Palestine, the furtherance of cultural Zionism, and the question of relations with non-Zionists.[3] The outcome of the struggle, however, had significant ramifications for Zionist foreign policy.

In the 1920s, when the Lipsky group dominated American Zionism, Weizmann paid some visits to the United States. On those occasions economic matters and internal Jewish affairs were central to his agenda. However, starting in 1930, when the Jewish-British partnership began to unravel, and during that entire decade, when the Brandeis group led

2   *Diary*, January 5, 1939, BGIA #27.
3   Melvin I. Urofsky, *American Zionism from Herzl to the Holocaust* (Garden City, N.Y., 1975), pp. 363–377, 417–424; Brandeis to Weizmann, October 10, 1940, in Louis D. Brandeis, *Letters of Louis D. Brandeis*, eds. Melvin I. Urofsky and David H. Levy, vol. 5, (Albany, N.Y., 1978), p. 646, n. 1. The preceding two books serve in this work as major sources for the history of American Zionism; and see n. 18 in chap. 7, below.

America's Zionists, Weizmann did not set foot in the United States, except for a brief visit in 1933 to participate in "Jewish Day" at the Chicago Exposition. Even during the two years of bitter Jewish disillusionment with British policy, 1938–1939, Weizmann stayed away.

Ben-Gurion's timetable was just the reverse. He did not come to America in the 1920s, whereas his political program made him a frequent visitor in the 1930s. One ought not make too much of the two leaders' reverse schedules; nonetheless, alignments ensued — Weizmann–Lipsky and Ben-Gurion–Brandeis — that affected later developments.

Ben-Gurion and Brandeis developed a warm personal and political relationship during the 1930s, marked by deep mutual respect. They had first met during Ben-Gurion's earliest stay in America, from 1915 to 1918, but they developed close contact in 1928 when Brandeis responded to a request to support the Histadrut — the General Federation of Jewish Labor in Palestine. In December 1930, during his first trip to the United States since World War I, Ben-Gurion again met with the American Zionist doyen, this time but a few months after the leadership of the ZOA had passed into the hands of Robert Szold, Louis Brandeis's spokesman on Zionist affairs. It bears emphasis that although Brandeis, who had been a Supreme Court justice since 1916, was not officially involved in the Zionist movement, he was quite active behind the scenes, his views and counsel carrying great weight.

Ben-Gurion's meetings with Brandeis in the summer of 1935 were particularly significant. Brandeis supported the pro-British foreign policy of the World Zionist Organization and went so far as to suggest that the Zionist movement emulate British statesmanship. Nevertheless, Brandeis and Ben-Gurion were at the same time considering the possibility of exerting some American pressure on London. Much of what they shared in common — the concept of Zionism as a pioneering and creative endeavor — was reflected in their commitment to the development of the Negev.

By his remarks and by the detailed memorandum he submitted, Ben-Gurion succeeded in winning Brandeis's enthusiastic and weighty support. Between this visit and the next, Brandeis had only the warmest praise for Ben-Gurion. In the summer of 1936, in response to Judah Magnes's attacks on the Palestinian Zionist leadership, Brandeis observed that "we have in Ben-Gurion and Shertok practical leaders of great ability, men of understanding, vision, and wisdom rare in government. We should give them unqualified, ardent support."[4]

Brandeis and the American Zionist leadership opposed the partition proposals of the Peel Commission, which Ben-Gurion and Weizmann accepted. In the autumn of 1937 Ben-Gurion traveled to the United States primarily, as he put it, "to keep up contact with Brandeis and his friends, [contact] shaken a bit with the partition proposal." In notes summarizing his visit, Ben-Gurion wrote: "Now I understand what underlies the opposition of the Brandeis circle to the partition plan. It is, or one source is, lack of confidence in Weizmann." Although Ben-Gurion had some success in convincing several members of the Brandeis group, he could not budge the older statesman himself from his position. Despite this, the two men parted on the best of terms.[5] During the dramatic autumn of 1938 Ben-Gurion involved the American Zionist leader in his assessments of the situation through detailed letters and reports. (Weizmann, in contrast, never turned to Brandeis.) The meeting of January 1939, then, can be seen as the high point of nearly a decade of contact.

If the lack of communication between Brandeis and Weizmann had personal and political roots, Brandeis's rejection of Jabotinsky (president of the New Zionist Organization) was a blend of an opposing philosophical outlook with repugnance regarding the Revisionist leader's tendency to view military force as central to Zionist progress and to sanction militaristic education. Jabotinsky's biographer recalls a meeting of the two men in Palestine in the summer of 1919: "The two clashed and that set the tone of their future relationship irrevocably. A deep rift divided them, one that was never breached: they remained distant from one another for the rest of their lives." During a visit to the United States in 1935 Jabotinsky was described by Brandeisian Zionists as having fascistic tendencies, and Brandeis gave his assent to that characterization.[6]

---

4   Brandeis, *Letters*, vol. 5, p. 571. The Ben-Gurion–Brandeis relationship sketched here is based primarily on Ben-Gurion's diary and the minutes of meetings (BGIA). See, as well, n. 3, above. An emissary returning from the United States at that time spoke of Brandeis as "an ardent admirer" of Ben-Gurion (*Diary*, June 24, 1936, BGIA #23).

5   *Diary*, September 4, 14, 1937, BGIA #24.

6   Schechtman, *Jabotinsky*, vol. 1, pp. 320–321. Brandeis to S. Wise, March 19, 1935, in Brandeis, *Letters*, vol. 5, p. 551.

It bears repeating at this point that Solomon Goldman, president of the ZOA since 1938, belonged to the Brandeis circle. As noted, Ben-Gurion and Goldman had excellent personal and political relations during the tense fall of 1938. This was one more factor that brought Ben-Gurion closer to the Brandeis camp.

The ZOA was not as deeply and extensively divided as it had been in the early 1920s. New issues, new groups, and new configurations had arisen. Still, the Brandeis group and the Lipsky circle (with Weizmann adherents) remained major centers of power within the movement.

During his American stay, Ben-Gurion cultivated his connections with an eye to the line-up of forces within the ZOA, especially those of Justice Brandeis and his followers. Ben-Gurion's most intensive contacts were clearly with the Brandeisians; it appears that he never met privately with Louis Lipsky, then an elected member of the American Zionist leadership and a resident of New York, Ben-Gurion's base of operations in the United States. One can also assume that he did not meet privately with Stephen Wise, even though the latter was the most prominent American Zionist of the era. Lipsky, leader of the anti-Brandeis camp, was a committed follower of Weizmann then and later. At the time of the schism, Wise had been in the Brandeis circle, but within a few years he moved over to the Lipsky-Weizmann camp. Although Brandeis and such colleagues as Felix Frankfurter and Ben Cohen influenced Roosevelt's government, the top echelons of the Democratic party and Roosevelt himself viewed Wise, too, as a leader. Nevertheless, it appears that Ben-Gurion turned away from Wise. Ben-Gurion, then, kept his distance from the Lipsky-Weizmann group (and disregarded completely the minuscule Revisionist circles), continuing his contacts with Brandeis and, through him, with Ben Cohen.

Because Ben Cohen was not much involved in Jewish life, there was no reason to discuss conference issues with him. As in his earlier talks with Cohen in London and Paris, Ben-Gurion focused on diplomatic strategy. Ben-Gurion's diary relates:

> When I told him [Cohen] of L.D.B.'s [Louis D. Brandeis's] optimism, he observed that the old man exaggerated America's willingness to help us. Good will was present — but great caution as well. I asked him if he would come to London.... I told him, "In

the final analysis, we have few things to work with, and America's position is an important consideration. Just as we must take care not to exaggerate this factor, so we must not undervalue it." Wise has all the good intentions in the world, but when it comes to politics he is infantile. We cannot depend upon the opinions of the non-Zionists. They suffer from an inferiority complex. ... Precisely because he [Ben Cohen] is much more cautious than L.D.B. he must be with us during these momentous negotiations, especially now that F.F. [Felix Frankfurter] will not be coming.[7]

Ben-Gurion took the time to visit the home of the ailing Julian Mack, a close ally of Brandeis in all Zionist affairs who had retired from Zionist activity because of poor health. "He, too, is confident that the President will help," Ben-Gurion noted in his diary, "though he, like Cohen, feels that L.D.B. is likely to exaggerate the parameters of such support. ... He is very much in favor of Ben Cohen's participation in the London talks. He is so very sorry — genuinely, I am sure — that he [Mack] cannot take an active role at my side at this difficult hour. A good Zionist!"[8]

On policy issues and questions of security for Palestinian Jewry, Ben-Gurion would confer at length with Robert Szold, Brandeis's right-hand man in all Zionist affairs. Although Szold was unwilling to involve European Jewry in the proposed conference, he sought as large a gathering as possible, the better to pressure Britain; and he held that the conference's impact would be all the greater were it to include non-Jews. On the other hand, as Ben-Gurion discovered, Szold was ready to depend on England more than had been expected: "I agree with him," Ben-Gurion wrote, "that our destiny is linked with England — but it is quite likely that, under present circumstances, we can win British aid and support only by mounting a fierce campaign against her; not like the Arabs, but in a way that suits Zionism, quintessentially — an *aliyah*

7   *Diary*, January 5, 1939, BGIA #27. That very day Roosevelt had submitted Felix Frankfurter's name for the post of Supreme Court justice, and ratification followed by the end of January. Under the circumstances, Frankfurter could not serve as a Zionist representative at the London talks, nor could he meet with Ben-Gurion that month. Nonetheless, Ben-Gurion assiduously cultivated his links with Frankfurter. (See Ben-Gurion to Frankfurter, January 5, 1939, and Frankfurter to Ben-Gurion, January 10, 1939, BGIA #27).

8   *Diary*, January 17, 1939, BGIA #27.

war." Eventually, through his exchanges with Szold, Ben-Gurion convinced the latter to see things his way — possibly because the distance between the two was slight at the outset, Szold holding the same view as "the chief" (Louis Brandeis). Both men agreed on the vast potential of American Jewry, a potential that could well be realized after the envisaged shift in American foreign policy. This talk most probably laid the foundation for the teamwork that was to characterize the two men's efforts months later at the St. James Conference.[9]

At the convention of the United Palestine Appeal in Washington, Ben-Gurion met with Abba Hillel Silver and spoke with him at length. Silver, who had at first sided with the Brandeis camp during the schism of 1921, began to cooperate with the Lipsky leadership and even drew close to Weizmann in the 1930s. Throughout, Silver was buttressing his independent position, using as his base his Cleveland congregation as well as the United Palestine Appeal, which he had headed since 1938. In his meeting with Ben-Gurion, Silver spoke enthusiastically of the prospects of American Zionism: "We are growing stronger. Large organizations like B'nai B'rith and others are drawing closer to us. The public is becoming more and more aware of Palestine; only the rich listen to the Joint [Distribution Committee, the non-Zionist philanthropic organization]."[10]

Ben-Gurion had not been scheduled to speak at the conference of the United Palestine Appeal; however, as a result of his talk with Silver, and to the great surprise of the delegates, he was given the honor of delivering the closing address. Although he raised no new points in his speech, the very act of taking the rostrum was of consequence. Stephen Wise refrained from attending the conference "supposedly because of toothache," Ben-Gurion wrote in his diary. Ben-Gurion's participation in Silver's "show" seemed to have irritated Wise. In speaking, Ben-Gurion gave himself a small exercise in acclimatization to the political realities of America. "I was told that many in the audience did not understand Yiddish," he recorded in his diary, "so I decided to speak in

9 R. Szold to S. Goldman January 7, 1939, ZAL, Szold Collection III/4; *Diary*, January 12, 1939, BGIA #27; R. Szold, interviewed by Yigal Donyets, New York, February 1 and 23, 1977, BGIA, Oral Documentation Section.

10 Brandeis to Frankfurter, October 21, 1920, in Brandeis, *Letters*, vol. 4, pp. 489–490; *Diary*, January 15, 20, 1939, BGIA #27.

English for the first time at a public meeting." In a letter to his wife he wrote: "The convention was good... I told the people what I wanted to say and they paid close attention, even though they were tired. I saw and realized that you can talk seriously even to an American audience."[11]

Other than Brandeis — who had withdrawn from active Zionist work — Ben-Gurion found no one in the ranks of the American Zionist leadership who could measure up to the needs of the hour. However, he did form a strong bond with Solomon Goldman. Although the Jewish Agency Executive chairman felt that Goldman lacked a statesman's vision and political initiative, he considered him to be of high moral and intellectual caliber and valued his immersion in Jewish and Hebrew culture. (The two corresponded in Hebrew.) During his visit to the United States in 1939, and thereafter as well, Ben-Gurion channeled his efforts at guiding American Zionists through Goldman — not only because of the latter's position as president of the ZOA but also, as we shall again see in the ensuing chapters for other reasons; and Ben-Gurion, rather than Weizmann, remained Goldman's conduit to the world Zionist movement.

As noted earlier, the wave of protest in the autumn of 1938 engulfed not only Zionists but influential non-Zionist circles as well. In his visit to the United States, Ben-Gurion tried to involve the latter in the proposed gathering. A letter sent by Maurice B. Hexter, non-Zionist representative to the Jewish Agency Executive from 1929 to 1938, to Cyrus Adler, one of the leaders of the non-Zionist and very influential American Jewish Committee, reflected the initial steps in these negotiations:

> I don't know whether you know, but Ben-Gurion arrived yesterday (January 2, 1939) in the States, and he spent last evening

---

11 *New Palestine* 29, no. 3 (January 20, 1939): 8, 5; *Diary*, January 15, 1939, BGIA #27; S. Wise to S. Goldman, January 17, 1939, CZA A 243/125; *Diary*, January 15, 1939, BGIA #27. The editor of *New Palestine* described Ben-Gurion's presentation as follows: "The closing [address] at the banquet [was given] by David Ben-Gurion, who had not expected to speak at all. Mr. Ben-Gurion gave an analysis of the political situation. He spoke English with difficulty, but the picture he painted had color and sharpness, and a sort of desperation" (*New Palestine* 29, no. 3 [January 20, 1939]:8); Ben-Gurion to his wife, Paula, *Diary*, January 16, 1939, BGIA #27.

with me. ... He is in this country to arrange for a conference to take place some time in March, not alone of American Jewry but of European Jewry as well. He wants to be able, on his return to England, to tell the [British] government of this contemplated conference in order that the government realize that any decision which the British government may come to — failing an agreed decision between Jews, Arabs and the British government — will have to run the gamut of American public opinion. He is going to see Justice Brandeis, and then wants to see you.[12]

Hexter pointed up the likely dangers of such a conference. Any attempt to rouse the American public against England would most likely fail, he maintained, as had been the case during the Czechoslovakian crisis. Americans had then been sensitive to the argument that they had no right to make demands on Britain — demands that would draw it into military action while America was not prepared to take any action whatsoever. Second, such a conference could perplex the generally sympathetic American administration. If a conference was called, Hexter added, it could not take place in Washington.

Hexter's position accorded with that of the American Jewish Committee in the 1930s: while the non-Zionist committee members increasingly accepted Palestine as a refuge for persecuted Jews, they maintained the tradition of *shtadlanut* (quiet diplomacy) for the furtherance of Jewish interests.[13]

Within a few days Ben-Gurion had met Adler to explain to him that "this is an ad hoc conference designed to strengthen our hand in the negotiations with the British and the Arabs. The Arabs have mobilized their monarchs. We have no monarchs or states, but there is a people... and we must mobilize that which we have."[14]

---

12   M. Hexter to C. Adler, January 3, 1939, AJCA, M. D. Waldman files. Hexter sent copies of this letter to Warburg, Strook, Waldman, and Karpf. For this point and general background, see Menahem Kaufman, *An Ambiguous Partnership: Zionists and Non-Zionists in America, 1939–1948* (Jerusalem, 1991), chap. 1.

13   Hexter to Adler, January 3, 1939 (see preceding note); Naomi Cohen's research on this point, if perhaps somewhat apologetic, is illuminating: Naomi W. Cohen, *Not Free to Desist: The American Jewish Committee 1906–1966* (Philadelphia, 1972), pp. 154–226, esp. pp. 188–192.

14   *Diary*, January 6, 1939, BGIA #27.

Ben-Gurion, then, sought a massive conference with maximal representation — precisely what the leaders of the elitist American Jewish Committee feared. In a letter to Hexter, reporting on a two-hour conversation with Ben-Gurion, Adler wrote:

> He [Ben-Gurion] laid before me a proposition that there should be held in America, some time in March, a general conference of Jews from all over the world; and that that should be agreed to in advance, so that it be used at the conference in London which is supposed to be taking place toward the end of January as a weapon of sorts, because he said that England is now very amenable to American public opinion. I asked him who was to call this conference and he said the Jewish Agency. I asked him how the conference was to be constituted. He thought of having great organized communities like Warsaw, etc., sending delegates. He was not very specific on that point. He wanted a great conference.

Put off by the notion of a mammoth conference, Adler proposed an alternative. "We talked along that line [about the scope of the conference] and about a good many other things," he wrote Hexter, "and finally I said to him that I would oppose, or at least certainly not take part in, such a conference; but that if the Council of the Jewish Agency desired to have a meeting in America, or the Council itself and the Administrative Committee [so desired] I would be very glad to take part in it. This seemed rather a new thought to him and I am inclined to think that he assented."[15]

Ben-Gurion wanted to invite representatives from outside the Jewish Agency Executive, particularly B'nai B'rith and the Jewish Labor Committee, and he felt that Cyrus Adler had given his agreement. Later, however, it became evident that this was the very bone of contention. Despite Ben-Gurion's many efforts, the American Jewish Committee leadership, fearing a broad and more democratic conference, did not change its position. At that time isolationism and anti-Semitism were on the rise, and some committee leaders were swayed by consultants' advice that they should distance themselves from Zionism and Jewish

---

15   C. Adler to M. Hexter, January 9, 1939, AJCA, Waldman Files. See also *Diary*, January 6, 1939, BGIA #27.

nationalism "and, above all, ... avoid notoriety or over conspicuousness."[16]

Paralleling his efforts to convince Committee circles, Ben-Gurion invested much energy in wooing two bodies, both of which in the 1930s were leaning toward affirmation of the Zionist enterprise in Palestine: the Fraternal Order of the B'nai B'rith and the Jewish Labor Committee. The latter in particular commanded Ben-Gurion's attention. He was quite familiar with the organization from his stint as chairman of the Histadrut and had met its leaders during his previous trips to the United States.

Ben-Gurion's efforts, however, were unsuccessful. The dogged opposition of the influential American Jewish Committee so caught him by surprise that he could not counterattack effectively. The weakness of the Zionist movement was a further reason. Despite a growth spurt in the 1930s, the movement was not central to American Jewish life. Solomon Goldman, for all his talents, was not accepted as a leader by the American Jewish community and even lacked the unified backing of the various heads of the Zionist movement.

During the great anti-British protest of mid-October 1938 Solomon Goldman founded the National Emergency Committee for Palestine, headed first by the leaders of the ZOA, Hadassah, Mizrachi, and the Labor Zionists; later these were joined by representatives of various non-Zionist bodies. Toward the end of 1938, with the waning of the protest movement, the National Emergency Committee broke up. Ben-Gurion eagerly sought an overarching framework that would enable Zionism "to win the people," as he put it, "to take control of American Jewry." To this end he proposed two structural changes in the Zionist movement — merging all Zionist organizations and linking the United Palestine Appeal to Zionist politics and education. He held that creating a common front would engender more support for Zionism and that the second measure would invigorate the movement. However, when he laid these proposals before the American Zionist leadership on January 11, 1939, at the Astor Hotel in New York City, the response was less than enthusiastic.[17]

16   *Diary*, (as in preceding note); Cohen, *Not Free to Desist*, pp. 202–204.
17   Shpiro, "Political Reaction of American Zionists," pp. 105–106, 116; Ben-Gurion's speech and ensuing deliberation: Extract from ZOA Executive Meeting, January 11,

At that same meeting Ben-Gurion emphasized the significance of American Jewish activism during the autumn of 1938: "Three months ago we were in a very great danger... the danger of stopping immigration into Palestine was a real thing at the time.... I can tell you that American action was very helpful... the American action strengthened the hands of our friends in the British government, and we have not many friends in the British government." In line with this same strategy, Ben-Gurion proposed the international Jewish conference in the United States, citing reasons that were to serve as the bedrock of his policy from 1938 to 1942.

> Now we are to have these discussions in London; we will be faced with the whole Arab world. ... We must mobilize what we can. We have only the unorganized, stateless Jewish people. The only logical place to organize the Jewish people is here in America. This is the only country in the world on which England is very largely dependent, in case of war. The fate of England hinges upon the actions of America.
>
> Fortunately, your President takes a broader view than many Americans do... . The more America is concerned with world affairs, the better our position is. England needs America and American sympathy. This is a democratic country. The Jews here bear some weight and there is some sympathy with the Jewish people here... . The question is, will England keep good faith? We think we will be strengthened as far as we can be strengthened in this very great struggle if the British government will know that the Jewish people in America and, to a certain degree, American public opinion, is watching them.[18]

Some participants in the debate, favoring a strictly American conference, questioned the need for allocating funds for delegations of

---

1939, BGIA, Protocols Division; *Diary,* January 1, 1939, BGIA #27. At the close of 1938, in the wake of *Kristallnacht* in Germany, Jewish charities in the United States, including the United Palestine Appeal (UPA), merged to form the United Jewish Appeal (UJA). The dominant force in the UJA 1939–1948 was the non-Zionist Council of Jewish Federations and Welfare Funds (CJFWF). See Marc L. Raphael, *A History of the United Jewish Appeal 1939–1982,* (Missoula, Mont. 1982), pp. 1–11.

18 Extract from ZOA Executive Meeting, January 11, 1939 (as in preceding note).

Jews from all over the world. Ben-Gurion often took the floor to espouse his view. "We want, in the first place," he stated, "to impress American public opinion by hearing from Jews representing German Jewry, Polish Jewry, and Palestine Jewry. We should let the American public hear that... only Palestine is suitable for settlement of Jewish refugees.... . We want the American public to hear directly from these representatives of Germany and Polish Jewry, what the situation is in countries of Jewish persecution; and by impressing American public opinion we hope to impress the British government."

The Jewish Agency Executive chairman emphasized that he did not seek an American conference but a pan-Jewish conference. The British government, he explained, would have to realize that the demands of the Jewish people were being sounded in "the greatest democracy in the world." His last statement in the debate was that "America should be the seat of judgment."[19]

Solomon Goldman, who chaired the session, and Louis Lipsky were instrumental in the passing of a resolution in the spirit of Ben-Gurion's proposal, calling for "a world pan-Jewish conference in March in order to obtain a general Jewish reaction to the position of the British government vis-à-vis the London deliberations." The minutes of the meeting state that Ben-Gurion felt this "reaction should come from the Jewish people as a whole, and it should be expressed in America." The resolution, however, seems to have been imposed upon the gathering. Members of the ZOA Executive were more wholehearted in their espousal of other, and relatively limited, resolutions. They spent a great deal of time on the promotion of ZOA activities and made decisions on various organizational matters. At least one of these decisions was significant — the establishment of a political bureau in Washington — and a committee was chosen to implement the project.[20]

On January 20, one day before he left the United States, Ben-Gurion received a coded cable from Weizmann, labeled "Confidential, for

19   Ibid. Ben-Gurion set down in his diary his major emphases at the meeting, including the following central statement: "We want the locus of the *entire* Jewish people's reaction to be here, so that the English understand *the American People*, too, hear what we are saying to them" (*Diary*, January 11, 1939, BGIA #27).

20   Minutes of the meeting of the ZOA Executive held on Wednesday, January 11, 1939, at the Astor Hotel, New York City, ZAL, ZOA collection.

closest colleagues only." Weizmann, then in London, reported on the possibility of an immediate outbreak of hostilities, noting at the close: "Sensitiveness of British government to American feeling increasing with [the] probability [of] war. This indicates necessity for closest possible watch Washington [on] our part."[21]

Ben-Gurion pushed for immediate implementation of the decision to set up a political office in Washington. He showed the cable to Wise, Lipsky, and Szold (all in New York) and sent copies to Brandeis and Solomon Goldman, reporting to the latter that it had been decided to open the Washington office immediately. Within a week the office was functioning. To be known as the American Zionist Bureau, it represented the entire Zionist movement in the capital for two years.

Weizmann saw the bureau primarily as a diplomatic conduit; Goldman and Ben-Gurion, however, also viewed it as a means of mobilizing public opinion against British policy in Palestine. In his attempts to convince Wise to set up the bureau, Goldman had called for a more organized, militant stance throughout America, one that would make life uncomfortable for the British.[22] Ben-Gurion summed up his position in a letter to Goldman:

> At this critical hour, increasing our strength, influence, vigilance and activity in America is perhaps Zionism's most burning mission, aside from strengthening the Yishuv. The Mufti [Haj Amin el-Husseini] is exploiting British fear of the Arab world — and we have no external support other than America. This international situation calls for two steps here: (1) bolstering our Zionist strength in America — through unifying the movement, mounting a major shekel campaign, recruiting young people and turning out hard-hitting publicity; (2) activating our friends in the government, in Congress, in the press, the church and in the labor movement. At this point we must take political action here [in the U.S.] regularly and systematically, not haphazardly. Next to London, this is our political front line.[23]

21   Weizmann to Ben-Gurion, January 20, 1939, in Weizmann, *Letters and Papers*, vol. 19, ed. Norman A. Rose (Jerusalem, 1979), p. 8; *Diary*, January 10, 1939, BGIA #27.
22   Weizmann to S. Goldman, March 10, 1939, in Weizmann, *Letters and Papers*, vol. 19, p. 28; S. Goldman to S. Wise, January 22, 1939, CZA A243/125.
23   Ben-Gurion to S. Goldman, *Diary*, January 20, 1939, BGIA #27.

Goldman's response was immediate: "We are setting out to implement your suggestions at once." After listing several steps that had been taken, he concluded, "I assure you that we shall stand guard here in order to strengthen your position in London." In a subsequent letter to Ben-Gurion he devoted a special section to public opinion and detailed systematically the work schedule of the bureau. Half of the report dealt with broad lobbying efforts through the capital's diplomatic channels, and the other half raised suggestions for varied and ambitious public efforts.[24]

Ben-Gurion's growing interest in America's potential contribution to the Zionist cause and his pursuit of ways to realize that potential led to his having a lengthy meeting with Henry Montor, executive director of the United Palestine Appeal, a man who had had his share of successes and frustrations in Zionist public relations. In Montor's estimation, Zionism in America was weak because its leaders did not appreciate the power of the press. "What is printed in the [New York] Times," he explained, "is more important than what is said verbally to the President or to a senator. Roosevelt reads the Times. A few years ago the papers were taking no interest in Palestine. Now almost every day the Times devotes hundreds of lines to [Palestine] news, mostly from Arab sources. Palcor [the Zionist news agency] is not doing its job. It does not give out enough news."[25]

Montor was critical of the Zionist establishment in London and of Weizmann: "The London Palcor is not simply inadequate — it is dangerous. They have no ties with American journalists. An Associated Press representative wanted to see Chaim [Weizmann] — and he just brushed him off.... [The A.P.] feeds all the papers in America. It is the

---

24   S. Goldman to Ben-Gurion, January 26, 1939, BGIA #67; S. Goldman to Ben-Gurion, April 6, 1939, BGIA #68.

25   Henry Montor worked as a representative of Palcor in the United States from the start of the agency's existence in 1934 (see CZA L 19); *Diary*, January 20, 1939, BGIA #27. Ben-Gurion's Palcor initiative and his involvement with the agency reveal a great deal about his tendency to influence policy making through public opinion (see the Palcor files for 1934 and onward, CZA L 19). Yehoshua Justman, interview with author, Jerusalem, April 23, 1979; Henry Montor, interview with author, Jerusalem, July 2, 1979; *Diary*, January 20, 1939, BGIA #27. The last entry is the source for the ensuing discussion.

primary source of influence. All the papers, including the [*New York*] *Times*, take its news. A talk with him [the A.P. representative] outweighs a talk with a minister." Ben-Gurion, who had been the moving force behind the creation of the Zionist news agency, asked Montor for a list of London-based American reporters at once.

If, compared with Weizmann, Ben-Gurion looked to public support to move his programs forward, in comparison with Ze'ev Jabotinsky, Ben-Gurion brought political calculation to bear in so doing. Jabotinsky's wooing of public opinion, dramatic as it was, lacked an effective political strategy. From the close of 1938 Jabotinsky had called for the immediate transfer of one million Jews to Palestine; but this appeal was addressed to Poland, which he hoped would somehow impose the scheme on its British sympathizer. One might say that Poland was to Jabotinsky what Turkey was to Weizmann. The Polish option, however, was barren. Poland was too anti-Semitic, too removed from Middle-Eastern affairs, and too weak. Jabotinsky's call, in the end, was essentially a sheer cry of protest.[26]

Jabotinsky confined his vision to Europe. He was known for his "policy of alliances" designed to gain political leverage in Eastern Europe. This orientation was reflected also in the Revisionist leader's lack of interest in America. He had visited the United States three times before 1938. During his first visit, in the winter of 1921 to 1922, he had written: "America is a boring country.... I have seen nothing here that would justify crossing the ocean for." His second trip, in 1926, did nothing to dispel his negativism, and he similarly summed up his third trip, in 1935, as "utterly useless."[27] Even in the face of *Kristallnacht* he was unable to break free of his European orientation. It is true that he tried to interest U.S. representatives in Poland and Rumania in the emigration of one million Jews, and when he attempted to organize the

26 Schechtman, *Jabotinsky*, vol. 2, pp. 354–363; Shavit, "Fire and Water," pp. 72–75.

27 Benjamin Akzin, "Jabotinsky's Foreign Policy" [Mediniut haḤutz shel Jabotinsky] in idem, ed., *Questions in Law and Statesmanship* [Sugiot beMishpat uviMedina'ut] (Jerusalem, 1966), pp. 90–96; Joseph Schechtman, "The Statesman" [HaMedinai], *Ha'Umah* 18, nos. 3–4 (September 1980): 359–367; Schechtman, *Jabotinsky*, vol. 1, pp. 388–389; vol. 2, p. 256, quotation on p. 271.

"Sejm (Parliament) for Zion," he considered a special appeal to the United States.[28] However, these gestures, rather than reflecting a valid political line, seemed to be accidental facets of a basically European-oriented policy.

To return to Ben-Gurion and his conclusions regarding his trip to America, aboard ship he wrote: "The agenda that I sketched before arriving in New York [January 1, 1939] was carried out in part, and in part, no; and in part — slightly." In the first section, reviewing the conference, Ben-Gurion noted the difficulties raised by the non-Zionists and the lack of enthusiasm of the Zionists, asserting that "the former feared the conference, and the latter were afraid of the ones who were afraid... . The Zionists can hardly do anything that the non-Zionists oppose." In the next section, on "security and ships," dealing with his proposed *aliyah* war, Ben-Gurion also noted that the outcome was mixed: "Obstacles to expanding the security effort were completely removed, I would say. The path has been laid for more vigorous activity. An understanding has been reached on the seriousness and urgency of the effort. Concerning the ships, up to now nothing has been accomplished."

The continuation contained additional items, one of them on a Jewish army: "The groundwork has been laid for a [Jewish] legion. There is no doubt that if war breaks out we will be able to muster men, if the government does not stop us. Generally speaking, people have begun to consider planning for serious eventualities. The idea of naval and air training fell on some receptive ears, but we still have a long path to hoe."

Ben-Gurion's conclusion was cautious but positive: "I became better acquainted with the American frame of mind, general and Jewish. I came to a deeper understanding of the status and needs of the Zionist movement. On the whole the trip was worthwhile, although its brevity set limits on what I could get done."[29]

Statements such as "an understanding has been reached," "impetus was given," and "the groundwork has been laid" characterize the

28   Schechtman, *Jabotinsky*, vol. 2, pp. 352–353, 359.
29   *Diary*, January 24, 1939, BGIA #27. We do not have, as of yet, a comprehensive, detailed history of Revisionist foreign policy.

sections detailing what was accomplished during Ben-Gurion's stay. The Jewish Agency Executive chairman saw in America a challenging and promising theater of action, and he felt that the lessons he had learned, together with the rise of proper leadership, could realize "the immense potential contained in this great community" (see Appendix I).

CHAPTER THREE

CONFRONTING THE
ST. JAMES CONFERENCE
AND THE WHITE PAPER

British machinations at the St. James Conference, surfacing almost from the start, made David Ben-Gurion more keenly aware of the need for American Jewish support. Seeing how Malcolm MacDonald was cooperating with the Arab delegation in furtherance of the White Paper philosophy, he wrote in his diary: "Our affairs are winding up — in London. The center of activity will soon shift to Palestine and America." In a conversation with MacDonald on February 18, 1939, Ben-Gurion emphasized the Yishuv's ability to withstand an attack of the Arabs of Palestine and neighboring countries, because, among other reasons, "there are governments that will help us in this... . We will be able to bring tens of thousands of people from America, too, and we can manage the Arabs by ourselves," which is to say, without Britain.[1]

The St. James Conference roused American Jewry to action. Besides launching a diplomatic effort, the community was mobilized for mass protest, largely under the leadership of Solomon Goldman, as in the autumn of 1938; and, as then, the divergent approaches of Ben-Gurion and Weizmann resurfaced. True to his political instincts, Weizmann rejected any "rallying of the masses." Eschewing more democratic avenues, he turned to the White House, directly requesting U.S. intervention.[2]

1 *Diary*, February 11 and 18, 1939, BGIA #27.
2 Urofsky, *American Zionism*, pp. 413–415; Shpiro, "Political Reaction of American Zionists," pp. 121–123, 126–130; Amitzur Ilan, *America, Britain and Palestine: The Origin and Development of America's Intervention in Britain's Palestine Policy, 1938–1947* [Amerikah, Britaniah ve'Eretz Yisrael: Reshitah veHitpat'hutah shel Me'oravut Artzot haBrit baMediniyut haBritit beEretz Yisrael, 1938–1947] (Jerusalem, 1979), p. 38.

Ben-Gurion, by no means averse to diplomatic activity, advocated mass action and the molding of public opinion. His diplomatic conduit was Brandeis — and Brandeis's circle — and leaders of the Jewish and general labor movements. For mass action he turned primarily to Solomon Goldman.[3]

The American-Zionist delegation in London consisted of Stephen Wise, Louis Lipsky, and Robert Szold. Wise's stance blended his distaste for militancy in America with a fear of the consequences of strident Jewish criticism of Britain. A few members of the Zionist delegation to the talks, mostly from Britain, asked Wise to launch a sweeping campaign against Britain on his return to America. Wise refused, insisting that American public opinion must not be stirred against the one power confronting Hitler and Nazism.[4]

Weizmann played a significant role in the crystallization of Wise's position. The minutes of the meeting of the Jewish Agency Executive from March 3, 1939, one day before the departure of the American delegation, read: "Dr. Weizmann... told him not to start an anti-British agitation in America. He [Wise] agreed that such a thing could not be done."[5]

As Moshe Sharett noted in his political diary:

> [During this meeting Wise] delivered an address disappointing and disheartening to all present. He announced that he had to return to America for personal reasons... and that he had to warn us in advance that he and his friends could not be expected to wage a bitter struggle against the British government. All during these last years they have called upon their government to stand by Britain in the world struggle between democracy and Nazism; and so long as Hitler exists they cannot change their position. To fight for Britain and against her in one and the same breath they cannot do.[6]

3   See, for example, Ben-Gurion to S. Goldman, February 8, 1939, S. Goldman to Ben-Gurion, February 14, 1939, ZAL, ZOA, BG File XLVIII/5.
4   Shpiro, "Political Reaction of American Zionists," pp. 123–124.
5   Minutes of the twenty-fifth meeting of the Jewish Agency Executive, March 3, 1939, CZA Z 4/302/23.
6   Ibid.

The debate was confused by Wise's analysis. Some answered him with preachment, others addressed the issue per se, and the two elements became tangled. Several participants called for breaking off the negotiations, whereas others were prepared to dissolve the panel and turn over the rest of the negotiations to the executive. Szold delivered the "directive" that he had received from America (apparently from Brandeis): "[I]f no change occurs in the position of the government, there is no reason for the delegation to remain in London." Berl Katznelson came down heavily on Wise and finished by moving that the British be informed that if they had no other proposals the Yishuv leadership was calling off the negotiations.[7]

Katznelson, who was not in the habit of noting in his calendar the contents of discussions, this time did so, apparently because of the weight of the topic and the severity of the clash. He wrote: "The meeting of the Zionists of the panel — Wise replies we can't fight England during Hitler era"; and he noted that he had taken the floor against Wise. Later, Rabbi Judah Fishman (Maimon) recorded Ben-Gurion's position at that meeting: "Wise delivered a speech to the executive and told them, 'You cannot depend upon America. The Jews of America fear for themselves, they are concerned about themselves; nothing can be done in America.' This had an unpleasant effect; then Ben-Gurion had some bitter things to say, until he [Wise] was insulted. He [Ben-Gurion] told him, 'You are Jews who look out only for your own skins'." Rabbi Fishman added here a comment of his own: "But that is indeed the fact." Moshe Sharett described the bleak close of this harsh debate: "The meeting was muddied up for a good while: the debaters spoke before ever-emptying chairs."[8]

That evening the finishing touches were put to a historic day's events. Sharett's political journal tells that from St. James they went to the Park Lane Hotel to take leave of Wise. They discussed the monies needed for the anticipated American conference. Sharett felt ill and left the

---

7   Moshe Sharett, *Political Diary* [Yoman Medini], vol. 4. (Tel Aviv, 1974), pp. 104–105, entry for March 3, 1939.

8   Berl Katznelson, appointment book for 1938–1939, entry for March 3, 1939, ILPA, Berl Katznelson collection; minutes of the meeting of the members of the Zionist Executive and alternates living in Palestine, March 23, 1939, CZA S 5/313; Sharett, *Political Diary*, vol. 4, p. 105, entry for March 3, 1939.

gathering in the middle of a discussion on the political note of American Zionists, an issue that remained, he felt, as clouded as before. "Weizmann was doubtful that he could participate in a conference that would be seen as mobilizing American public opinion against the British government; but without Weizmann there is hardly any reason for the conference."[9]

The account of Blanche Dugdale ("Baffy"), prominent English-woman and close friend of Zionism, sheds light on the evening's denouement. Sharett was the only representative of the Yishuv at that farewell gathering; after he left it was easier for Weizmann to take charge and set his own tone. Thus, a situation was created in which only Weizmann and Wise were speaking. Dugdale, who was present, ends her account sharply: "Chaim's injunction was: 'Do not make anti-British propaganda.' And Wise agreed."[10]

"Chaim's injunction," the Weizmann line, was rooted largely in his profound philo-Anglicism. He believed that the Zionist movement could attain its goals in the international arena through its links with one power primarily — Great Britain. At the London conference itself it would appear that, as a result of this basic outlook, he was prepared to discuss curtailing immigration to Palestine. In opposition to pressure from MacDonald and Halifax, Sharett and Ben-Gurion made a successful joint effort to reassert the basic position of the Zionist delegation.[11]

Although Weizmann's instructions were clear-cut, there was another side to the Zionist statesman's policy. He did at times "play the American card," especially in private encounters. A report on the London conference reveals that in his talks with the British Weizmann

9   Sharett, *Political Diary*, vol. 4, p. 106, entry for March 3, 1939.
10 Dugdale, *Baffy*, p. 129, entry for March 8, 1939: "I was in the room when Dr. Wise came in for a few last words with Chaim before going to the U.S.A. and Chaim's injunction was...".
11 Leonard Stein, *Weizmann and England* (London, 1964), pp. 6–32; Isaiah Berlin, *Chaim Weizmann* (New York, 1974), pp. 37–55; idem, *Zionist Politics in Wartime Washington: A Fragment of Personal Reminiscence*, The Yaacov Herzog Memorial Lecture, delivered at the Hebrew University, Jerusalem, October 2, 1972, pp. 25–29; Cohen, *Palestine*, p. 70; Sharett, *Political Diary*, vol. 4, pp. 122–124, entry for March 7, 1939.

twice argued that the Americans were abandoning the negotiations. "The Americans want to leave London," he said, "and return home to call a Jewish conference, and I will go there, for there is nothing left me but to report these matters to American Jewry." Weizmann also initiated contacts with American diplomats in Europe.[12]

To accuse Wise of cowardice, as Ben-Gurion and others did, is to do him an injustice. One must grasp his stance in a wider context. Dov Joseph's report included an explanation:

> Stephen Wise... said that he and his friends in America could not declare war upon England; for years he and his American colleagues have been fighting to convince American public opinion of the need to march shoulder to shoulder with England in the war against fascism; he could not deviate from this position, even if the Zionist cause suffered. The movement toward Anglo-American cooperation in the war against fascism, a menace to the entire world, could not be threatened. Wise said that he could not give up this war [against fascism], even for Zionist interests.[13]

Stephen Wise, who had protested German anti-Semitism as far back as the 1920s, was a path breaker in the general Jewish struggle against the danger of Nazism and Hitlerism. His Zionist outlook was imbued with a special concern for Jewish communities wherever they might be. In 1936 he founded the World Jewish Congress, whose major goals were the guaranteeing of the rights and status of Jews and Jewish communities, especially where Jews were persecuted or in danger, and the promotion of Jewish culture and creativity throughout the world. Wise headed the World Jewish Congress until his death in April 1949. Undoubtedly Wise's sensibilities and a felt obligation to combat world fascism underlay his ardently pro-British commitment. It is difficult to determine precisely when the growing influence of Wise's Congress activities began to be reflected in his Zionist foreign policy. Perhaps the

---

12   Sharett, *Political Diary*, vol. 4, pp. 21, 72–76, entries for February 6 and 22, 1939; quotation: Kaplan Report, minutes of the meeting of the Mapai Political Committee, March 6, 1939, BGIA. See, for example, Weizmann's letter to William Bullit, April 24, 1939, in Weizmann, *Letters and Papers*, vol. 19, p. 41.
13   Minutes of the meeting of the Mapai Central Committee, February 22, 1939, BGIA.

events of 1938 — the annexation of Austria, the Munich accords, and especially *Kristallnacht* — marked the genesis of his view of Britain as the unquestioned bastion of international democracy.[14]

An important landmark along this ideational journey was Wise's efforts in setting up the General Jewish Council in the summer of 1938. Besides his Congress work, his activities in combating anti-Semitism embraced the non-Zionist B'nai B'rith, the American Jewish Committee, and the Jewish Labor Committee. At the close of October the World Jewish Congress met in New York, under the leadership of Stephen Wise and Nahum Goldmann, primarily to deal with anti-Semitism, Jewish refugees, and the future of democracy. In the wake of *Kristallnacht*, Wise redoubled his efforts to strengthen the embargo against German goods, a movement he had initiated years before. In the process, his identification with Britain grew ever deeper.[15]

In January 1939 Wise wrote frankly to an American Zionist friend: "I confess that I see in Hitlerism such an overwhelming imperilment of everything we are and cherish that hardly anything that could happen in Palestine short of absolute betrayal would keep me from England's side."[16] Thus Stephen Wise, a participant in the London talks in February 1939, was totally prepared to accept Weizmann's dictates on international issues, and that at once. Chaim Weizmann's directive "not to start an anti-British agitation" in the United States meshed with Wise's political logic and with his most deep-seated fears.

Furthermore, Wise's loyalty to Roosevelt led him to cleave unswervingly to the president's cloudy assurances to Zionists and to avoid complicating matters for the president through public protest. A biography on Wise has the following summary statement:

[F]rom that time [Roosevelt's hosting of Wise in the executive mansion in January 1936, with the presidential campaign] until his

14   Melvin I. Urofsky, *A Voice That Spoke for Justice: The Life and Times of Stephen S. Wise* (Albany, N.Y., 1982), pp. 260–331; [A. Leon Kubowitzki], *Unity in Dispersion: A History of the World Jewish Congress* (New York, 1948), pp. 45–73; Natan Lerner, "World Jewish Congress," *Encyclopedia Judaica*, vol. 16 (Jerusalem, 1972), p. 637. The conclusion arrived at here is based on issues of *Opinion* and *The Congress Bulletin*, 1938–1941.

15   *Congress Bulletin* 5, no. 2 (October 14, 1938): 2, 5; no. 5 (November 4, 1938): passim.

16   S. Wise to S. Goldman, January 20, 1939, CZA A 243/125.

death, Wise gave to Franklin Roosevelt the unswerving loyalty he had once reserved for Woodrow Wilson.... One of the truly strong traits of Wise's character was loyalty, and at times it blinded his judgment. Because Roosevelt had done great things, because he had opened the door for reconciliation, and... the President frequently expressed himself as sympathetic to Jewish problems, Wise ignored the less appealing facets of the Roosevelt personality [and his willingness] to be all things to all people.[17]

On returning to the States Wise delivered a lukewarm speech — compromising, in fact, from a Zionist perspective — on relations with Britain. The British ambassador informed Whitehall that Wise's remarks were unusually warm, displaying an extraordinary lack of incitement against the British government. Indeed, the phraseology of the British ambassador reads, almost word for word, like Weizmann's instructions to Wise on the eve of the latter's return home. In the aftermath of the St. James talks, Wise published several articles in his journal, *Opinion*, proposing — again in the spirit of Weizmann's diplomacy — that the quintessential Zionist response to Britain must be the continued upbuilding of the national home. In these pieces he emphasized settlement activity, to the near exclusion of the political potential of American Jewry.[18]

Although the Wise-Weizmann approach became clear to the participants in the St. James Conference, it was not an express item on the agenda; hence it is difficult to determine individual positions. Some few days after his arrival in England, Louis Lipsky cabled Solomon Goldman demanding that the protest movement in America be restrained. Lipsky's stands during the delegation's deliberations suggest that he inclined toward the position of the president of the World Zionist Organization. Following his return from the London talks, he made a statement in the American Jewish Congress bulletin — for which he

17   Urofsky, *A Voice for Justice*, p. 256.
18   Shpiro, "Political Reaction of American Zionists," p. 124; *Opinion* 9, no. 6 (April 1939): 8–10.

often wrote, along with Wise — for the most part praising the democracy and humanism of Great Britain.[19]

Sharett's diary and the conference protocols reveal that Robert Szold took a relatively strong stand against British machinations during the St. James negotiations, often siding with Ben-Gurion when votes were taken. Later Szold was to report that his positions on Zionist foreign policy crystallized during the St. James Conference. In these talks he came to a deep understanding of David Ben-Gurion, one that was to endure over the years. Upon returning to the United States, Szold sent Ben-Gurion a copy of his letter to Brandeis, stating: "There was great participation [in the March 19 meeting of the ZOA Administrative Board.] Wise, Lipsky and I reported on the London conference. The atmosphere was excellent. There wasn't a trace of defeatism; to the contrary, enthusiastic agreement was the position of the Palestinian and American delegates. The platform of 'reject and redouble efforts' was put forward in your name by [Solomon] Goldman."[20]

During the London talks Solomon Goldman urged the American Zionist delegation not to kowtow to the British. On March 6, for example, he sent a telegram expressing his concern lest the U.S. delegates be dragged into formal negotiations and water down their position. Both Jews and Christians, he asserted, were absolutely opposed to any compromises. On the following day Szold sent a cable, in Brandeis's name, opposing the lukewarm stance of the London executive. In addition, he noted with satisfaction that a strong American opposition was eager for battle.[21]

Interestingly, Brandeis himself, the revered leader of Solomon Goldman and Robert Szold, underwent a change of heart in 1939,

19   L. Lipsky to S. Goldman, February 16, 1939, CZA Z 4/17055; minutes of the meeting of the Panel Executive, February 8–March 16, 1939, CZA S 25/7643, Z 4302/23; *Congress Bulletin* 5, no. 24 (March 17, 1939): 1.

20   See, for example, Sharett, *Political Diary*, vol. 4, entries for February 6, 1939 and March 7, 1939, pp. 23 and 116–118; R. Szold, interviewed by Y. Donyets, New York, February 23, 1977, BGIA. Hadassah leader Rose Halprin put Szold at the center of Ben-Gurion loyalists in the United States (see R. Halprin, interviewed by Y. Donyets, New York, May 2, 1977, BGIA); quotation, R. Szold to Ben-Gurion, March 20, 1939, BGIA #68.

21   S. Goldman to L. Lipsky and R. Szold, March 6 and 7, 1939, BGIA #68.

bringing his stance rather close to that of Stephen Wise. His philo-Anglicism, together with his marked antifascism, led him to view Britain more and more as the defender of civilization, including the Jewish people and their particular fate. Still, it would seem, his views did not coalesce fully with Wise's: on the eve of the outbreak of World War II Brandeis was still considered throughout the Zionist world as the authority behind the militants.[22]

Ben-Gurion sent the Jewish Agency Executive a long letter summarizing the London talks, devoting considerable space to the American position. Roosevelt, he maintained, must be influenced through public opinion, even though "American public opinion was backward and weak in regard to international affairs." Regarding the president himself, he wrote that as a fast friend of England, like every progressive American, Roosevelt was very concerned about Britain's safety and situation: "He is not prepared to put pressure on a friendly state in such time of trial, as we would like him to do. But without this pressure I see no prospect whatsoever for any change in the current direction of the [British] government." Despite this objective difficulty — perhaps because of it — Ben-Gurion, then in London, composed a long letter to Solomon Goldman, one day after writing the preceding assessment. Toward the letter's close he asked to be informed "of everything that is being done in America and of the activities of the Washington [American Zionist] Bureau. The main question now," he stated, "is, what can we expect from America?"[23]

Answering his own question, Ben-Gurion suggested three arenas for action in the United States — the government, public opinion, and the Jewish community. Solomon Goldman correctly summed up this request as a tendency "to lean heavily on us [American Zionists] politically and financially," and he responded affirmatively. Answering

22   Urofsky, *A Voice for Justice*, pp. 263–269; Brandeis, *Letters*, vol. 5, pp. 603–636. Ben-Gurion corresp. with Brandeis voiced the latter's support for the Jewish Agency Executive's programs for settlement and illegal immigration (ibid., p. 68). See also *New Palestine* 29, no. 19 (May 19, 1939): 6. World Zionist Organization, *The Twenty-First Zionist Congress* [HaKongress haTzioni ha'Esrim ve'Eḥad], Geneva, August 16–25, 1939, stenographic report (Jerusalem), pp. 114–115.

23   Ben-Gurion to members of the World Zionist Executive in Jerusalem, March 22, 1939, BGIA #68; Ben-Gurion to S. Goldman, March 23, 1939, *Diary*, BGIA #28.

Ben-Gurion's letter point for point, he proposed a meeting with President Roosevelt and discussed public opinion, the Washington office, and the internal situation of the movement. In the last section he analyzed the American Jewish community. First he considered the processes of assimilation and how they were weakening the potential for American Jewish influence; then he emphasized the positive prospects.

> What, then, ought to be done? Shall we despair of American Jewry? I think we must pull our forces together and forge a mass movement, which, with a huge membership and strong discipline, will affect even the non-affiliated. However, in order to forge such a popular movement we must find a way to reach the masses. The first step is to minimize any differences we present to outsiders. The party system in American Zionism is more than folly, it is a mortal danger.... . What is needed here is one federation, or at least a united federation of men and women.... . What I have managed to accomplish with the political office in Washington ought to be done in all Zionist business... . I am sure that unified and organized we can become, in two or three years, the decisive force in American Jewry.[24]

In the face of the threatening British proposals of March 1939 the Zionist leadership came forward with alternative programs revolving about a Jewish state, or the assurance of *aliyah* and settlement. There were roughly three positions. Weizmann advocated diplomacy alone. He felt that the expanding, constructive labors of the Yishuv, and especially the settlement effort, would suffice to snap the chain of the White Paper. The majority of the Mapai leadership, on the other hand, vigorously advocated the additional effort of illegal *aliyah*. Going beyond both, a minority in Mapai — headed by Ben-Gurion, Berl Katznelson, and Eliyahu Golomb — called for pressuring Britain through the use of force, including disturbances in Palestine.[25]

---

24   Ben-Gurion to Goldman, see preceding note; S. Goldman to S. Wise, April 5, 1939, CZA A 243/125; S. Goldman to Ben-Gurion, April 6, 1939, BGIA #68.
25   Bauer, *From Diplomacy to Resistance*, pp. 43–62; Yehudah Slutsky, *The Book of Haganah History* [Sefer Toldot haHaganah], vol. 3 (Tel Aviv, 1972), pp. 19–88.

In April-May Ben-Gurion coined the phrase *tziyonut loḥemet* (militant, or fighting, Zionism) to represent a necessary and new phase in the movement's history, the realization of Zionism through Jewish sovereignty. In fact, herein Ben-Gurion continued the same approach that he had adopted toward the close of 1938 after *Kristallnacht*. The goal of "fighting Zionism" included the setting up of special squads to complicate the implementation of the White Paper (but not, as some have posited, to drive the British from Palestine). Here, it seems, Ben-Gurion meant to stir up public opinion in both Britain and America, in hopes of involving the American people in the Zionist struggle. Though the international dimension of Ben-Gurion's program was only hinted at in his guidelines, that dimension became patent in the Jewish Agency Executive chairman's remarks, actions, and directives, from the St. James Conference until the outbreak of World War II.[26]

At the meeting of the Political Committee of Mapai on April 5, Ben-Gurion reported on a cable he had received from Solomon Goldman, suggesting Roosevelt's possible intervention against the White Paper. Doubtful whether this would happen, Ben-Gurion stressed that "the value of American aid cannot be dismissed; during these weeks we must make a concerted political effort in this direction." Later in the discussion he observed: "If we can bring home to the world community, and particularly America, what England intends to do and what we are fighting for, perhaps we can manage to block the danger.... This calls for our calculating when to begin; but if they shoot at Jews trying to break through to Palestine, the world will surely be outraged."[27]

On April 9 Ben-Gurion noted in his diary the new edict empowering the British high commissioner in Palestine to determine the scope of *aliyah*. He wrote that a letter opposing the law "must be prepared to serve our battle in Parliament, the Mandate Committee, America and [world] Jewish communities." Two weeks later he wrote in a similar vein: "I doubt that England would dare carry out a policy that rests on bayonets, when in England itself that policy has met with opposition; and public opinion throughout the world, especially in America, would

26   Bauer, *From Diplomacy to Resistance*, pp. 43–44, 57–60. Ben-Gurion, "Guidelines for Action," Jerusalem, May 24, 1939, BGIA #68.

27   Minutes of the meeting of the Mapai Political Committee, April 5, 1939, BGIA.

view such a policy as a breach of faith, a betrayal of assurances and promises tendered the Jewish people.... Through active rejection we will safeguard the support of the Jewish people and win public opinion in England and America."[28]

On April 21 Ben-Gurion summoned David Hacohen of Haifa, a leader in the Histadrut and a Haganah activist, after the detention of two illegal vessels in Haifa port and the expulsion of ships from Palestine with no Jewish reaction whatsoever. Ben-Gurion instructed Hacohen to see to it that "Haifa knows no calm whenever such a new opportunity arises. Arrange a demonstration, a riot, a newsworthy protest for the foreign press.... I am particularly interested in the British and American press."[29]

In a meeting of the Jewish Agency Executive that same month Ben-Gurion clashed with David Werner Senator, who represented the non-Zionists, on the role of America. Senator read and supported Wise's remarks opposing any American Jewish diatribe against England, America's partner in the war against fascism, and emphasized that without American Jewry's political support any violent struggle against British policy would be a wasted effort. While agreeing that the political factor was a vital consideration, Ben-Gurion did not rule out the use of force: "We are in constant contact with our colleagues in America," he said, reminding his listeners that he had suggested a conference in the United States — one that, to his regret, did not take place. Ben-Gurion went on though to propose the vehicle of militancy, through which "we will win America's friendship, in addition to England's." He expressed his regret that Weizmann did not go directly to America from England, inasmuch as "one man there can save us — President Roosevelt."[30]

At the meeting of the Zionist General Council in Jerusalem at the close of April 1939 Ben-Gurion delivered his thoughts on the constraints of British policy, which left room for Zionist maneuvering and pressure: "The British empire is not based solely upon suppression and force of arms. England depends upon America, depends upon her [own] reputation, deserved or undeserved, and she invests a great deal of

28   *Diary*, April 9 and 20, 1939, BGIA #28.
29   Ibid., April 21, 1939.
30   Minutes of the meeting of the Jewish Agency Executive, April 16, 1939, BGIA.

energy in maintaining it.... We have support in America. ... If the Yishuv fights, with the Jewish people behind it, we will find sympathy in America. Our struggle will gain us friends. The same holds true for England."[31]

The date of the White Paper's issuance was not known in advance, and American Zionists had taken vigorous mass action shortly before that; hence, public action in the weeks preceding May 17 was weaker than what had been hoped for in Jerusalem. Ben-Gurion's disappointment was tempered by understanding. Still, he maintained that besides Palestine, "there was no value to any public meeting except in the United States." On May 7, representing the Jewish Agency Executive, he took leave of a colleague from that body who was returning to the States, of Hadassah leader and ex-president (1930–1932 and 1935–1937), Rose Jacobs. Praising American Zionists for their intensive efforts in the preceding autumn — "If the White Paper comes out now, it cannot be said that it is because of our colleagues' inaction" — the Jewish Agency Executive chairman emphasized that the Yishuv could not succeed without the strong backing of world Jewry. Ben-Gurion detailed the areas wherein American Jews could be of help: (1) involving the American press in the fight against British policy; (2) educating the American Congress; (3) rendering economic aid; and (4) preparing Jewish America for the eventuality of war: "Tens of thousands of young Jews should register at once in order to make *aliyah* to Palestine and fight for her."[32]

Some mass action had taken place; and after the issuance of the White Paper, Solomon Goldman, at a ZOA conference, called for increased sophistication and intensification of public efforts. He also encouraged the Yishuv to continue its stubborn fight, including illegal *aliyah*. This attitude, among other factors, encouraged Ben-Gurion to suggest, as he had done in the fall of 1938 and in the London talks, a struggle relying heavily on the forces of American Zionism. In a long cable sent to Solomon Goldman and Louis Brandeis in the wake of the White Paper,

31   Minutes of the meeting of the members of the Zionist General Council being in Palestine, April 24, 1939, BGIA.

32   Remarks of Ben-Gurion at the meeting of the Zionist Executive, May 3, 1939, BGIA. Minutes of the meeting of the Jewish Agency Executive, May 2 and 7, 1939, BGIA.

he proposed an unceasing illegal *aliyah* effort and called for funding of the same, with the purpose of overturning British policy, strengthening the Yishuv, and preparing for war. Additional cables brought this agenda home forcefully.[33]

David Ben-Gurion's foreign policy during the months following the St. James Conference up to the outbreak of World War II became ever more focused through intense debate and argument in the various Mapai bodies. The Mapai Council meeting of April 1939 was especially important in this regard. After Ben-Gurion's opening remarks, Berl Katznelson observed:

> Now, when we have been left so isolated in the world, when our traditional political leaning post has broken, we must — I won't use the word "revise" — re-examine what this [American] exilic community is, what is its strength and its value, and what we give it. To my deep regret, I must say that in this matter we have not shown enough depth and breadth of vision... . We have not yet forged a new mentality for ourselves, that here we have outposts to be taken; that we have here a revolutionary task, a conquest like any other. And now I shall talk not only of ourselves, but also of the top Zionist leadership. In these bitter times... we know that London can offer no salvation... and if there is some other political address where we should exert pressure and where we can exert pressure... it is Washington... . And I ask: In these days, have the needed forces been marshalled for America, both within the Zionist camp and on the political front?[34]

Eliyahu Golomb followed Katznelson and spoke in a like vein, emphasizing the need to supplement the Yishuv's forces. Decrying many colleagues' disparagement of the democracies, he asserted that England and America "comprise the force with which and through which we can, I hope, render our effort more effective. I tell you that we cannot rely on our strength alone. ... Sometimes we concentrate [our] forces in London

---

33 *New Palestine* 29, no. 18 (May 12, 1939): 3; no. 19 (May 19, 1939): 1, 6; no. 24 (June 23, 1939): 9–13; Ben-Gurion to S. Goldman, May 24, 1939, BGIA #69.

34 Minutes of the Mapai Council, April 14–16, 1939, BGIA.

and sometimes we leave London bare [of our presence]. Sometimes a shout goes up for action in America, but we have not taken pains to set up a continuing, formal effort; and we must."[35]

A position different from Katznelson's and Golomb's was put forward by Mapai's militant, kibbutz-sprung group (destined to establish Faction B). Its members regarded American Jewry as potential settlers and defenders. Aharon Zisling called for "work... in the actual area with renewed strength." The "actual area" meant for him the inherent strengths of the Yishuv, made up of immigration, settlement, and defense. Yitzhak Tabenkin insisted that "the true political phenomenon is only that which creates facts, not that which is formal and juridical. There are political facts. Our political fact is not the Balfour Declaration or the Peel Declaration or the Woodhead Document. Our political fact is the 400,000 Jews who are here. That is a political fact. Beyond this there are no political facts." The problem confronting the Zionist movement, he asserted, was not one of orientation. Up to that time, he claimed, progress had been effected by independent acts. The call of the hour was to teach the movement that Zionist realization would continue without British sponsorship. Finally, he dismissed the political potential of American Jewry. Even as Jews could not remain in Germany or Poland, he warned, so one could not be certain "that we are assured a long-range stay in either England or America."[36]

Not a single resolution of the Mapai Council addressed American Jewry directly. The general call to the Zionist movement "throughout the exile" was couched largely in the language of Faction B: "Do not lose heart or despair! The builders will build; the defenders, defend; and the *olim* [immigrants], come. The building up and the struggle will continue under any and all circumstances. And as for you — do not content yourself with small acts. Equip and strengthen the *olim*, the builders and the defenders; then, conquer we shall!"[37]

This frame of mind — that the role of the Zionist movement "throughout the exile" was to "equip and strengthen" Palestinian Jewry

---

35   Ibid.
36   Ibid.
37   For a position paper of the Mapai Council, see *HaPoel haTza'ir* 10, no. 22 (March 21, 1939): 1, 2.

— found expression as well in a statement issued by several of the session's participants, who emphasized the economic significance of American Jewry. In the next chapter we shall see how wartime developments led ever-growing circles in Mapai to realize that the role of the world Zionist movement was more than providing Palestinian Jewry with equipment and encouragement.

Meanwhile, in the summer of 1939 Solomon Goldman visited Palestine at the urging of Ben-Gurion, who had cabled him on the eve of the issuance of the White Paper: "Promulgation White Paper seems inevitable. Yishuv have to face British bayonets. Suggest several colleagues and leaders inform [U.S.] President they leaving for Palestine join Yishuv as victims fall resisting proposed new regime." Goldman had additional motives for this trip beyond accommodating the Palestinian leader, with whom he had been in intimate contact over a full, stormy year. Having been re-elected ZOA president in June 1939, he needed a firsthand acquaintance with the realities of Palestine, as had been the case following his election in 1938. In addition, the visit would provide him with needed background for the upcoming Twenty-First Zionist Congress.[38]

Goldman met with Ben-Gurion at least twice during his stay. They first talked on July 25, a few hours after his arrival. "[Goldman is] optimistic," Ben-Gurion noted. "Roosevelt helped and is willing to help. He also had a good talk with [Joseph] Kennedy [the U.S. ambassador to Britain]." Of the second meeting, two weeks later, Ben-Gurion recorded: "Goldman thinks that not one American will support my position on ways of combatting the White Paper."[39] Ben-Gurion's urge to use force against British policies was thus tempered by the twofold message brought home by his American Zionist ally — that although the U.S. government was a tremendous source of potential support, it would not countenance violent anti-British tactics.

In contrast with the warm and intense working relationship Solomon Goldman enjoyed with Ben-Gurion, the American Zionist leader's association with Weizmann was tenuous and abrasive. In his dealings with Goldman, Weizmann acted in consonance with his own

38   Ben-Gurion to S. Goldman, May 9, 1939, BGIA #69; *New Palestine* 29, no. 25 (July 7, 1939): 1.
39   *Diary*, July 25, August 9, 1939, BGIA #28.

instructions to Stephen Wise during the St. James Conference. In the fateful months of the spring and summer of 1939 all Weizmann's requests to Goldman were confined strictly to the diplomatic sphere; any exception to this rule involved fiscal matters. Weizmann's remarks to the ZOA convention in July 1939 assigned no political role whatsoever to American Zionism.[40]

Toward the close of the summer of 1939 Weizmann, together with the diplomat St. John Abdullah Philby, an Anglo-Arab romanticist and a friend of Ibn Saud, began to weave a program for a Jewish state. In exchange for a Jewish loan to Ibn Saud, and with Britain's blessing, the desert monarch would become the leader of the Arab world and a sympathizer of the Zionist program. This diplomatic pursuit of Weizmann's, which lasted more than four years, closely resembled his Turkish initiative, discussed previously. Both were predicated on the faith that quiet negotiation with world leaders could produce a Jewish state, both relied on the weight of a Jewish loan, and both catered to British imperial interests in order to gain sovereign rights. The Turkish program, it will be recalled, followed the Woodhead Report; the Saudi plan, the issuance of the White Paper. Both plans show how Weizmann severely limited his range of action by his single-minded attachment to Great Britain.[41]

Ze'ev Jabotinsky, too, was left with precious little room in which to maneuver, and for the same reason — albeit the Revisionist leader tended, as a result of his political frustration, to look to military action, rather than to diplomatic negotiation à la Weizmann. As the events of 1939 unfolded, Jabotinsky grew ever closer to the Irgun Zvai Leumi, the military component of the Revisionist movement. In the wake of the London talks, that group had initiated a series of anti-Arab terrorist actions and, after the White Paper, moved against government targets and public property as well. In August 1939, in Switzerland, Jabotinsky allegedly handed an emissary of the Irgun Zvai Leumi an envelope containing the first stage of a planned military campaign against Britain,

40   *New Palestine* 29, no. 25 (July 7, 1939): 2.
41   Bauer, *From Diplomacy to Resistance*, pp. 224–228, 250–252.

one designed to evoke broad public reaction. The plan called for a takeover of British government offices in Jerusalem, raising the national flag, holding firm for twenty-four hours with complete disregard for casualties, and proclaiming a provisional government that would continue to function abroad.[42]

A careful historical examinition of the hazy and unrealistic "proposal for revolt" on the eve of World War II — shows that the plan was the result of militarist pressures from within the Irgun Zvai Leumi and Betar, the Revisionist youth movement. To the extent that it was a serious proposal at all, it comprised a temporary deviation from the traditional thought of Jabotinsky. Still, one cannot understand Jabotinsky's readiness to engage in so demonstrative and bloody an effort merely as a result of intensive internal Revisionist pressures. Rather, it would seem that his lack of any realistic outlet and his political strategy's weakness led the Revisionist leader to agree to the scheme. Jabotinsky's political world was hopelessly bounded by Europe, primarily Poland and England, as has been noted. Perhaps for this reason his diplomatic stance was doomed to collapse in times of great pressure. Put otherwise: for Jabotinsky, when there appeared to be no possibility of winning allies on the diplomatic front, a response of bravado — one that would supposedly yield swift results — loomed ever larger. The "proposal for revolt" of August 1939, then, sprang from a combination of militarist inclination and ineffectual foreign policy.[43]

At the outset of 1939 Ben-Gurion hoped that Roosevelt's failure to change the neutrality laws would indirectly bolster American Zionism and help convert it into a political factor, as had been the case in the autumn of 1938. Actually, the effects of Roosevelt's debacle were complex. After the liberal president's attempt was thwarted in the House and then in the Senate (July 11), conservative and isolationist forces gained great strength in America, leading to a rise in anti-Semitism — a

---

42 Schechtman, *Jabotinsky*, vol. 2, pp. 475–484.
43 Shavit, "Fire and Water," pp. 230–235. For the ineffective Revisionist foreign policy of a later period, see Menaḥem Begin, *The Revolt: Memoirs of the Commander of the Irgun Zvai Leumi in Palestine* [HaMered: Zikhronotav shel Mefaked haIrgun haTzevai haLeumi beEretz Yisrael] (Tel Aviv, 1974), chap. 3.

movement that remained potent at least until the entry of the United States into the war.[44]

The retreat of the liberal camp, together with the growing influence of anti-Semitism, made for a muted and diluted American Zionism. The U.S. delegates to the Twenty-First Zionist Congress in Geneva (August 16–25), headed by Abba Hillel Silver, were a very subdued group. Silver and Solomon Goldman gave no voice to anti-British sentiment beyond what Weizmann was prepared to say, nor did they speak of any dependence on American involvement in the world conflict. Still, in one closed session Barnett A. Brickner, an American Zionist and a distinguished Reform rabbi, had a radical message to deliver; and in his closing speech Solomon Goldman, seeking to correct the impression that the American delegates had made on the Congress, vowed to eschew a defeatist stance.[45]

That the Zionist Congress did not relate to the great potential of American Zionism, as expressed in the autumn of 1938, can be attributed to four factors: Roosevelt's setbacks in June and July 1939, the rise of anti-Semitism in the United States, the muted tones of the representatives of American Zionism, and the approaching clouds of

44   Minutes of the meeting of the Mapai Central Committee, July 5, 1939, BGIA; William L. Langer and S. Everett Gleason, *Challenge to Isolation: The World Crisis of 1937–1940 and American Foreign Policy* (New York, 1952), pp. 142–147, 185–192; Charles H. Stember et al., *Jews in the Mind of America* (New York, 1966), pp. 110–111; Donald S. Strong, *Organized Anti-Semitism in America: The Rise of Group Prejudice during the Decade 1930–1940* (Washington, D.C., 1941), pp. 21–190.

45   Remarks of Solomon Goldman, August 18, 1939, World Zionist Organization, *The Twenty-First Zionist Congress* (see especially the conclusion on pp. 114–115); remarks of Abba Hillel Silver, ibid., pp. 134–136; remarks of Weizmann, August 17, 1939, ibid., pp. 33–47. "On August 21 the congress's political committee met: their deliberations were confidential so that one could speak openly. Dr. Barnett Brickner, from the United States [Cleveland], announced that American Zionist opinion was not that heard by the Americans in the congress; rather, 'It accords in general with the lines of Ben-Gurion and Ussishkin'" (Ben-Gurion, "En Route to the Army and the State of Israel" [BaDerekh laTzavah veliMedinat Yisrael], *Davar*, October 11, 1963). It was Berl Katznelson who delivered the sharpest critique of the American Zionist position on August 20: see World Zionist Organization, *Twenty–First Congress*, pp. 147–152. Note S. Goldman's muted tone and acknowledgment of responsibility for the realization of the Zionist endeavor in his closing remarks at the twelfth session, on August 24, ibid., pp. 241–242.

war. As well, and for the same reasons, the Congress did not take into account the possibility of American intervention in the world struggle. The debates and resolutions of the Congress focused mainly on the methods and scope of the struggle against the White Paper regime. Ben-Gurion, too, held to this focus.[46]

Yet, again, it would be erroneous to assume that all American delegates simply threw up their hands and sank into inactivity. From the evening of the close of the Zionist Congress until the dawn of the next day, the members of the Histadrut Executive Committee met with representatives of Poalei Zion and, for most of their deliberations, with the American delegates. During this nonpublic session decisions were reached on organizing a voluntary military effort from the States and on encouraging illegal *aliyah*.[47]

46   See "Political Decisions," in World Zionist Organization, *Twenty-First Congress*, which contained a special section on "addressing the British People," pp. 249–251; remarks of Ben-Gurion, August 18, ibid., pp. 80–87.

47   Minutes of the meeting of the Histadrut Executive Committee in Geneva on the eve of the closing session of the Twenty-First Zionist Congress, August 25, 1939, HECA.

CHAPTER FOUR

CHARTING THE COURSE
TOWARD A JEWISH STATE

One week after the outbreak of the war and three days after America's declaration of neutrality, David Ben-Gurion presented the Haganah command with his proposals for the establishment of a Jewish state, pro-British in orientation, through Jewish force of arms. He pinned his hopes for success, though, not just on the power of the Yishuv but also on the support of American Jewry. "England knows," he asserted, "that America holds the key to victory in this war of Gog and Magog. While the Jews of America comprise only four percent of the population, their weight and influence... are many times greater... the friendship of American Jewry can be a great blessing to England in her war of survival."[1] This observation, made at the very beginning of World War II, reflected a close acquaintance with American realities and revealed as well the kernel of a new approach — a Zionist foreign policy linked not solely to England but to the Anglo-American world.

At the first meeting of the Mapai Central Committee (September 12) following the outbreak of the war, Ben-Gurion summed up the complexities of the Yishuv's relationship with Britain in a famous sentence: "We must help the [British] army as if there were no White Paper, and we must fight the White Paper as if there were no war." If at the St. James Conference his proposal for establishing a Jewish state had been one of several possibilities, that notion was now central. "We need a light shining on history's horizon," he claimed, "to show us the way through the tangled paths that await us. To my mind, this political

---

1 Ben-Gurion, "[Remarks] at a Social Gathering with Friends," Tel Aviv, September 8, 1939, BGIA #159.

compass is — *advancement toward the creation of a Hebrew state in Palestine.*"[2]

The Jewish Agency Executive chairman proposed two guidelines for the requisite revolutionary struggle: autonomy ("We ourselves will establish the state") and avoidance of headlong confrontation with England. Herein Ben-Gurion was not sounding a new Zionist note. His innovation lay in his assessment of the vast potential of American Jewry because of the circumstances of the world war. "It is doubtful whether we can even hold our ground by our own strength," he maintained. "Certainly we cannot win new positions without a great deal of outside help; and right now there is no outside other than America. ... The vast amount of help needed to set up an army, redeem the land, settle, and maintain our position can only come from North America. In constituting a Jewish army, too, America will have to play a major role.[3]

Ben-Gurion believed that despite America's neutrality, a Jewish legion could be set up in the United States. Although acknowledging that fear of anti-Semitism was paralyzing American Jewry and Zionism, he maintained that the pluralistic character of America was designed to meet the need of the hour:

> It would seem that American Zionist leaders hesitate to set up a Jewish legion because they are in the grip of fear. The day the war broke out I cabled our colleagues in America on the need for setting up the legion. You needn't strain to guess the advice I received: wouldn't that be dangerous, contribute to burgeoning anti-Semitism, fuel the accusation that Jews are lacking in loyalty to America? Not only are assimilationists in a panic — Zionists are, too. Now, the Irish are not afraid of openly helping their fellows in Ireland: they were not timid in the least about collecting money for the anti-English rebels; but as for us — a Zionist leader is afraid to aid illegal *aliyah*. And because America is neutral, our Zionist leaders fear organizing a Jewish Legion. These people do not understand that precisely by acting as Jews and only as Jews they will win respect in America, gain sympathy from the public at

---

2   Minutes of the meeting of the Mapai Central Committee, September 12, 1939, BGIA.

3   Ibid.

large. America will be able to respect the Jews' wish to fight Hitler as Jews.[4]

For American Jewry to act courageously, patriotically, and Jewishly, Ben-Gurion asserted, there is "an urgent need for a high-level delegation to be sent from Palestine to America...." The Zionist struggle and the situation of the Yishuv were complex matters, he held, and "America has not one leader who is expert in these matters. ... American Zionism will not overcome its inner weaknesses and will not extend us moral, political and financial help without Palestinian leadership, without the guidance of strong, known figures who will impose their opinions and wishes on American Jews and Zionists."[5]

Ben-Gurion concluded with a concrete proposal for such a delegation: "An aggressive and multi-talented 'emissarium' is a necessity — not for the short range, but for the entire course of the war." The crucial role Ben-Gurion assigned American Jewry is further indicated by the remarks of David Remez in that same Mapai Central Committee meeting: "For about ten days now [since the outbreak of the war] I have been hearing from Ben-Gurion about the need for an emissarium in America.... I would like to open the parentheses and decipher the meaning of this 'emissarium' in America."[6]

From September to November Ben-Gurion, both in the councils of Mapai and in the Jewish Agency Executive, actively promoted the idea of sending a high-level delegation to the United States; his chief candidate was Berl Katznelson. The Jewish Agency Executive chairman supported his proposal by asserting that "the sole source of help that we need, political and fiscal, is only in America." And he added in this vein that "we require people who can guide the American leaders. I would not seek the agreement of persons in America for this delegation at all." Of a conversation he had at the end of October with Menaḥem Ussishkin, chairman of the Jewish National Fund Executive, he reported: "[Ussishkin] asked me if I would be prepared to take the trip. I told him that at this time there could be no question of my leaving the country; but if it should be required — I would be prepared to travel. I suggested Berl

4   Ibid.
5   Ibid.
6   Ibid.

Katznelson, [Ussishkin] himself and Professor Rutenberg."[7]

In the first meeting of the Jewish National Fund Executive after the outbreak of war, an aggressive policy of land acquisition, depending largely on American Jewish support was suggested. Katznelson supported these proposals even though he, according to Ben-Gurion, "sees the future of American Judaism and Zionism as bleak in the extreme." Critical of Katznelson's stance, Ben-Gurion held that "it is a mistake to conclude that American Judaism and Zionism are a lost cause. The fault is our own.... If we raise a mighty cry here, we might meet with a response."[8]

Ben-Gurion and Katznelson, both of whom were activists *vis-à-vis* Britain and maximalists in their land policies, did not differ fundamentally on the significance of American Jewry. At the Mapai Central Committee meeting of September 21, Katznelson, although acknowledging the centrality of London on the international Zionist map, argued that "we must get someone to America — I propose [Eliyahu] Golomb — to get things moving for the Jewish Agency on the question of the Jewish brigades.... We mustn't dawdle. If we don't create the nucleus of a volunteer movement, others will fill the vacuum. Jabotisnky might have left for America already."[9]

In the end it was Eliyahu Golomb who left for the United States. As far as Katznelson was concerned, sending Golomb was tantamount to sending his personal political representative. The memoirs of Yosef Yizre'eli, sent as a Mapai emissary to America (arriving in November 1939), also show that Katznelson was particularly receptive to the notion of activating American Jewry.[10]

Nonetheless, it was David Ben-Gurion, rather than Berl Katznelson, who was clearly determined to seek strong Jewish and international support; and it was this clear vision and determination that made him much more the statesman of the two. At the meeting of the National Committee of the Yishuv during the latter half of September, Ben-

---

7   Minutes of the meeting of the Jewish Agency Executive, October 15, 1939, BGIA; *Diary*, October 24, 1939, BGIA #29.

8   *Diary*, October 18, 1939, BGIA #29.

9   Shapira, *Berl*, pp. 285–293, 334; minutes of the meeting of the Mapai Central Committee, September 21, 1939, BGIA.

10 Yosef Yizre'eli, *On a Security Mission* [BiShlihut Bit'honit] (Tel Aviv, 1972), p. 18.

Gurion delivered a policy statement (originally titled "Our Policy during the War" and later titled "Looking Ahead," in the newspaper *Davar*). He closed the address with a long section in which he called on American Jewry to mount a significant international political effort:

> At this point European Jewry is, for the most part, wounded and imprisoned. Outside of Palestine there is but one Jewish center capable of taking up the heavy burden of rescuing our people and homeland — the Jewish center in America. Europe stands on the threshhold of enervation and ruin as a result of the war. Whether America stays neutral — and she will undoubtedly retain her neutrality for some time — or whether she joins the fighting democracy in Europe, the disaster will not touch America or the Jews of America... . Bread for the hungry and shelter for the refugees in Europe, strengthening the productive and military forces needed to settle the land, and political-military mobilization, within the international constellation, in preparation for our war of independence — these are the tasks that the present hour lays upon the Jews of America.[11]

Ben-Gurion later published a similar article in the ZOA's *New Palestine*. Part of the article dealt methodically and at length with a military alliance with Britain, whereby aid would be offered not by individual Jews but by a force organized for independence, by "Judea." And the concluding section contained the above-quoted message to the Jews of America.[12]

With the outbreak of the world war, the leaders of the ZOA, carried out the directives of the Twenty-First Zionist Congress: they set up an emergency committee whose task it was to represent the World Zionist Executive and further the Zionist cause in America under the new circumstances. Weizmann, president of the World Zionist Organization, understood that this committee would be subservient to him and thus readily approved the initiative and called for the inclusion of Mizrachi, Hadassah, and Poalei Zion, besides the ZOA. The representatives of

11   Ben-Gurion, "Our Policy during the War" [Mediniyutenu biTekufat haMilḥamah], *Davar*, September 22, 1939.
12   *New Palestine* 29, no. 33 (September 27, 1939): 5.

these four organizations, together with other persons added subsequently, constituted the Emergency Committee for Zionist Affairs, a body authorized to run a united American Zionist effort for the duration of the war.

For a few months Solomon Goldman chaired the meetings of the Emergency Committee, but then he resigned. During the year before the war he had tried, generally, to rouse American Jewry to fight British policy in Palestine openly, but the war had created a new hierarchy of sorts among American Zionists wherein he was pushed aside. First, the Emergency Committee operated under the aegis of Chaim Weizmann; as a result, Louis Lipsky and Stephen Wise quickly became the dominant forces. In addition, American anti-Semitism, strengthened by the outbreak of the world war, inhibited active, political Zionism. Under these conditions, the divergent approaches within the Emergency Committee hardly surfaced. Wise and Lipsky generally had the upper hand in the minor confrontations that emerged within the committee; it was only natural that the latter should begin chairing the committee's meetings from the outset of 1940. Paralleling Lipsky's control of the Emergency Committee, the committee became by and large synonymous with Stephen Wise, president of the ZOA before Solomon Goldman's tenure and the regnant figure within American Zionism.[13]

Goldman remained consistent in his criticism of the Weizmann-Wise line but only occasionally exploited public forums to advance his views. In an address to the Hadassah national convention in October, he lashed out at the semi-paralysis of American Jewry's "self-negation." He urged public demonstrations in London, Paris, and Washington and called on American Jews to seize the reins of leadership in the new circumstance confronting the Jewish people.[14]

It is difficult to determine Brandeis's precise position on Jewish activism during the first few months of the world war. In any event, he consistently supported Goldman, showing special enthusiasm over the dissemination of a radical address the latter delivered in June, excoriating the White Paper. In that speech, it will be recalled, Goldman called for *aliyah* by all means possible. Robert Szold, Brandeis's loyal

13 Minutes of the meetings of the Emergency Committee, September 10, 1939–February 6, 1940, ZAL.
14 *New Palestine* 29, no. 33 (September 27, 1939): 1–3.

supporter and the man responsible for fiscal affairs on the Emergency Committee, spoke in much the same vein as Goldman, generally supporting the latter's motions at Emergency Committee meetings.

The militant wing of American Zionism was significantly bolstered by the return of Emanuel Neumann to the United States in December 1939 after a seven-year stay in Palestine, where he had been allied with the more nationalistic, anti-Weizmann, General Zionist B group. Toward the end of the 1920s Neumann had been a member of the ZOA leadership. Having closely allied himself with the Brandeis group at the time, he maintained contact with that circle during his years in Palestine. In October 1938 he sent Brandeis a wide-ranging letter, which read in part:

> I was in London on the Friday when they telephoned to New York to save the situation. Only America, only America could save us — that was the refrain; and I couldn't help recall with bitterness the short-sightedness with which our leadership in London has discouraged if not suppressed our efforts to build up America as a political force for our cause.... . More and more, England must look to America as the only great power to which it could look for help in case of war; and more than ever America can demand certain things from England... it's *America*, America alone that can save us. We must have a new birth of Zionism in America which will grip all... . The five million Jews of America can and must do the trick politically and financially.[15]

Two months later, in light of the encouraging, vigorous American Jewish reaction, Neumann wrote a long letter to Robert Szold spelling out the need for Brandeis's leadership of the world Zionist movement rather than Weizmann's. Neumann considered the willingness of Zionist leaders to participate in the St. James Conference to be appeasement under the prevailing conditions. In August 1939 at the Twenty-First Zionist Congress, Neumann spoke with Abba Hillel Silver, his friend from childhood. Neumann relates in his autobiography:

---

15   Emanuel Neumann, *In the Arena: An Autobiographical Memoir* (New York, 1976), pp. 95–148; and see Neumann to S. Wise with copies to Brandeis, Mack, Frankfurter, B. Cohen, and R. Szold, October 23, 1938, CZA A 243/131.

I said something about the desperate political and international situation and then added that our only hope lay in America: only if the United States could be moved to oppose the White Paper actively and exert pressure upon Britain might it be possible to avert the worst.... . He [Silver] replied that the proper moment had not yet come, but that eventually America would enter the war which was about to come, and then the time would be ripe for America to wield her full weight and influence. "At that point," he said, "I may do what you suggest." I was encouraged by his reply and added that I would then want to be at his side and join in his effort. I never forgot that brief conversation, nor, I believe, did he. It was an unarticulated pact to which both of us eventually adhered.[16]

One doubts that this conversation contained all the elements recalled by Neumann. Had Silver felt the need to exert American pressure on Britain through public demonstrations, given the unfolding events of the world war, his remarks at the Congress would have reflected that belief; but his speeches, like those of the other American delegates, neither struck an anti-British note nor hinted at any future American involvement in the fighting. Silver even opposed the illegal *aliyah* effort. On the other hand, during Congress deliberations, Goldman repudiated the accusation of defeatism while speaking on his own behalf and Silver's. Assuming that Silver and Neumann's close and lasting friendship did have a political dimension, it might well have been Neumann who drew Silver to a critical stance on Weizmann's policies during this period (1939–1940). Perhaps it is in this light that we should understand that historic conversation at the Twenty-First Zionist Congress.

On returning to the United States at the close of 1939, Neumann saw no opportunity for his immediate integration within the leadership of the movement. He relates in his memoirs: "Now not only was the Brandeis group out of office, but its opponents in the pro-Weizmann 'Lipsky group' seemed to be in full control of the organization and had no

---

16 Neumann to R. Szold, December 19, 1938, and January 30, 1939, CZA A 243/131; Neumann, *In the Arena*, p. 147. See also Marc L. Raphael, *Abba Hillel Silver: A Profile in American Judaism* (New York, 1989), pp. 77–80.

particular interest in me; in fact, from their viewpoint, I was in the enemy camp."[17]

According to Neumann, this state of affairs arose despite the fact that ZOA president Solomon Goldman "had, in fact, developed very good relations with Justice Brandeis." Neumann had no prospects at that time of becoming an influential figure in American Zionism, especially because he had no desire to be active in the ZOA; rather, he sought, a position on the Wise-Lipsky–dominated Emergency Committee, which he felt would become American Jewry's most important body.

At the outset of November 1939, David Ben-Gurion told the Jewish Agency Executive of his intention to visit London to assess what was happening there and to consult with Weizmann, who was slated to visit the United States. Before leaving, Ben-Gurion heard a report from Berl Locker, who had represented Mapai in England. Put off by Locker's Pollyanna account of Weizmann's status and achievements in the British capital, Ben-Gurion criticized the Zionist representatives in London for lack of courage in the face of Colonial Secretary Malcolm MacDonald's intransigence in implementing White Paper policies. Moshe Sharett, who had also been in the British capital during that period, likewise dissociated himself sharply from what he perceived as Weizmann's hesitancy and weakness in contacts with the British. When Ben-Gurion arrived in London, he took a more aggressive stance.[18]

By early 1938 Ben-Gurion was eager to see Weizmann go to America. Indeed, all of Mapai's leaders who had had any contact with Weizmann pressured him incessantly during 1938 and 1939 to do so. Berl Katznelson, who had been in London for the conference of the Zionist General Council at the close of 1938, urged that Weizmann had work to do in Washington. At the end of January 1939, a few days after his arrival in London from America, Ben-Gurion again tried to convince the world Zionist leader of the wisdom of this course of action. The Yishuv leader noted in his diary: "Weizmann told [me] that he is exhausted.

---

17   Neumann, *In the Arena*, pp. 149–150; this is the source of the ensuing discussion.
18   Minutes of the meeting of the Jewish Agency Executive, November 6, 1939, BGIA; *Diary*, November 8–15, 1939, BGIA #29; Sharett, *Political Diary*, vol. 4, pp. 373–518, entries for October 6–November 20, 1939.

When the talks end he will return to Palestine. He won't go to America. He is sixty-five already. Sixty is retirement age."[19]

This kind of procrastination was rather typical of Weizmann from the time of the Woodhead Report to the issuance of the Land Regulations. That trait was undoubtedly among the main factors contributing to Weizmann's eclipse and the elevation of Ben-Gurion in the period covered by this study. On the eve of the promulgation of the White Paper, Zalman Shazar (Rubashov — a future president of Israel) declared: "The Palestinian Pavilion [at the New York World Fair] has invited Weizmann to attend the opening and he has declined. This time, however, the party [Mapai] has to make a special effort to convince Weizmann to agree to go.... . He just might get there before the White Paper is issued.... . If we are turned down again, we needn't necessarily lay this task on Weizmann. It might well be worth our while to bring in someone else, from Palestine; and that, as quickly as possible."[20]

On the very day that Shazar had attacked him for not going to the United States, Weizmann met with Ben-Gurion, who questioned him on several matters, including the trip issue. Weizmann relented; in any event, it was the fiscal rather than the political aspect of the trip that concerned him. Later, when contacting American Zionists to look into the visit, he was cold-shouldered by Solomon Goldman, most likely at the instigation of Brandeis. Ben-Gurion, conversely, exerted heavy pressure on the ZOA leadership to extend an offical invitation. He cabled Goldman at the end of May that he felt it would be calamitous if Weizmann's offer to proceed to America were to be declined.[21]

In the fall and winter of 1939 Weizmann planned his American expedition in close consultation with ministers and high officals in London. He met with Winston Churchill, then secretary of the navy and a staunch pro-Zionist, with whom he enjoyed a long-standing and close relationship; he also conferred with Lord Halifax, the foreign secretary and one of the shapers of the White Paper policy. At a meeting on September 18, Halifax urged Weizmann to act with Lord Lothian, the British ambassador to Washington, while in America. Early in October

19   *Diary*, January 31, 1939, BGIA #27.
20   Minutes of the meeting of the Mapai Central Committee, May 2, 1939, BGIA.
21   Ben-Gurion to H. Montor for S. Goldman, May 29, 1939, BGIA #69.

Weizmann again saw Halifax, at the latter's request; and they met yet again toward the end of the month. Weizmann's close cooperation with Whitehall was entirely logical within his frame of reference. He consistently held that in the international arena the Zionist movement could attain its goals through reliance primarily on one power, Great Britain, and he believed that any activity in America should be undertaken in such a way as not to threaten Britain's relationship with the United States. According to Sharett's diary, Weizmann, in his last meeting with Halifax before leaving for America, said: "I am leaving now for America, for our sake even as for yours. My colleagues remain here and my conscience oppresses me for leaving them in the face of all that looms ahead of us — do you be a father to them." Halifax, however, had his own notion of the paternal function. Before Weizmann sailed, the British minister sent him a long letter in which he resolutely advocated continuation of the White Paper policies.[22]

Weizmann's mission was further limited by his idea of America's role during and after the war. As Ben-Gurion recorded a summary discussion he held with Weizmann on November 20, before returning to Palestine: "Chaim lectured me on the situation as he sees it: this war will not last long, not for years, perhaps it will end this year. America will not take part in the war (unless Westminster is destroyed) — she will only provide weapons, and she will not have much of a say in establishing the peace. The dominions, however, will play a larger role."[23]

Moshe Sharett's diary, reporting that same meeting, corroborates Ben-Gurion's entry on this decisive issue:

> Chaim spoke of his reflections. He spent the weekend on [Lord] Marks' estate and did some thinking. He is going to America. He will speak with the President about the Palestinian solution to the Jewish question. He fears that American influence on the outcome of the present war will be less than her influence after the last war, unless she will enter the fighting. It is almost certain that she will not, since at bottom it is not men that are needed but equipment,

22   Sharett, *Political Diary*, vol. 4, pp. 421–422, entry for October 23, 1939; Halifax to Weizmann, December 19, 1939, BGIA #71.

23   *Diary*, November 20, 1939, BGIA #29.

and that America has to spare. On the other hand, we can assume that the dominions' power will increase.[24]

When Ben-Gurion reported to Mapai's Political Committee on his doings in London, he noted Weizmann's estimate that "we cannot count on American help following the war" but dissociated himself from that judgment. Often critical of Weizmann's flaccidity in confronting the British, Ben-Gurion again concluded that Weizmann's "capacity to act, the value of what he does and his direction all depend upon one thing — if there is someone to guide him."[25] The differences between the two leaders on America, which had taken shape in the autumn of 1938, reemerged, if not quite so sharply on this occasion.

What were Weizmann's goals on this trip? At an early stage of planning he weighed action furthering the creation of a Jewish army. However, after William Bullit, the American ambassador to France, explained that such a project would be considered illegal in neutral America and might well stir up anti-Semitism, Weizmann retreated. During his aforementioned summary talk with Ben-Gurion and Sharett the subject was not even raised. In his autobiography Weizmann notes, "I had nothing too specific in mind. It was to be an exploratory trip, to get my bearings. I was, in a sense, merely laying the groundwork for later trips."[26]

Much is plausible in these remarks. This was Weizmann's first politically oriented trip to the United States in a decade, and he needed to feel his way as it were. Weizmann set himself two primary goals, fiscal (a loan) and political. The political effort was to have been strictly diplomatic — a meeting with the president and his advisers to prove the justice of the Zionist cause to the American leader and to explore how far the president might go in dissociating himself from the White Paper. This diplomatic role of explicator and pleader was sketched by Moshe Sharett in his report to the Jewish Agency Executive on the situation in

24 Sharett, *Political Diary*, vol. 4, p. 510, entry for November 20, 1939.

25 Minutes of the meeting of the Mapai Political Committee, November 27, 1939, BGIA.

26 Sharett, *Political Diary*, vol. 4, pp. 491, 535–536, entries for November 14 and 29, 1939; Chaim Weizmann, *Trial and Error: The Autobiography of Chaim Weizmann* (New York, 1966), p. 418.

London and the plans of the president of the World Zionist Organization. "Dr. Weizmann intends to meet with President Roosevelt and to point out that even though America is not at war, there is a Jewish question, which is a world-wide question, and there is the problem of evacuating Jewish masses; and that Roosevelt's search for all sorts of islands is fruitless. He [Weizmann] will present him [Roosevelt] with the solution that can be realized in Palestine alone." Ben-Gurion's reports, as well, cited (critically) Weizmann's willingness to deal with the idea of a Jewish state in western Palestine in preparation for his trip to America, basing himself on the Philby initiative.[27]

As suggested in the preceding paragraph, the atmosphere in America during the early phase of the world war was distinctly inimical to Zionist activity, for Jews and non-Jews alike. Given his temperament and outlook, Weizmann was quite sensitive to this state of affairs. Of this visit he wrote in his memoirs: "America was, so to speak, violently neutral, and making an extraordinary effort to live in the ordinary way. One had to be extremely careful of one's utterances.... I was frustrated both in my Jewish and general work."[28]

Weizmann's itinerary for the United States, including his departure date, was coordinated — often quite closely — with the British authorities. The conference with President Roosevelt was arranged through Lord Lothian, who was an active participant at that meeting. Though friendly, Roosevelt did not obligate himself in the slightest to any course of action; he emphasized, rather, the overriding need to win the war. Weizmann spoke of a possible federation to solve Jewish-Arab relations, a suggestion seconded firmly by Lord Lothian. At the meeting's close Weizmann expressed the hope that an appropriate American would be designated to be involved in finding a solution to the problem.[29]

27   Sharett, *Political Diary*, vol. 4, pp. 509–512, entry for November 20, 1939; Weizmann, *Trial and Error*, pp. 418–420; minutes of the meeting of the Jewish Agency Executive, December 26, 1939, BGIA; minutes of the meeting of the Mapai Political Committee, November 27, 1939, BGIA.

28   Weizmann, *Trial and Error*, pp. 419–420. Weizmann's trip extended from January 12 through March 5, 1940.

29   "Memorandum of Conversation between President Roosevelt, Dr. Weizmann, and Lord Lothian, February 8, 1940," ZAL, Jewish Agency File XVI/2.

Weizmann's trip did not result in any softening of the internal rivalries of the ZOA or in any real improvement in his own relationship with Brandeis. The two did meet, in the presence of Solomon Goldman (as reported by Goldman in *New Palestine*); that no thaw occurred was most likely due to Brandeis's intransigence. Following Weizmann's departure, the ZOA, in its inner counsels, weighed extending an invitation for another visit. Brandeis wrote Robert Szold that all should know of his vigorous opposition to anyone's "joining with the Lipsky crowd" and concluded with the harsh statement, "No 'appeasement' for me."[30]

All during Weizmann's stay, Solomon Goldman maintained no more than a proper relationship with the ZOA's honored guest; likewise, Weizmann followed the advice of his American advisers not to trust Solomon Goldman, since he was being backed by Brandeis and Hadassah. The outbreak of the war, together with the Weizmann visit, drew Stephen Wise closer to the world Zionist leader. Toward the end of February, the Jewish Institute of Religion bestowed an honorary doctorate on Weizmann. On that occasion Wise delivered an address acclaiming the recipient's Zionist leadership, thus shocking and angering the Brandeisians. Two months later Kurt Blumenfeld, a staunch follower of Weizmann then in the United States, sketched for his leader a map of the ZOA forces. After warning of opponents, Blumenfeld wrote that Lipsky and Wise could be counted on and that Wise especially had gone over to Weizmann's side. At the same time (the summer of 1940) Brandeis, instructing Robert Szold, spoke of "the Lipsky-Wise contingent."[31]

The Mandate's draconian Land Regulations, promulgated during Weizmann's American trip, exposed opposing forces in the American Zionist movement. Solomon Goldman found himself torn between two options — sending an American Jewish legation to London or organizing mass protests in America; in the end, he chose the latter path,

---

30 *New Palestine* 30, no. 6 (February 9, 1940): 2; Brandeis to Szold, April 10, 1940, in Brandeis, *Letters*, vol. 5, p. 638.

31 M. Weisgal to Arthur Lourie, March 11, 1940, WA; Kurt Blumenfeld to Weizmann, April 29, 1940, WA; Urofsky, *A Voice for Justice*, p. 313; Brandeis to R. Szold, April 5, 1940, in Brandeis, *Letters*, vol. 5, p. 643.

cabling Weizmann to that effect on February 29. Weizmann chose to ignore the message; at no time during his visit did he advocate public protest. In a Zionist address delivered in Boston after the promulgation of the Land Regulations, he focused on the subject of the loan, contenting himself with an expression of support for the statement issued by the Jewish Agency Executive. A protest meeting led by Lipsky and Wise did take place in New York — but it was a half-hearted effort, it would seem. George Landauer of Mapai, then on an economic mission to the United States, later reported to the Histadrut Executive:

> You should have seen the gathering of America's Zionists at Carnegie Hall to protest the Land Regulations.... The hall was not full; the press gave no coverage to the meeting: they had no interest in it. The speakers, our colleagues among them, declared, "It is true that England has wronged the Jews, but we dare not damage British prestige at this time. Nonetheless, we must register our protest over British policy in Palestine." Stephen Wise, after he had finished his speech, sent me a note, "We have to shout in low tones."[32]

This "low-toned shout" was accompanied by a series of low-toned articles in Wise's *Opinion*. Prior to Weizmann's arrival, Wise stated his position clearly: Jewish interests should be seen as identical to those of the fighting democracies; even after the Land Regulations he concluded that "it is for peoples who are, and for men who would remain free, their most sacred obligation to render moral, political and material aid and furtherance to Britain and France."[33]

During the first six months of the world war Brandeis shifted from the position that he had previously conveyed to Ben-Gurion — "Don't

---

32   S. Goldman to A. Lourie, February 27, 1940, WA; Goldman to Weizmann, February 29, 1940, ibid. In a letter to Stephen Wise dated February 1, 1940, Goldman supported both a delegation to London and public protest, noting that "if we pull our people and American sentiment into an acceptance of this betrayal we shall be helpless at the peace table" (CZA A 243/126). See also Weizmann to S. Goldman, February 29, 1940, in Weizmann, *Letters and Papers*, vol. 19, p. 240; *New Palestine* 30, no. 10 (March 8, 1940): 6; minutes of the meeting of the Histadrut Central Committee, May 9, 1940, HECA.

33   *Opinion* 10, no. 3 (January 1940): 5; no. 5 (March 1940): 5.

yield!" — moving more or less toward Wise's "We have to shout in low tones." Eliyahu Golomb, the Mapai emissary to the United States (from mid-November 1939 through the end of February 1940), had a two-hour meeting with Brandeis, during which he was greatly taken with Brandeis's personality, knowledgeability, and dedication to the Zionist cause. The veteran American Zionist leader expressed his fundamental approval of the Palestinian activist's approach; nonetheless he also reflected a certain cooling to mass action, probably because of his close relationship with Roosevelt, who often sought his advice on Zionist affairs. Whatever the justice's reasons, when it came to reacting to the Land Regulations in February of 1940, Golomb found Brandeis and Weizmann to be of one mind. Both felt that "we dare not react to the law in the press: they [the American Zionists] did not even want to hold protest meetings." Golomb fought this approach and, according to what he wrote, succeeded in effecting a compromise of sorts.[34]

During his trip to the United States Weizmann began to formalize his relationship with Meyer Weisgal, whom he had known for a decade. Weisgal became in effect Weizmann's personal representative in America. He had begun his public career under the tutelage of Louis Lipsky, whom he admired all his life. "Lipsky was my first mentor and teacher, [Max] Reinhart [the Jewish stage director] my second, and Weizmann my third and last," he wrote in his lively autobiography. Before leaving America Weizmann wrote Weisgal a long letter in which he asked his lieutenant to further two projects — obtaining the loan and fostering public support after the war, primarily by publishing a book on Zionism aimed at the educated public. Obviously, then, Weizmann was aware of the weight of American Jewry and the importance of public opinion. But these were not central to his vision; his was a sporadic and strictly educational effort rather than a persistent attempt to exert political pressure through mass action.[35]

Eliyahu Golomb's mission to the United States has already been

34   E. Golomb [to M. Sharett?], December 16, 1939, BGIA #71; Brandeis to B. Flexner, October 29, 1949, in Brandeis, *Letters*, vol. 5, p. 628; E. Golomb, report on his mission to America, in minutes of the meeting of the Histadrut Central Committee, March 28, 1949, HECA.

35   Meyer W. Weisgal, ...*So Far: An Autobiography* (New York, 1971), pp. 98–104, 164ff., quotation on p. 284; Weizmann to M. Weisgal, March 3, 1940, in Weizmann, *Letters and Papers*, vol. 19, p. 244.

mentioned. He found sympathetic ears among the younger American leadership — the Brandeis group and various opponents of Stephen Wise. Some ten days after arriving in the country he met at length with Silver, who revealed himself as more militant than had been thought. (Silver had given Weizmann full cooperation during the latter's stay in the United States.) Golomb also mentioned Solomon Goldman and Robert Szold as leaders with whom he spoke a common language.[36]

The observations and conclusions drawn by Eliyahu Golomb contributed in no small way to sharpening Ben-Gurion's perceptions of the American scene. At the close of Ben-Gurion's stay in London in November 1939 (discussed earlier), he rushed a letter to Golomb, from the island of Rhodes, citing what he perceived to be the weakness of the Zionist representatives in London, emphasizing that "the [White Paper] regime lives on" and concluding: "And what have you found in America?" Shortly after Ben-Gurion's arrival, Golomb sent him a cautiously worded report, positive in tone. Despite problems and difficulties, Golomb had the impression that the Zionist movement might well be able to command a public response. In that connection, he noted the challenge of Revisionist activity in the United States and returned to that theme in a second letter from America.

> [Benjamin] Akzin has worked intensively with the intellectuals, Rabbi [Louis] Newman is trying to break through to monied circles. They speak of national daring, of the rescue of Jews; and at times they are impressive. They have also made inroads in schools... It seems to me that we stand on the threshold of a major breakthrough to a vital Zionist movement. The groundwork has been laid by the destruction of European Jewry, on the one hand; and, on the other, the blow delivered Communism with the attack on Finland, more grievous than the blow delivered by the Stalin-Hitler pact.[37]

36   E. Golomb to Ben-Gurion, November 27, 1939, BGIA #71; TA, Weizmann File, 1939–1940; S. Goldman to E. Golomb, February 9, 1940, HHA, Letters of E. Golomb, File 4109; E. Golomb, report on his mission to America, minutes of the meeting of the Histadrut Central Committee, March 28, 1940, HECA; R. Szold to Brandeis, January 31, 1940, *Diary*, BGIA #71.

37   Ben-Gurion to E. Golomb, November 23, 1939, *Diary*, BGIA #29; E. Golomb to Ben-Gurion, November 27, 1939, BGIA #71; E. Golomb [to Ada Golomb], December 9, 1939, BGIA #71.

Golomb concluded that, at bottom, the Zionist movement could succeed if it launched independent action by dissolving the partnership between the United Palestine Appeal and Joint Distribution Committee circles: "There can be no freeing ourselves from this weakness [of Jewish public action in America]... I would venture, except through the unrestricted action of Zionist bodies. In the absence of such activity, I very much fear for the future of the Zionist movement here and see the groundwork being laid for burgeoning Revisionism.... It is my feeling that stepping free of our partnership with the Joint is the right road to follow to an expanded Zionist effort and a growing Zionist movement." In a letter written one week later, Golomb was more emphatic. Highlighting the prominence of Revisionist activity, he unequivocally recommended an independent course for the Zionist fund (the UPA): "Separating the Palestine appeal means the salvation of American Zionism."[38]

The aforementioned letters made their way to Ben-Gurion, although only some had been written to him personally. Of special significance is Golomb's response to Ben-Gurion's Rhodes letter, depicting Revisionist infiltration of various segments of the Jewish and non-Jewish public. Given that situation, he explained, he had met with the Revisionists' leading body — the American Friends of Jewish Palestine. Golomb expressed great concern over "our" Mapai's weak efforts. About half of the letter contained his description of the great opportunities awaiting American Zionism and his assertion that, to that end, it must break free of the United Jewish Appeal. From his experience, he concluded it was "not difficult to imbue Zionists, as well as broad Jewish circles, with an awareness of Palestine's needs and with a proper respect for the work now being done, and that can be done, in Palestine." He urged sending out major leaders as emissaries for lengthy periods.[39]

Typical of Golomb was his positive assessment of Hadassah, the Women's Zionist Organization of America. In a letter to Dov Hos, a copy of which was sent to Ben-Gurion, he wrote: "I urged Weizmann to extend the olive branch to Hadassah and to Brandeis." On the one hand, Golomb saw Hadassah as firmly under Brandeis's influence; on the

---

38   E. Golomb [to Ada Golomb], December 16 and 22, 1939, BGIA #71.
39   E. Golomb to Ben-Gurion, December 29, 1939, BGIA #71.

other, as ideologically diffuse and open to the influence of voices calling for appeasement to the Arabs. Still, Golomb found the movement to be very well intentioned and concluded that it comprised "fertile ground worthy of labor."[40]

Golomb was critical of the political direction that Stephen Wise was giving to the Emergency Committee and to various Zionist projects. A public meeting chaired by Wise in the latter half of December 1939 struck Golomb as politically ineffectual. No concrete resolutions were put forward for the rescue of the oppressed Jews of Europe, and no demands were made of the U.S. government. His critique of the Emergency Committee was scathing. In a letter addressed directly to that body he wrote:

> Every individual, every group [on the Emergency Committee] is out for a special post... but there is no one to bear the burden of Jewish and Zionist responsibility... if it does not fall within the framework of run-of-the-mill activities.... We can rescue tens of thousands of Jews from Nazi countries, strengthen our position in Palestine, there are ideas for taking advantage of the implementation of the Land Regulations; but all these are doomed from the start, because no one will do anything outside his sphere of activity and everyone knows in advance that nothing will be done.[41]

Golomb undoubtedly exaggerated the scope of Revisionist activity in the United States. Benjamin Akzin, who lived in America for a number of years and was intimately acquainted with the Revisionist movement, concluded that at least until the spring of 1940 it was a tiny, marginal group. When the war broke out, Jabotinsky himself rushed from Paris to the capital of the world power that comprised his basic political address — London. He stayed there for more than six months attempting a rerun of what he had effected during World War I. Straight upon his arrival in Britain, Jabotinsky turned to Colonel John Patterson, who had

40   E. Golomb to Dov Hos, January 18, 1940, BGIA #72.
41   E. Golomb [to Ada Golomb], December 16, 1939, BGIA #71; E. Golomb to the Emergency Committee, January 28, 1940, HHA, Letters of E. Golomb, File 4109.

commanded the British battalion that contained the Jewish Legion. "Within an hour of England's declaration of war on Germany on September 3, 1939," recalled Patterson, "I was rung up on the phone, and, answering the call, heard Jabotinsky's excited voice eagerly urging that we should once again cooperate as we had done almost a quarter of a century previously, and throw ourselves heart and soul into the creation, not of a legion this time, but of a fully mechanized Jewish army, to fight side by side with the Allied forces." For six months Jabotinsky, together with Patterson, tried to move the British government to set up such a force, one that would fight on all fronts.[42]

After much hesitation and soul searching, Jabotinsky decided to head for the United States. During the last weeks that preceded his journey he wrote a book broad in scope, *The Jewish War Front*. Except for one positive mention of Roosevelt at the Evian Conference, neither the United States nor its Jewry was cited as an element in a Zionist strategy. His hesitancy and inconsistency were reflected in a letter to an active Revisionist in the United States. He wrote: "*If* (I underline the 'if' as heavily as I can) there is a force that still can place the Jewish problem in the forefront and compel the Allies to treat us at least as they do Danish bacon (they pay for it!) that force can only come from within American Jewry."[43]

It was Jabotinsky's intention to confine his efforts in the United States to the creation of a Jewish army. He hoped that by campaigning for American involvement in the global conflict alongside the Allied powers he would oblige Britain to create this force. When Hillel Kook, an Irgun Zvai Leumi activist, gingerly moved toward contacting the American ambassador in London, Jabotinsky — hidebound by his own game plan — cut the effort off and gave him stern warning not to proceed. After the Revisionist leader reached the United States (March 13, 1940), he met with the British ambassador to Washington, Lord Lothian — very much as Weizmann had done — and tried to coordinate his efforts with him.

42   Benjamin Akzin, interviewed by Sandy Koros and David Shpiro, December 15, 1977, Jerusalem, BGIA; Schechtman, *Jabotinsky*, vol. 2, p. 371.

43   Vladimir Jabotinsky, *The Jewish War Front* (London, 1940); Schechtman, *Jabotinsky*, vol. 2, p. 371.

Jabotinsky, however, did not show any sensitivity to the American political mind by, for example, qualifying Revisionism's claim to "both sides of the Jordan." This dogmatism, again, reflected the lack of any meaningful interest in a Zionist-American alignment.[44]

The Land Regulations, designed to effect the goals of the White Paper by drastically reducing Jewish acquisition of land in Palestine, were promulgated on February 28, 1940. The Yishuv was outraged because the British government was taking the time and effort during the war to put teeth into the White Paper; outraged over the death decree declared on the Zionist effort; and outraged over the degradation that this law entailed. At the meetings of the Jewish Agency Executive and the Zionist Executive one day after the issuance of the Land Regulations, Ben-Gurion announced his resignation from the Jewish Agency Executive. March and early April witnessed a growing rift in Mapai, apparently bringing the party to the brink of a split between moderates and activists (vis-à-vis Britain). Ben-Gurion held, on April 8, that the war on the White Paper had to take precedence over everything else and that opposition to that document had to be effected through "politics B" — fomenting "prolonged and serious unrest in Palestine."[45]

But just the day after, on April 9, Germany invaded Denmark and Norway (and then the Lowlands); and Winston Churchill came to power in Britain on May 10. These world events removed the grounds, at least temporarily, for a head-on anti-British kind of struggle. Ben-Gurion resumed his position as chairman of the Jewish Agency Executive. However, more than a description of the debate between activists and

---

44   Schechtman, *Jabotinsky*, vol. 2, pp. 384–388; Hillel Kook, interview with the author, Kfar Shemaryahu, November 11, 1983; Schechtman, *Jabotinsky*, vol. 2, p. 389. W. Murray to C. Hull, March 15, 1940, and W. Murray — B. Akzin corresp., March 1940, NAUS, RDS #19.

45   Slutsky, *Haganah History*, vol. 3, pp. 133–145; minutes of the meeting of the Zionist Executive, February 29, 1940, BGIA; see also minutes of the meetings of the Mapai Central Committee, March 13, April 9, and April 14, 1940, BGIA; quotation is from minutes of the meeting of the Jewish Agency Executive, April 8, 1940, BGIA. This was the last meeting of the Jewish Agency Executive in which Ben-Gurion participated prior to his departure for England and the United States.

moderates would be required to convey the political ferment within Mapai, its growing political sophistication. and the attitude of Ben-Gurion himself.

Eliyahu Golomb's reports on his visit to America helped root a new political perspective within Mapai. On March 28, 1940, Golomb gave the Histadrut Executive Committee a broad report on his mission. At the outset of his remarks he emphasized that "there now obtains a Zionist consciousness in America. There is a disillusionment with other plans to resolve the Jewish question. Communism has suffered a severe setback within the broad American public; perhaps not quite so starkly among the Jewish working class, but there, too, the decline is palpable." He described Revisionist successes in America and called for spirited competition: "We must not seek an outlet in a war against Revisionism, but in the revival of Zionist efforts in the same areas in which the Revisionists are working."[46]

Reporting on the status of the organizational program of Ben-Gurion and Solomon Goldman, Golomb was optimistic: "We sought a joint effort of all the Zionist organizations. Solomon Goldman, chairman of the Zionist organization, wanted this especially — herein he saw the means of reviving Zionism. However, the idea met with tremendous opposition from the Zionist establishment: the principle of taking on another burden was accepted, but the principle of joint effort was not. Still, we must not despair. Even here we have a beginning, of sorts, of joint endeavor."

Golomb sensed that sympathy for the Zionist effort in Palestine (not necessarily for Zionist ideology) had by now spread to wealthy Jews who were non-Zionists by their own definition, and to the masses, organized in Jewish unions. "I think that in the wake of the great Jewish tragedy there is now room for action," he observed, though he warned that "doors are not opened readily and we ought not predict a victorious campaign in America, either to amass new members or more funds." In his summary remarks he emphasized the prospects for "a good job of winning hearts" and proposed establishing a formal institute to prepare emissaries for missions in the United States.[47]

---

46 Minutes of the meeting of the Histadrut Executive Committee, March 28, 1940, HECA. This is the source for the ensuing discussion.
47 Ibid.

Eliyahu Golomb's report twelve days later at a large and tense meeting of the Mapai Central Committee, attended by Ben-Gurion, seemed an even weightier affair. Golomb pointed out the gap between the limited achievements of the Zionist movement and the huge pro-Yishuv potential of American Jewry, emphasizing that the pursuit of an activist policy within Palestine could make this potential a reality:

> It seems to me that things can be changed. Zionist sentiment among American Jewry is very strong; there is grave disappointment over other solutions to the Jewish question. ... Had we inculcated the Jewish masses with greater faith in the possibility of Zionist action and a war for Zionism, then we could do great things in America. The question is, how to inculcate this faith.... . It seems to me — also based on my experience in America, based on talks with Jews, both Zionist and non-Zionist — that only if the Jews of Palestine stand up and fight for their lives will Zionist consciousness and action be stirred up among the Jews. The Jewish street and perhaps the non-Jewish, too, can be won by successful Zionism or militant Zionism.[48]

Eliyahu Golomb held that Zionism had a chance of setting its mark on non-Jewish public opinion. He maintained that minorities were being regarded more and more favorably and that anti-Semitism was declining: "I remember that Ben-Gurion, upon his return from America, told us that fear of revived anti-Semitism had gripped America's Jewish and Zionist leaders, and that as a result we could not hope for very aggressive promotion of Jewish-Zionist concerns. That sentiment, I believe, has markedly weakened."[49]

Moshe Sharett, too, at that same meeting contributed to a heightened awareness of the growing importance of America and its Jewry during the world war and on its conclusion. He cited Weizmann's positive assessments, which focused on the economic potential of American Jewry, in the wake of his visit to the United States, but was critical of Weizmann's reluctance to stir up public opinion:

---

48   Minutes of the meeting of the Mapai Central Committe, April 9, 1940, BGIA.
49   Ibid.

It is not simply a question of harnessing American Jewish power to influence the American government (though that in itself is most important); but, as well, a question of harnessing American Jewish energy to creating an American Jewish lever on the English government. But thus far, this has not been done. While the British government is sensitive to the mood of the American public — and she is decidedly so — she does not feel that America's Jews comprise a power bloc or that they are bold enough to use their strength.... . Early and late we must broadcast to the American public — and through them, to England — that what England has done to the Jewish people in the very thick of this war is akin to what Hitler has done — Hitler, whom Britain is fighting — to a number of nations, and what he would like to do to the entire world.[50]

Special weight was given the remarks of Golda Meir (Meyerson), who had come on *aliyah* from America. Meir abjured "theoretical debate... rather, I suggest we deal with the concrete steps that lie ahead of us, and first and foremost — action in America." All in all, a dominant activist-leaning trend then developed within Mapai, its proponents had had some sort of American experience and were particularly sensitive to the importance of American Jewry. Ben-Gurion, Berl Katznelson, and Eliyahu Golomb were the prominent members of this trend; Golda Meir was singular in the strength of her American background; Dov Joseph, whose background and status resembled Meir's, was destined to take over Ben-Gurion's role in the United States within the space of one year and in the process buttress his position within Mapai; and Eliezer Livneh (Livenstein) began to gain prominence during this period for his analyses of the significance of American Jewish support.[51]

One week later the Mapai Central Committee concluded its series of deliberations on the Land Regulations. The decisions taken not only

50   Ibid.
51   Minutes of the meeting of the Mapai Central Committee, April 9, May 26, 1940; Jewish Agency Executive, February 21 and May 25, 1940, BGIA. See Livneh's outspoken piece, "The Underpinnings of Our Opposing Stance" [Mishe'enet leHitnagdutenu], *Davar*, March 17, 1939, and his reflective essay, "Palestine and the Zionist Diaspora" [HaAretz uTefutzot haTzionut], *Davar*, April 18, 1940.

called for combating the decree but also signaled a major political shift in the direction of America. The second (of five) resolutions supported "a systematic propaganda and protest effort against the White Paper, designed to stir up public opinion in the world, and especially in the United States, against the British government's betrayal of the Hebrew people."[52]

This decision and the new political climate obtaining in the corridors of Mapai were largely the work of Ben-Gurion. At the meeting of the Jewish Agency Executive preceding the promulgation of the Land Regulations, he maintained, hewing to the political line that he had held since the autumn of 1938, that focusing Zionist political efforts in London would not be very helpful: "The principal reaction can only come from the United States. It were best for America's Jews to prepare to react accordingly and send an appropriate delegation to the British ambassador to warn him that American Jewry will not tolerate such racial discrimination [the Land Regulations]."[53]

At the next meeting, still before issuance of the decree, Ben-Gurion suggested that, as a political response to the Land Regulations, the Zionist General Council should meet in America. With Dov Joseph and Pinḥas Rutenberg in strong support, the motion carried, and the proposal was cabled to Weizmann, then in the United States. Weizmann and the Emergency Committee were not prepared to accept the suggestion, and Ben-Gurion continued to press for such a step in the meetings that followed issuance of the new law.

Ben-Gurion's appearance at the Jewish Agency Executive meeting of March 24, 1940, was of special significance. At that gathering the Executive heard a broad survey from Rose Jacobs, then visiting Palestine, who had been among the founders of Hadassah and had served as its president. Jacobs delivered a very negative assessment of American Zionism's prospects. Toward the end of her remarks she observed that America's Zionist leaders during World War I — men such as Brandeis, Mack, and Frankfurter — no longer headed the

---

52   Minutes of the meeting of the Mapai Central Committee, April 14, 1940, BGIA.
53   Minutes of the meeting of the Jewish Agency Executive, February 18, 21, and 25, and March 7, 1940, BGIA; the minutes of these meetings are the source for the ensuing discussion.

movement and had turned their backs on the new forces that had taken over in the 1930s. As for America's role in the war, she claimed that no one could foresee what the results of the war would be.

Ben-Gurion took the floor to deliver a strong rebuttal to Jacobs; he was the only person present who could do so effectively and authoritatively. The meeting's protocols reveal his assertion that he, too, had a great deal of American experience. Having lived in the United States for three years, he was not prepared to accept the analogy with World War I. When he had arrived in the United States at the outset of that war, he pointed out, there had been widespread persecution of the Jews of Palestine, and American Jewry at that time had been led by assimilated Jews who were opposed to Zionism and the Yishuv. Moreover, the newspaper *Forverts* was on the assimilationists' side, and the Zionist Organization of America was not Zionistic. Finally, Ben-Gurion asserted, the monies that had been sent to Palestine then were far less than those currently being sent. "The question is," he pressed, "what will the future bring?" In his opinion, the war had only just begun. Eschewing Jacobs's pessimism, he denied that the situation obtaining at the time determined the future. "Everything depends on us.... There are five million Jews in America, most of whom are interested in the question of Palestine, and if they see the avant-garde prepared to fight for Palestine, all of them will be with us."[54]

Ben-Gurion's prognosis and dynamism contrasted sharply with Jacobs's position:

> To my mind, the assumption of our Zionists there, that since America is neutral American Zionists must remain neutral, is an anti-Zionist position. This has nothing to do with loyalty. There are Irishmen in America, too, very loyal to the government and very influential in American politics. But in everything pertaining to Ireland the Irish Americans have their own politics and to date no one in America has told them that their involvement in Ireland's internal affairs contravenes the American Constitution. Our efforts must be aboveboard, and American Jewry must know that, where internal issues are concerned, she can and must speak out, and defend her position. The United States is a free country,

54   Minutes of the meeting of the Jewish Agency Executive, March 24, 1940, BGIA.

and its Jews, United States citizens, are obligated to help their brothers — as Jews.[55]

Ben-Gurion concluded his remarks by emphasizing that the most important help that American Jewry could render was not in the economic sphere but in "political warfare." American Jewry needed political guidance today as then, he maintained, alluding to Jacobs: "Louis Brandeis rendered an historic service during the last war, but who knows what American Jewry would have done had it not been for the late Shemaryahu Levin, who preached Zionism day and night. That America's present situation must dictate tomorrow's is an unacceptable conclusion."[56]

Indeed, at the aforementioned meeting of the Jewish Agency Executive on April 8, when Ben-Gurion called for "prolonged and severe unrest in Palestine," he also presented a series of political proposals for the international front.

He suggested, among other things, "organized activity in the United States vias the press, and unrelenting demonstrations all during the war." As a result of his diplomatic stance, the decisions of the Jewish Agency Executive contained a special section emphasizing the need to win over American public opinion.[57] This decision (adopted by the Mapai Central Committee on April 14, as well) and others required the authorization of the Zionist Executive.

Following publication of the Zionist Executive's position on the Land Regulations, that body gathered for a series of three closed meetings on the political situation. The first meeting, in mid-March, began with members rising to their feet to honor three victims of the struggle against the new law. The atmosphere was bleak in the extreme. It seemed clear that Britain had proved its determination to convert the Yishuv into a shrunken corner of the Diaspora on the shores of the Mediterranean. Ussishkin, chairman of the Zionist Executive exclaimed in his opening address: "Upon whom can we depend in our struggle for the future of Palestine? ... Can we depend upon England? ... Can we depend upon America, on Roosevelt's elegant smile, on his handshake with

55   Ibid.
56   Ibid.
57   Minutes of the meetings of the Jewish Agency Executive, April 8 and 14, 1940, BGIA.

Weizmann? Is that enough? On whom can we depend? ... On the Jewish people in America, afraid to open its mouth and demand its full rights, as it did twenty-five years ago? Upon whom?" His reply, one of near desperation, was: "The only force [we have] is the half million Jews in Palestine and the one-and-a-half million dunams beneath our feet."[58]

Ben-Gurion, too, opened his remarks feelingly: "Gentlemen, this time I approach the clarification of a political situation with a trepidation whose like I have never known." Asserting that Zionism had to strike out on a new course, unchained to Britain and looking beyond the immediate suffering of the Jewish people, he declared: "We must not judge this situation from the perspective of the hell of German Jewry, Polish Jewry or any other Jewry, but only from a Zionist perspective.... I wish to address you strictly on the Zionist aspect of our political path. My analysis is strictly Zionistic, for a general Jewish analysis is also possible, nor can it be denigrated — looking at the situation of Palestinian Jewry [alone].... A Zionist assessment raises one question and one question only: will this make possible, will this facilitate the transfer of masses of Jews to Palestine and enable them to strike roots in the land? No other facts, figures or calculations enter the picture" (see Appendix II).

At this historic meeting Ben-Gurion emphasized two major elements in Zionist policy: the attitude toward Britain and the gravitation toward new international factors. He elaborated on the question of the Yishuv's relations with Britain in connection with the war effort. The Jewish community of Poland, he asserted, was dearer to his heart than that of Palestine; but the Yishuv was defending Zionism and had to do so "as though there were no war in the world." He was a staunch supporter of England, he continued, but denigrated the stand of those Jews who were prepared "to put themselves in England's shoes" — a barb aimed doubtless at Chaim Weizmann and his camp. Thus far, Ben-Gurion's position was indistinguishable from that of Ussishkin; but in the second part of his speech he proceeded to lay out a program, or at least a direction.

Ben-Gurion maintained that the time for the unseating of the Chamberlain government had arrived, that for the first time since the

58   Minutes of the meeting of the Zionist Executive, March 14, 1940, BGIA; this is the source for the ensuing discussion.

outbreak of the war, this was an attainable goal. Viewing the Land Regulations as a grievous blow to England's war effort, the British opposition had voiced its readiness to bring down the present government, despite the war. Ben-Gurion urged his listeners to contribute to that effort by adopting an effective policy. He proposed as the power base for such a policy American Jewry, a free community, not subservient to England. Until that juncture, the Yishuv leader asserted, American Jews had been warm sympathizers of England because of its Zionism, but now England had abandoned Zionism and delivered a serious setback to the Jewish people.

Ben-Gurion addressed the ethnic nature of America. "There are all kinds of people living in America," he declared, "there are Germans, there are Irish — sworn enemies of England. The Germans of America are more numerous, but the Irish have more influence. There are also pure-blooded Americans who have not yet forgotten what the English did to them." Ben-Gurion went on to note the strength of American Jewry. "And this America holds, as well, a community of four to five million. Now it is true that that is not much for America; but when we consider the situation, they are concentrated in a few states, mostly in cities; hence their influence is greater."

The Yishuv leader envisaged a scenario in which American Jewry could threaten Britain with the adoption of an independent stance, isolationist to all appearances, that posed the question: "Can you [English] afford to put such a factor into jeopardy, even if it is not decisive? Can you allow yourselves do it?" The Land Regulations were deeply offensive to world Jewry, including American Jewry: "They [the Jews] had the land of Israel, it's their home; so they will then tell the English, 'What need do we have of all this?'" And the reaction would be that "In every city, in every town where there are Englishmen, they will have an address, and they will set up pickets: England broke faith with the Jewish people, the English are our enemies in Palestine, England is scheming against the Jewish people. If the Jews do that throughout the cities of America, it would be very dangerous for England."

In this fashion the Jewish Agency Executive chairman proposed a stance sprung from a new international and Jewish situation as he understood it. He hammered home the logic of seeking support in American Jewry's political strength. Ben-Gurion hoped that this Jewish community, acting in tandem with the Yishuv, would bring the Zionist cause to the press and the public through dramatic, extreme action and that England, subject to such pressure, would have to change course. It was largely on the question of tactics in the struggle against the British that members of the Zionist Executive differed with Ben-Gurion; on the question of American Jewry they agreed with him, for the most part. Yehoshu'a Suparsky, one of the leaders of General Zionist B Group, recalled the disservice of Stephen Wise, who during the St. James Conference would not hear of activating American Jewry. Suparksy held that a direct, on-the-spot appeal to American Jewry was crucial. Daniel Syrkis from the activist wing of Mizrachi, the religious Zionist party, discerned a change of line on Ben-Gurion's part. In the process of excoriating Weizmann's policies, he asked Ben-Gurion whether the Yishuv leader had won others to his new approach. "If your [Jewish Agency] Executive follows the path you are proposing," Syrkis told Ben-Gurion, "if it changes its line entirely — then we must go to America and stop taking England into account."[59]

While most members of the Zionist Executive tended to agree with Ben-Gurion on his American orientation, few interpreted his international outlook as radically as did Syrkis and Suparksy. Prominent activists in Ben-Gurion's party, those destined to constitute Faction B, showed no great interest in American Jewry's political potential and in the international ramifications thereof. In a manner characteristic of this group, Israel Bar-Yehuda lashed out at the moderates but did not broach any alternative political stance.[60]

Moshe Sharett's speech at the concluding session of this dramatic series of meetings expressed more or less the consensus of Mapai party members and the members of the Zionist Executive who had attended the sessions. There was no room for a shift toward an anti-British policy. Sharett pointed out that England still controlled Palestine and was, therefore, the appropriate focus of action. At the same time, he noted, avenues affecting England should be sought, especially in America. Doubtless, the question of Palestine would be raised at the peace conference, and that "would relate, of course, to the question of our status and activity in America, not only towards the end of the war, but

59   Ibid.
60   Minutes of the meeting of the Zionist Executive, March 26, 1940, BGIA.

during the war as well." He emphasized that "America would exercise tremendous influence at the war's close, and that England was, in certain ways, sensitive to American opinion." Sharett brought the decisions of the Jewish Agency Executive before the Zionist Executive.[61]

In his closing address, Ben-Gurion stressed the strength of the Zionist enterprise in Palestine and the consequences of the Yishuv's struggle against democratic England. The English government, he claimed, could not strike out at Palestinian Jewry at will. In his preceding speech, Ben-Gurion had stressed that a militant American Zionism could open new political horizons for the Yishuv. Now he emphasized, here seconding Golomb's position, that a determined Yishuv struggle against the White Paper could awaken the empathy of American Jewry and foster the growth of allies. Militant Zionism, he exclaimed, would save American Jewry.[62]

At a meeting held on the morning of April 19, Yitzḥak Gruenbaum read the proposed resolutions of the Jewish Agency Executive. These included a section emphasizing the need for "a systematic propaganda and protest effort against the White Paper, aimed at rousing world opinion, and especially in the United States, against the British government's betrayal of the Jewish people."[63] These resolutions, which passed by a large margin, expressed a certain continuity in Zionist policy: Britain continued to be an addressee for Zionist grievances and hopes. At the same time, and particularly against the background of David Ben-Gurion's remarks at the Jewish Agency Executive and his first speech at the Zionist Executive meeting, they reflected a significant shift — a withrawal from traditionally exclusive orientation on Britain and a move toward growing reliance on the political potential of American Jewry and the United States. This change marked the genesis of a Zionist foreign policy aimed at the Anglo-American world; and the activism of Ben-Gurion and his associates thus gradually became both sustained and restrained by this new foreign policy.

---

61   Minutes of the meeting of the Zionist Executive, April 18, 1940, BGIA.
62   Ibid.
63   Minutes of the meeting of the Zionist Executive, April 19, 1940, BGIA.

CHAPTER FIVE

ZIONIST ASPIRATIONS
AND ANGLO-AMERICAN DEMOCRACY

At Weizmann's request Ben-Gurion left for London, arriving May 1, 1940. Nine days later Chamberlain resigned, making way for a new government led by Winston Churchill. A fresh era in the Yishuv's relationship with Britain seemed imminent. Churchill was not only a foe of appeasement but also a staunch friend of the Zionist movement. Given the new set of circumstances, it appeared that there was no longer any place for serious differences of opinion between Ben-Gurion and Weizmann. However, the composition of the Churchill government, which included ardent advocates of the White Paper policy, did not allow for a pro-Zionist stance on England's part. Both in his letters to Palestine and in his memoranda to the London Zionist leadership Ben-Gurion warned against any hope that the new government would radically alter the White Paper policy. His assessment grew all the bleaker following meetings that he and Weizmann held with Lord Lloyd, the new colonial secretary and an old-time anti-Zionist. Ben-Gurion was particularly concerned at the lack of any real progress on the question of the Jewish army. With Italy's declaration of war on England and France on June 10, Ben-Gurion viewed the raising of a Jewish force as vital to the security of the Yishuv. In the latter half of August he concluded that "our business has gotten just about nowhere; I have decided to leave. I realize that under present circumstances almost nothing can be done here, so I am going back to Palestine."[1]

1   Gavriel Cohen, *Churchill and Palestine, 1939–1942* [Churchill uShe'elat Eretz Yisrael biTeḥilat Milḥemet haOlam haShniyah, 1939–1942] (Jerusalem, 1976), chaps. 1, 2; Ben-Gurion, "Short Note of Interview with the Right Honorable The Lord Lloyd, Colonial Office, Wed. 15th May 1940," BGIA #73; idem, "Additional Notes on the Present Situation," May 17, 1940, BGIA #73; Ben-Gurion to Paula Ben-Gurion, August 23, 1940, *Diary*, BGIA #30.

Relations between Ben-Gurion and Weizmann had grown progressively more strained, with the former maintaining that the president of the World Zionist Organization did not show the requisite skill and aggressiveness in negotiations over the Jewish army. "I have decided to break with Chaim once and for all," the Jewish Agency Executive chairman wrote in his diary, "but in a friendly way. I wrote him a farewell message that should make him understand I have no intention of seeing him again." Although their parting notes were couched in friendly tones, there were additional, strident meetings. Weizmann hinted at the tension in a brief comment to his wife: "Ben-Gurion has gone off, and so — an irritant less."[2]

Historians who focus on Ben-Gurion's "aggressive" or "Palestinian" bent, as compared with Weizmann's, to explain the former's initial stay in London from May to September and the conflict between the two men omit an essential element from their analysis — Ben-Gurion's social philosophy. The fall of the Chamberlain government and Churchill's rise to power further entrenched Ben-Gurion's faith in the strength of public opinion in the English-speaking democracies. In a letter from England during his fifth month there, the Palestinian leader wrote: "Few countries have attained to a truly democratic regime and among these none show a democracy as deep-rooted as England's. It is democracy that has stood by this nation in its greatest hour of trial. But for [England's] democratic regime, free parliament and free press — even while a war was going on — Churchill never would have come to power nor would England have become what she now is!"[3]

The Yishuv leader's further observations on this point shed light on the relationship between his political thought and activity:

> I recall the argument I had at the outset of the war with the members of HaShomer haTza'ir [a Marxist-Zionist movement] —

---

2   *Diary*, September 11, 1940, BGIA #30; Weizmann to Ben-Gurion, September 9, 1940, in Weizmann, *Letters and Papers*, vol. 20, ed. Michael J. Cohen (Jerusalem, 1979), p. 38; Ben-Gurion to Weizmann, September 9, 1940, *Diary*, BGIA #30; C. Weizmann to Vera Weizmann, September 23, 1940, Weizmann, *Letters and Papers*, vol. 20, p. 45.

3   Ben-Gurion to Paula, September 8, 1940, *Diary*, BGIA #30; this is also the source of the next quote.

we have some Shomer HaTza'irniks in our party, too — who tried to prove to me that present-day England meant Chamberlain. They wagged their heads in pity at my "thickheadedness" when I spoke of public opinion in England. According to the "Marxist" theology of HaShomer haTza'ir there is no such thing as unshackled public opinion outside of Soviet Russia... and because they are unable to read the book of life, rich in mutation and change — they chant mummified sentences from rotting tomes. But democratic England, in her hour of need, demonstrated the tremendous power of her "public opinion," and though the Chamberlain government had a large parliamentary majority, it collapsed like a pack of cards in a breeze... . This redemptive change — which I do believe can free mankind, can save it from the leprosy of Nazism — was possible only because England had a democratic regime, which is to say, a free regime. The Labour party has rendered England and the world an incalculable service in effecting this change while there was yet time.[4]

During his last months there, this deep-seated and augmented faith in the power of public opinion to sway governmental policy underlay all Ben-Gurion's efforts from London to rouse American Jewry. At the outset of his British trip he refrained from so doing, most likely because of Weizmann's imminent journey. But one week into his stay in England, Ben-Gurion, who felt himself far more grounded in the American reality than did the head of the World Zionist Organization, wrote disparagingly of Weizmann's having "'rediscovered' America — Jewish power and the great Zionist potential of American Jewry." In any event, Ben-Gurion summed up his qualified assessment for cooperation: "As regards the American agenda for action — we are almost in total agreement... . If his wish [for prolonged activity in America] stays constant throughout the year, and if his current plan is carried through — then his trip will surely be of great use."

Ben-Gurion's internal memoranda shows how set he was in his American orientation from the start of his Whitehall contacts. Following a disappointing meeting with Weizmann and Lloyd in mid-May, the Yishuv leader wrote four pages of "Additional Notes on the

4   Ben-Gurion to Paula, May 7, 1940, *Diary*, BGIA #30.

Current Situation," which included the following special paragraph: "It must be made clear to the British government and, so far as possible under war conditions, to British public opinion, that the Jews, mainly in Palestine and in America, are not to be taken for granted; that we constitute an independent, though perhaps not very important, factor; and that if our cooperation and help is valued and required, that cooperation cannot be one-sided only." The next paragraph called for resistance: "We must react in Palestine and in America to any infringement of our rights or interests."

After one month of Churchill's premiership, Ben-Gurion wrote Eliezer Kaplan, then in the United States: "In my opinion there is a need for pressure from America. You must meet the British ambassador. The time is now! A demand issuing from Washington now... will have decisive value." After a short while he sent a cable, stating "no progress on central issue [Jewish army] because firm opposition Egyptian [the Zionists' code-word for Lord Lloyd]. Without your maximum help see no prospect rapid success."[5]

During the ZOA conference in Pittsburgh at the close of June 1940, David Ben-Gurion sent a 1,600-word cable calling on American Jewry to perform two tasks: employ all its strength to see that the Yishuv could defend itself militarily and prepare the Jewish youth of America for war. Ben-Gurion was thinking of American Jewry's political responsibility as well as its military potential when he wrote at the end of this message: "European Jewry for time being practically ceased exist and apart from Palestine hope our people rests mainly on American Jewry. Am confident that under Zionist guidance Jews of America will again rise to height their responsibilities."[6]

In the latter half of August Ben-Gurion decided to return to Palestine via the United States for several reasons: his failure to promote a Jewish army, his lack of faith in Weizmann's ability to stand up to the British in negotiations, Weizmann's recurrent deferrals of his trip to the United

5   Ben-Gurion memorandum, April 17, 1940, "Additional Notes on the Present Situation," BGIA #73; Ben-Gurion to Eliezer Kaplan (cable), June 26, 1940, BGIA #73.

6   Ben-Gurion to the president of the Pittsburgh Zionist conference, June 28, 1940, BGIA #73.

States (he arrived there only at the beginning of March 1941), and his plan to lay the groundwork for raising a Jewish force in America.[7]

At Ben-Gurion's final meeting with Lord Lloyd a bitter exchange ensued over the issues of Yishuv defense and the Jewish army. When the chairman of the Jewish Agency Executive raised the danger of a German invasion or the infiltration of the German Officers Corps into the Near East, Lloyd reacted: "Oh, I have an agreement with Dr. Weizmann. In Palestine itself you will have 'parity' — though he [Weizmann] does not like it." Ben-Gurion's opposition on this score and his concerns over the Jewish army did not elicit any substantial response; on the second issue Lloyd was clearly coordinating his efforts with the then-war secretary and confirmed anti-Zionist Anthony Eden. Proving more rigid than Chaim Weizmann, Ben-Gurion informed Lloyd that in leaving for America he was continuing their argument. While he would inform the American public sympathetically of Britain's war posture, he also intended to find out how American Jewry — this, of course, in the face of Lloyd's opposition — could contribute to the establishment of a Jewish army.[8]

Ben-Gurion's American journey had significance extending beyond the aforementioned reasons: he was launching an overall effort to broaden Zionism's base through realizing the political potential of American Jewry. The Yishuv leader did not state this purpose explicitly, but it emerges from the letter spelling out the reasons for his trip and particularly from his description of his clashes with Lloyd. The political dimension stood out, for example, in his emphasis on the role of America's expanding aid to Britain. Perhaps it was Ben-Gurion's embarkation for America on September 22, leaving behind a vacillating Chaim Weizmann, that signaled the start of a historic process destined to change the top leadership of the Zionist movement.[9]

7   Ben-Gurion to Paula, August 21, 1940, *Diary*, BGIA #30.
8   In the late 1920s and early 1930s the Zionist movement proposed parity between the two nations in Palestine — i.e., that neither would rule or be ruled by the other in the autonomous institutions of the country. For a description of this plan, see Ben Halpern, *The Idea of the Jewish State* (Cambridge, Mass., 1969), pp. 340–343; memorandum of Ben-Gurion, "Note on Interview with Lord Lloyd, Colonial Office," London, August 26, 1940, CZA Z 4/14606.
9   Ben-Gurion to Paula, August 21, 1940, *Diary*, BGIA #30. This is the source for the ensuing discussion.

The timing of Ben-Gurion's departure hints at the trip's political aspect. He reached his decision during the week of August 15 to 21, after concluding that the war had taken a decisive turn. Contrary to Hitler's pronouncements, the Führer had not succeeded in bringing Britain to its knees; rather, he had suffered his first great setback. The Yishuv leader's decision also fell on the day following a rousing speech by Churchill that expressed for Ben-Gurion "the victory of courage, self-confidence and the brave liberty of a free nation that seeks to remain free at all costs." These external circumstances and personal proclivities undoubtedly encouraged Ben-Gurion to promote a more independent Zionist policy.

The negotiations conducted by Weizmann in June 1940 with Brendan Bracken, then Churchill's parliamentary private secretary (and minister of information in his government from 1941 to 1945), highlight the differing approaches of Ben-Gurion and Weizmann to the British leadership. At the outset of the month Bracken telephoned Weizmann on Churchill's behalf, asking the Jewish statesman to leave as soon as possible for the United States and to use all the influence at his command to promote full American Jewish support for U.S. aid to the Allies in the war effort. Weizmann's reply, orally and in writing, was, "Such a request, at such a time, is equivalent to a command." In his letter to Bracken, Weizmann added that in order for his labor to yield results in the United States, he had to arrive there having effected changes in British policy. (He called for the use of Palestine as a supply base for the war effort and for the establishment of Jewish military units.) In consequence, the president of the World Zionist Organization remained in London for almost a year following those contacts with Churchill's circle, attempting to make Zionist inroads. In his efforts to activate American Jewry from England, he focused on the economic sphere. Once in America, Weizmann adhered strictly to Bracken's guidelines.[10]

Ben-Gurion took quite a different, even an opposite, tack. Seeing that

---

10   Weizmann to B. Bracken, June 11, 1940, in Weizmann, *Letters and Papers*, vol. 19, p. 287. It would seem that Weizmann's political frustrations, rather than spurring him to a rethinking of his position, drove him to more intensive chemical research for the war effort; see Weizmann, *Trial and Error*, pp. 422–425; see also Weizmann's remarks at the close of his visit to the United States, Special Meeting, July 17th 1941, Astor Hotel (Final Conference Preceding Dr. Weizmann's Departure for London), WA.

Whitehall offered no response to crucial Zionist demands, he decided to leave for the United States to gauge the strength of those forces that could exert pressure from afar on the Mandatary.

One must bear in mind international realities to appreciate what united Ben-Gurion and Weizmann at that time — a basic leaning toward Britain — and what divided them. The United States still held resolutely to its neutrality, declared after the outbreak of the war, and aided the Allies only slightly and cautiously. In addition, very few voices in the United States could be heard calling for American involvement. One observer likened the political climate in the country at the outset of the winter of 1940 with that which had prevailed in pre-Munich England. Effectively and consistently the State Department cast a blind eye on the Zionist movement's struggle against Britain. President Roosevelt was not prepared to swerve from this line, as Weizmann had learned in his meeting with the president. All these considerations compelled Weizmann and Ben-Gurion to view Britain as their safest ally. However, as has been said, the Jewish Agency Executive chairman did not bind himself to Whitehall. Even as he inclined toward Britain he began to sow the seeds of independent Zionist political action within American Jewry.[11]

On September 9, while Ben-Gurion was in London awaiting travel arrangements to the United States, Italian planes bombed Tel Aviv, killing more than 100 persons. London, when bombed, answered vigorously with cannon fire and air attacks; but now its largest circulating English paper, the *Times*, Ben-Gurion pointed out in anger and distress, disregarded the fact that Tel Aviv and the victims were all Jewish. The Yishuv leader's frame of mind was mirrored more succinctly in a memorandum entitled "Our War Program," written in the aftermath of the bombing. The memo contained a proposal for the "authorization of the Jewish Agency for the purpose of enlisting Jewish Air Squadrons in neutral countries, especially in America." A special section suggested that, together with the establishment of a Jewish army, an unofficial body would be set up in America, "which, without

---

11   Phillip J. Baram, *The Department of State in the Middle East, 1919–1945* (Philadelphia, 1978), pp. 245–269; Manuel, *Realities of American-Palestine Relations*, pp. 305–309.

infringing the neutrality laws, should seek out some practical methods of mobilizing Jewish youth in the Americas, and/or organizing large-scale military training for all services, but especially for the Air Force."[12]

The months May to September, marked by agreements and disagreements between Ben-Gurion and Weizmann, were not particularly placid for America's Zionists either; many confrontations and battles took place in the ZOA and the Emergency Committee, some with far-reaching effects.

Brandeis remained firm in his support of Solomon Goldman for leadership of the organization. In a letter sent to Robert Szold in April 1940 the retired justice even offered to provide financial support for Goldman in the approaching contest for the ZOA presidency, observing that he knew "no one who would be [more] competent and willing to clean out the Lipsky gang and to worthily represent American Zionism." During this same period Brandeis groomed Rabbi Isadore Breslau, the ZOA's executive director. After Solomon Goldman gave his final refusal to stand for the presidency of the ZOA a third time, the Brandeis circle supported the candidacy of Edmund Kaufmann, a Washington businessman loyal to them. On Kaufmann's election to the presidency in early July, Brandeis cables Robert Szold in his laconic style: "Congratulations to you, Goldman, Kaufmann. Now take a good rest." In fact, the "chief" did not allow his followers a prolonged vacation. Less than a week after this cable Brandeis informed Szold of his concern over the make-up of the Emergency Committee, which was "much worse" than he had previously thought. He assigned Szold to ensure the appointment of five suitable men to all the slots open on the committee. "And should not our nominees be," he asked rhetorically, "of the young men who fought resolutely against the Lipsky-Wise contingent?" He went on to demand that not one of the Lipsky group be drawn into the ZOA's top echelon.[13]

The intermediary between Brandeis and those "young fighters" was,

---

12   *Diary*, May 12, 1940, BGIA, #30; Ben-Gurion memorandum, "Our War Program," September 12, 1940, London, section 7/3, 8/2, BGIA #73.

13   Brandeis to R. Szold. December 7. 1939, April 10. 1940, and July 17. 1940, in Brandeis, *Letters*, vol. 5, pp. 632–633, 644–645, 683; Brandeis to R. Szold (cable), July 2, 1940, in ibid., pp. 643–644.

as hinted, Robert Szold. Szold recalls 1940 as the most significant year in the crystallization of a new, aggressive group within the ZOA:

> I think we [Robert Szold and Ben-Gurion] saw eye to eye in 1939 at the London conference. I know... in 1940, when things were getting more critical and it was important for the Zionists in America to take a stand, the group around Solomon Goldman, which was a maximum position and against Weizmann's trust in Great Britain — that group played a big influence in the forties. There was [Maurice] Boukstein, there was [Leo] Guzik, [Irving] Lipkowitz, they were powerful in stiffening the American organization... that [the influence of Ben-Gurion's position] was *selbst verstandlich* [self-understood].[14]

The first of these younger men mentioned by Szold, Maurice Boukstein, states in his memoirs:

> At the close of 1939 and the outset of 1940 we began organizing in preparation for the annual ZOA conference in Pittsburgh in June of 1940. As a matter of fact, we began organizing in Baltimore in 1939. Our goal was to change the ZOA's regime, and that for a number of reasons: (1) We were a group of youngsters, the "oldsters" among us comprising Robert Szold, Louis Rocker, Louis E. Levinthal and Jimmy Heller. We were in our thirties then and they were forty-five to fifty, but every one of those "oldsters" had occupied an important post in the Zionist organization. We felt that the Zionist administration in America was not active enough, lacked all political direction, had not penetrated the community and was poorly organized.... By the way, Ben-Gurion knew of this, we had written him, and he encouraged us because he knew that Brandeis stood behind us, and that was indeed the case. The Brandeis group tried to take charge so we conferred with the "old man" [Brandeis] on everything we did. After the Pittsburgh conference I took the "young Turks" to Brandeis's house and presented them.[15]

After taking the presidency of the ZOA, Brandeis's young followers

---

14   R. Szold, interviewed by Y. Donyets, New York, March 21, 1977, BGIA.
15   M. Boukstein, interviewed by Y. Donyets, New York, March 21, 1937, BGIA.

displayed a zeal that rivaled their mentor's. In a systematic purge, trampling the objections of Lipsky, they reshaped the ZOA Executive Committee and replaced the editor of the movement's journal, *New Palestine*. These changes met with the opposition of Stephen Wise, who, standing above the contending factions, could still serve as a mediator at times.[16]

The aforementioned clashes had significant ramifications for the tug-of-war within the World Zionist Organization. The Lipsky-Wise group, it will be recalled, was pro-Weizmann, whereas the "young Turks" looked askance at Weizmann and mistrusted his lieutenants. Throughout 1940 the young Brandeisians, chilly to the idea of Weizmann's anticipated visit to the United States, contributed to his reservations and the trip's deferment. The appointment of Meyer Weisgal as Weizmann's semi-official representative in the United States stirred criticism of Weizmann within the ZOA beyond pro-Brandeis circles. When Eliezer Kaplan, a moderate Mapai leader and a consistent supporter of Weizmann's policies, reached America during the summer on an economic mission, he was tendered an angry reception by the Brandeisians, the more so for what they considered his meddling in internal American affairs.

In a letter to Robert Szold, Brandeis expressed his displeasure with Kaplan's involvement. When informed later of Kaplan's pending departure, he observed with satisfaction: "It is fortunate that he is leaving us." It is not clear whether Brandeis's followers were actively engaged at this period in bolstering Ben-Gurion's position in the World Zionist Organization in opposition to Weizmann. However, in practical terms, some of the most prominent among them (Brandeis himself, Solomon Goldman, Robert Szold), including the younger element (such as Maurice Boukstein), forged very warm relations with Ben-Gurion, thereby fostering increased respect for the Palestinian leader and greater receptivity to his ideas within American Zionist circles.[17]

16   R. Szold to Brandeis, August 21, 1940, ZAL, Szold Collection, IX/29; minutes of meeting of ZOA Executive, August 15, 1940, CZA A 243/34; S. Wise to E. Kaufmann, August 21, 1940, CZA A 243/136; S. Wise to B. Brickner, August 30, 1940, CZA A 243/34.

17   Brandeis to R. Szold, December 7, 1939, and April 10, 1940, in Brandeis, *Letters*, vol. 5, pp. 633, 639; Albert K. Epstein to Weizmann, June 17, 1940, WA; Brandeis to R. Szold, July 5 and 17, in Brandeis, *Letters*, vol. 5, pp. 644–645.

The tensions that gripped the ZOA that summer were as much personal as political or ideological. Although Solomon Goldman generally stood for militance and greater public involvement than the Lipsky group, he did not choose to voice his policies on the pages of *New Palestine* or at the ZOA convention. Brandeis claimed that the Zionism of his supporters was broader and more educative than that of their rivals. That was true insofar as Solomon Goldman was concerned, but Brandeis's claim was never raised in open debate. Moreover, the Zionism of Edmund Kaufmann, another Brandeis loyalist and Solomon Goldman's successor, was shallow.[18]

The debates that racked the ZOA in the summer preceding Ben-Gurion's arrival in America were grounded in no small measure in past rivalries, differences of cultural background and social rank, and personal animosities. Of course there was an undeniably political dimension to ZOA infighting. The Brandeisians, and especially the younger element among them, tended to emphasize the significance of American Jewry and its new responsibilities. They saw little value in continuing Zionism's historic partnership with Britain and looked with a jaundiced eye on the London Zionist establishment. As they grew ever more convinced of the correctness of their position, they drew away from Stephen Wise and his leadership.

As I indicated, in the summer of 1940 Stephen Wise, who stood far above his colleagues in the American Zionist movement, began to act as an ally of Chaim Weizmann. This tendency grew stronger as the year progressed. The more the dimensions of the Jewish tragedy in Europe became known, the greater became Wise's commitment to embattled England, as was evident in his organ, *Opinion*. In the Jewish New Year issue of October 1940, the month of Ben-Gurion's arrival in the United States, he published a systematic and summary article, linking the awesome blows raining down on one European Jewish community after another with the heroic resistance of England, defender of the Judeo-Christian heritage and the democratic Anglo-Saxon tradition.

---

18 Edmund Kaufmann to S. Wise and R. Szold, May 17, 1940, CZA A 243/136. On S. Goldman, see Jacob J. Weinstein, *Solomon Goldman: A Rabbi's Rabbi* (New York, 1973). E. Kaufmann, a businessman, straightforwardly declared, before assuming office, that he intended to fulfill his duties strictly as an administrator (E. Kaufmann to S. Wise and R. Szold, May 17, 1940, CZA A 243/136).

Concluding that "America must give the fullest moral, material, political support to England," he went on to assert:

> For once I would have my fellow Jews be more American than America; more democratic than democracy; as sacrificial on behalf of the victory of England as Englishmen themselves. I am ready to lay down the principle as a way of life for Jews everywhere that there is nothing that England needs which Jews should withhold. Our readiness to give can only be measured by England's need. The time has come to put aside all irrelevant and trivial questions, to forget everything save that England shall not perish, and that if England perish, the light of life itself may be extinguished for generations.[19]

Given this orientation, Wise held that the creation of a Jewish army was not vital. Of greater importance was the actual Jewish military contribution, in whatever form, to Britain's struggle, the struggle of all mankind. He agreed that the Yishuv had the right to defend itself and be incorporated within the British forces separately, but he did not press the issue as a particular Jewish interest nor did he view the scheme as a fulcrum for the attainment of Jewish sovereignty. The goal of victory over Nazism, he wrote at the end of his programmatic piece, was the flowering of freedom, the restoration of human dignity, and the holiness of human life. "What greater glory, what holier benediction," he concluded, "could the new year hold?"[20]

As noted, in the winter of 1939–1940 Abba Hillel Silver tried to shake loose the image of moderate that had adhered to him following his appearance at the Twenty-First Zionist Congress. In June 1940 he moved further into activism in asking President Roosevelt to set aside a segment of the monies for war refugees that were allocated by Congress to aid Jews fleeing Europe for Palestine. After one and a half months he got a reply directing him to the American Red Cross. (It will be recalled that during this period America's gates were all but closed to immigrants from countries that had fallen beneath Nazi rule.) In the meantime there had been the Italian bombing of Haifa (July 24) and then of Tel Aviv

---

19   *Opinion* 10, no. 12 (October 1940): 10–12 (quotation is on p. 12).
20   Ibid.

(September 9). Unlike Wise, Silver viewed these events above all as *Jewish* tragedies and reacted by calling for a strengthening of both the Yishuv and world Jewry. He and Henry Montor began to exert formidable pressure on the American Red Cross to free monies for Jewish refugees and the victims of the bombings. On September 23, on the basis of a telephone conversation with Norman H. Davis, head of the American Red Cross, Silver felt so confident of receiving a sizable sum from that organization that he shared the good news with others. He was in for a rude surprise, however.[21]

On September 27 Davis and his lieutenant, Ernst Swift, met with Edmund Kaufmann, Rabbi Isadore Breslau, and Henry Montor in Washington. To the consternation of his listeners, Davis announced that the State Department had intervened, warning him against giving any preferential aid to the Jews (in the Haifa bombing, Arabs, too, had been wounded). The Zionist leaders, representing the victims of Nazi-Fascist atrocities, suddenly found themselves on the defensive. The State Department did not stop at that, however. The American consul in Jerusalem, George Wadsworth, coordinating his effort with the Mandatory governor, informed the American Red Cross that after having made detailed inquiries he had concluded that there was no need for aid of any kind. Swift conveyed this news to Henry Montor on October 2. On October 7 Silver informed the Emergency Committee of these disheartening developments. The next day at noon Breslau and Montor again went to Washington to meet with Davis and Swift.[22]

21 Minutes of the meeting of the Emergency Committee, August 6, 1940, ZAL. Even the meager and discriminatory quota allowed by U.S. immigration laws had not been filled (Feingold, *The Politics of Rescue*, pp. 126–166); cable of A. H. Silver to the Jewish Agency Executive, September 9, 1940, TA, UPA 10–3–17. For a discussion of Silver's role at this juncture and later, cf. Monty N. Penkower, "Ben-Gurion, Silver and the 1941 UPA National Conference for Palestine: A Turning Point in American Zionist History," *American Jewish History* 69, no. 1 (September 1979): 73–76. See also minutes of the meeting of the Emergency Committee, September 18, 1940, ZAL; A. H. Silver to Israel Goldstein, September 23, 1940, TA, UPA 10–3–15.
22 Memo of Henry Montor, September 27, 1940, ZAL, Szold Collection IX/29; memorandum of H. Montor, October 2, 1940, ibid.; memorandum of H. Montor, October 8, 1940, TA 10–3–4. On the American consul in Jerusalem and the State Department see the comments of the knowledgeable Eliahu Elath, *The Struggle for Statehood* [haMa'avak al haMedinah], vol. 1 (Tel Aviv, 1979), pp. 32–43; Baram, *The Department of State*, pp. 245–275; this is the source for the ensuing discussion.

At this point the two American officials openly avowed the growing delaying tactics of the State Department. The Zionist representatives now understood that the Red Cross spokesmen had been sincere in their efforts and that it was indeed the State Department that was creating obstacles. Consequently, Breslau and Montor met that very afternoon with officials of the department's Division of Near Eastern Affairs. These officials, headed by Wallace Murray, laid out their motives cynically, in bald disregard of the fate of the Jewish victims: they were determined not to stir up the least bit of Arab ill will against Britain or the United States. Silver, who had orchestrated the Zionist effort for the refugees and the air-raid casualties and had been kept informed of all developments by Montor, met with a stone wall of hostility and indifference. On the evening of that same day, October 8, he sat down to a historic meeting with David Ben-Gurion, who had just arrived in America. Before this meeting is discussed, however, two other aspects of Silver's public activity should be considered.

Most of Silver's life and communal activity since 1917 had passed in Cleveland, Ohio, a stronghold of Republicanism and isolationism in America. There his independent political course gradually developed. In 1932 and 1936 Silver had voted for Roosevelt, supporting his New Deal and, of course, the president's wish to involve the United States in the international conflict. Nonetheless, in the elections of 1940 Silver endorsed Wendell Willkie. The Zionist leader's basic opposition to a third term for Roosevelt explains his behavior only partially. He supported the Republican candidate in order to forward Zionist interests by intensifying Democratic-Republican competition for the Jewish vote (this was his rationale for the same tactic in the election of 1944). Isaiah L. Kenen, editor of the political section of the *Cleveland News* from 1926 to 1943 and the holder of several responsible Zionist posts in the years following, analyzed Silver's election behavior:

> [Silver identified] with the Republican Party, a posture he adopted in 1940, when a group of us met in Silver's home and he decided to support the Republican candidate for president because he felt that Rabbi Stephen S. Wise, a veteran Democrat, was delivering American Jewry to President Roosevelt, undermining the bargaining power of the Jewish community... .
> We sat in Silver's lovely home in Bratenahl, an extremely wealthy

enclave in the city of Cleveland inhabited by the ultra-rich, including the famous Mather family. An active Jewish leader in the Cleveland Republican organization, James L. E. Jaffe, invited a group of us to meet with Silver in his home. He strongly argued that Jews should support the liberal Republican candidate, Wendell Willkie, a candidate for the Republican nomination for the presidency, who won it away from Robert A. Taft of Cincinnati. I do not remember any of the dialogue that night, but Silver made it quite clear that he intended to become involved as a Republican.[23]

It is difficult to determine whether Silver had decided on this tactic following the State Department's bald coercion of the Red Cross or prior thereto; it is probable that both processes took place during the same months. In August 1940 Silver came out for Willkie. Prominent ads published Silver's support for the Republican candidate, with long quotes of the latter's commitment to safeguard the world's democracies and the future of the Jewish people. Silver's initiative constituted a new tack for American Zionism and an approach more dynamic and independent than that of Stephen Wise, "Roosevelt's man."[24]

Yet another context can explain Silver's radicalization. As chairman of the United Palestine Fund, a post he held from 1938 to 1943, he had become very aware of the Yishuv's economic and political potential. Despite the economic hardships of the years of the Arab rebellion, Palestinian Jewry had emerged stronger, riper for independence, and brimming with confidence. One can assume that Silver, more than other American Zionist leaders, was influenced by this new Palestinian reality

---

23 Raphael, *Silver*, pp. 109ff. Zvi Ganin, *Truman, American Jewry, and Israel, 1945–1948* (New York, 1979); James T. Patterson, *Mr. Republican: A Biography of Robert A. Taft* (Boston, 1972), pp. 280–283; I. L. Kenen to the author, July 14 and 23, 1980.

24 After Roosevelt's electoral victory Silver noted with satisfaction that America's global pro-British policy would continue and expressed confidence that such would also have been the case had Willkie won. See his Sunday sermon, "After the Election — What?" November 14, 1940, TA. In its preelection issue, *New Palestine* devoted a full page to an editorial titled "As Dr. Wise Sees the Election," containing excerpts from Wise's article in the November issue of *Opinion*, calling on readers to vote for Roosevelt (*New Palestine* 31, no. 3 [November 1, 1940]:20).

and came to hold the Yishuv and its acknowledged leader, David Ben-Gurion, in high regard.[25]

In the spring of 1940 Emanuel Neumann made a major effort to convert his political calling card into a ticket of entry to the American Zionist leadership. In a twelve-page memorandum reviewing his political and business activities in Palestine, he emphasized his membership in Group B of the Palestinian General Zionists and his adherence to that group's line. The document was originally intended for Brandeis, but copies were sent to several other Zionist leaders. At this time Neumann, in everything he undertook, scrupulously consulted persons whom he took to be members of the Brandeis circle. At the Pittsburgh conference of the ZOA he was elected to the Executive Committee with the backing of the Szold-Kaufmann group. At the deliberations of the Executive Committee he supported the Washington-based Rabbi Breslau's efforts to influence the formation of American foreign policy — efforts that won no serious backing from the Emergency Committee and met with no success. At the close of July 1940 Neumann sent a letter to Silver, with whom he enjoyed an intimate working relationship, laying out his positions and detailing his connections with his colleagues. In this letter he stated his intention to write a book titled *Integral Zionism* to educate American Zionists politically. In this same letter he bitterly complained about the efforts of Nahum Goldmann to deny him any base of power in the ZOA.[26]

Goldmann occupied a very different position than Neumann in the spectrum of the ZOA. He had first come to the United States in 1931 at the invitation of Stephen Wise to lay the groundwork for the World Jewish Congress, and since that time, while living in Europe, he had

25   For the historical context, see Slutsky, *Haganah History*, vol. 2, pp. 1073–1080, and vol. 3, pp. 7–543; Elhannan Orren, *Settlement amid Struggles: The Pre-State Strategy of Settlement, 1936–1947* [Hityashvut biShnot Ma'avak: Istrategiah Yishuvit beTerem Medinah, 1936–1947] (Jerusalem, 1978), chaps. 2 and 3; Dan Horowitz and Moshe Lissak, *The Origins of the Israeli Polity: Palestine under the Mandate* (Chicago, 1978), chap. 3. See also discussion of this point in introduction and chapter 1, above. This suggestion is strengthened by Rabbi Feuer's letter to the author of July 3, 1980.
26   "Justice, Mr. Louis D. Brandeis," memorandum of E. Neumann [March 1940] CZA S 25/1874; minutes of the meeting of the ZOA Executive Committee, August 22, 1940, CZA A 243/34; E. Neumann to A. H. Silver, July 30, 1940, TA UPA 10–3026.

enjoyed the closest ideological and personal relationship with Wise. From 1935 on he served as a member of the Zionist Executive, although his primary base was the World Jewish Congress. Returning to the United States in June 1940, he joined the second rank of Zionist leadership, sitting in on the meetings of the Emergency Committee as the representative of the World Zionist Organization. Although in preceding years he, like Stephen Wise, had favored the democratization of Jewish life and believed in an informed and assertive public, under the conditions of wartime America he changed tack. Again like Wise, he channeled most of his energies into diplomatic activity.[27]

In his memoirs Goldmann clarifies his approach. The application of Zionist pressure on the molders of American policy was legitimate, he held, in the framework of American politics. But "diplomatic officials abroad," he explained, "do not like to have their plans disrupted by domestic considerations, by protests and delegations or by intervention on the part of political parties or even the White House. This makes them resentful and bitter." Goldmann concluded that "in exerting political pressure at home, one must always be cautious and tactful or risk incurring the hostility of influential diplomatic figures."

Having come to doubt the efficacy of public pressure, Goldmann went one step further and suggested that American Jews avoid as much as possible any engagement of the president or the secretary of state in negotiations: "In practice the [foreign policy] decision is often actually made by the man who writes the reports, assembles the data, and submits the proposals [rather than the aforementioned officials]." For this reason, Goldmann explained, he took pains to cultivate pleasant and even friendly relations with State Department personnel.

In all his efforts in Washington, Nahum Goldmann acted in the spirit described and in full cooperation with Stephen Wise. The Wise-Goldmann modus operandi revealed itself in their reaction to the State

---

27 Nahum Goldmann, *The Autobiography of Nahum Goldmann: Sixty Years of Jewish Life* (New York, 1969) pp. 122–123, 188–189, 206–207; this is the source for the ensuing discussion. After Goldmann had spent several months participating in the meetings of the Emergency Committee, his position was summed up as follows: "As a member of the [Jewish Agency] Executive [he] was in that capacity cooperating with the [Emergency] Committee in all political matters" (minutes of the meeting of the Emergency Committee, October 29, 1940, ZAL).

Department dictate to the American Red Cross. In a detailed memorandum Wise told Henry Montor that the exclusion of Jews from the State Department was repugnant and intolerable and had to be fought resolutely. The war proposed by Wise, however, involved no public outcry or mounting of barricades — quite the opposite: through sophisticated diplomatic efforts the Zionists were to infiltrate an able Jew, loyal to the cause, into the State Department, thereby providing a counterbalance to Wallace Murray, a foe of the movement. At the October 10 meeting of the Emergency Committee, Wise formally proposed this plan as the American Zionist response to the anti-Zionist and antihumanitarian policies of the State Department.[28]

In sum, the year 1940 ushered in several significant developments and changes within the ZOA. Robert Szold, the "young Turks," Solomon Goldman — groups and individuals whose names were linked with Louis Brandeis (with the exception perhaps of Edmund Kaufmann) — all tended to emphasize the significance of American Jewry and its beckoning political role. Neumann was vocal on this score, and toward the end of the year Silver began to adopt a similar tone. Stephen Wise, still the uncontested leader of American Zionists, continued to target Britain as the source of the movement's aid and the address for all Zionist grievances. Nahum Goldmann, who articulated the Zionist political consensus, identified in effect with Wise's position. All in all, one cannot speak of the existence in 1940 of two clearly defined political camps within the ZOA. Factors other than political, such as personal rivalries, cut across the various groupings. Intense animosity obtained between Solomon Goldman and Silver, two of the most prominent figures in the emerging activist wing of the organization. On the other hand, one cannot view the internal situation of the ZOA as an illogical muddle. Indeed, there existed some currents of political thought linked to various groups and positions held in the world Zionist movement.[29]

---

28   Goldmann, *Autobiography*, pp. 204–205; editor's comment in Brandeis, *Letters*, vol. 5, p. 644 (this topic has yet to be researched); S. Wise to H. Montor, October 10, 1940, TA, UPA 10-3-4; minutes of the meeting of the Emergency Committee, October 10, 1940 ZAL.

29   I. L. Kenen to the author, July 14, 1980; R. Szold, interviewed by Y. Donyets, New York, February 23, 1977, BGIA.

While the ZOA found itself in the ferment of preparation for fresh and innovative activity, America's tiny Revisionist camp was marking time. Jabotinsky's presence in the United States from mid-March until his death in August 1940 did nothing to breathe life into the movement. During his brief "American period" the Revisionist leader was steeped in a depression whose roots ran deeper than the trauma of estrangement from his wife, who had remained in London. Jabotinsky's malaise seemed to stem from his distance from the Jews and politics of Europe.[30]

Jabotinsky, it will be recalled, had intended his American journey to persuade Britain, through appropriate diplomatic contacts, to raise a Jewish army. He had no clear perception of the growing potential of American Jewry to influence international affairs; consequently, his proposals during his public appearances differed in no meaningful way from those prevalent in official American Zionist circles. *New Palestine*, surprised at this phenomenon, politely asked Jabotinsky what justified the separate existence of his New Zionist Organization. The journal's first strong critique of the Revisionist leader came in June, with a protest over his movement's claims for a greater share of Mandatory immigration permits. Shortly thereafter, *New Palestine* took Jabotinsky to task for propagandizing for a Jewish army in a way that suggested inviting American Jewish enlistment in contravention of American law.[31]

On August 4, following his disregard of medical advice, Jabotinsky died of a heart attack. His early demise (he was not yet 60) was a tragic postscript to a remark he had made to Berl Katznelson in the autumn of 1939 after the outbreak of the war: "You have won. You have America, a rich Jewry. I had only impoverished Poland. I have lost the game." Egotism and simplistic sociology aside, this brief observation couched a profound truth. Jabotinsky had indeed "played" only in Europe; he was unable to translate his fears for his people's future into a political agenda

---

30   Benjamin Akzin, interviewed by Sandy Koros and David Shpiro, Jerusalem, December 15, 1977, BGIA; Schechtman, *Jabotinsky*, vol. 2, pp. 394–395; Shmuel Katz, *Days of Fire* [Yom haEsh] (Tel Aviv, 1966), pp. 119–124 (the revised English version [New York, 1986] ignores Jabotinsky's depression); Hillel Kook, interview with the author, Kfar Shemaryahu, November 11, 1982.
31   *New Palestine* 30, no. 12 (March 22, 1940):4; no. 14 (April 5, 1940):1.

in a nation far removed from the European theater, a nation in which he felt lost from the outset.[32]

On October 3 Ben-Gurion arrived in the United States on a visit that was to last three and a half months. Through November 5 his tactics were dictated by the American presidential elections. He followed with deep concern the tight race between Roosevelt and Willkie, viewing the latter's camp as a hotbed of isolationism and reaction. Although his judgment might have been exaggerated, it is a fact that the American public was in anything but a saber-rattling mood. Roosevelt was taking pains to avoid any mention of American involvement in the hostilities; indeed the exigencies of the election campaign precluded any action in that direction. Ben-Gurion viewed the presidential contest as a fundamental clash of values, part of a world-wide struggle, and a far cry from the contest of 1916 between Woodrow Wilson and Charles Hughes, which was devoid of any such combat. Fearful of hurting Roosevelt's chances for victory, Ben-Gurion kept a tight lid on his plan for American involvement in raising a Jewish army, and he was confirmed in this judgment by Brandeis, Frankfurter, and Ben Cohen. He devoted most of his time in the preelection period to acquainting himself with the country's mood and its young Jewry, Zionist groups especially.[33]

What was the condition of American Zionism on Ben-Gurion's arrival? One historian cites 1940 as a nadir for the movement, characterizing the Emergency Committee's Zionist deliberations as "stagnation and disintegration." The rise of anti-Semitism in the United States precisely after the outbreak of war, the research suggests, led to a

32   Schechtman, *Jabotinsky*, vol. 2. pp. 394–398; minutes of the meeting of the Mapai Central Committee, September 21, 1939, BGIA. At the close of 1941 Irgun Zvai Leumi activists in the United States, not the Revisionists, set up the Committee for a Hebrew Army. For the perfurmance of this particular group headed by Hillel Kook see Ganin, *Truman, American Jewry, and Israel*, pp. 5–6 and passim.

33   On October 6, 1940, Ben-Gurion stated with confidence that Roosevelt would be reelected (*Diary*, October 4, 1940, BGIA #30). However, shortly thereafter he learned of Frankfurter's great concern that Willkie might win (*Diary*, October 15, 1940, BGIA #30); quotation and thereafter derived from *Diary*, October 15 and November 9, 1940, BGIA #30.

reticence on the part of American Jewry and a new low in Zionist activity. For one thing, ZOA membership in 1940 did not exceed that of the preceding year. The Zionist scene in America, however, was more complex than met the eye; it was decidedly not static.[34]

On his very first day in the United States Ben-Gurion sat with the Poalei Zion leadership. "They held unanimously," he recorded in his diary, "that there was no hope of raising a Jewish army from among American Jewish youth. They are wallowing in personal problems, afraid of what the non-Jews will say. I am not yet prepared to accept this devastating verdict." The next day he met with Yeḥezkel Sacharoff (Sahar), who was on an arms mission to the United States. He, too, assessed the situation bleakly. Yet Ben-Gurion wrote in his diary following the meeting: "Somehow I am unconvinced by all this pessimism." As was his practice, he sought out younger, emerging forces within the Zionist movement. About one week after his arrival in the United States he began to hear what he was after. One of the leaders of Junior Hadassah, he wrote, was "more optimistic regarding the youth. She believes that young people will respond if called upon. She has committed herself to action." Two days later he met with representatives of various Zionist youth movements. "Their reaction was better than that predicted by our colleagues," observed Ben-Gurion. "They are ready to volunteer... . They willingly accepted the idea of aerial training... . Some of them expressed willingness to volunteer at once for [service in] Palestine [only asking] — just how? At any rate the impression they made on me differed greatly from the notions held by our colleagues here." Ben-Gurion tried to gain firsthand impressions, to learn the facts from persons on the scene. Thus, at the suggestion of one young person who took part in the meeting, he devoted fully three hours

---

34 David H. Shpiro, "The Role of the Emergency Committee for Zionist Affairs as the Political Arm of American Zionism, 1938–1944" [Tahalikhei Binyanah shel Mo'etzet haḤerum haTzionit... 1938–1944], Ph.D. diss., Hebrew University, Jerusalem, 1979, chap. 3, esp. pp. 176–193. After arriving in the United States, Ben-Gurion became more optimistic, even though his impression was that an atmosphere of fear, even semi-paralysis, had gripped American Zionists generally. See *Diary*, November 9, 1940, BGIA #30; Ben-Gurion's reports on returning to Palestine — for example. minutes of the meeting of the Jewish Agency Executive, February 16, 1941, BGIA; Halperin, *American Zionism*, p. 327.

to a conversation with William Ziff, a well-to-do writer who had been an assimilationist but became a radical Zionist after witnessing anti-Semitism in Chicago.[35]

During the month preceding the American presidential elections, Ben-Gurion took a close look at the American Zionist leadership. Revealingly, as in 1939 he refrained from personal and political contact with Stephen Wise, the prestigious leader of the American Zionist movement at that time. Although Wise had been the first person to greet Ben-Gurion on his arrival in America and helped him as well — having strong and variegated ties with the administration — it is highly doubtful that the two conducted any political business. In his diary Ben-Gurion characterized Wise as, "this dear youngish-old fellow."[36]

Eager to maintain his working links with the Brandeis circles, Ben-Gurion acted on what he had heard during his first week in the country — that Wise had "distanced himself and had been distanced" from this group. Apparently Ben-Gurion avoided having a serious private meeting with Louis Lipsky as well, even though Lipsky was chairman of the Emergency Committee and ran most of its meetings during Ben-Gurion's stay in America. The Palestinian leader did keep in constant touch with Nahum Goldmann, who represented the World Zionist Organization on the Emergency Committee. He did not identify himself, however, with Goldmann's appraisal of the leadership of the Emergency Committee as a group destined to set American Zionism on its proper course.

Miriam Cohen (Cohen-Taub), a close friend who served as Ben-Gurion's secretary during his tirps to America in the early 1940s, has identified those among the ZOA leadership of the period whom he particularly trusted. She has emphasized his excellent relationship with Robert Szold and Solomon Goldman (in that order): "He got along famously with them and had a great rapport with them." Similarly she noted that he had a fine relationship with Louis Levinthal and Edmund Kaufmann. Cohen's observations shed additional light on Ben-Gurion's tactic of keeping Stephen Wise at arm's length and further corroborate the assumption that he cultivated primarily Brandeisian circles.[37]

35   *Diary*, October 4, 6, 8, 10, 11, and 13, 1940, BGIA #30.
36   Ibid., October 3 and 6. These are the sources for the ensuing discussion.
37   ˙ Miriam Cohen-Taub interviewed by Y. Donyets, New York, April 27, 1977, BGIA.

This notwithstanding, Ben-Gurion's links with the Brandeis camp were not uniform. First, he found Kaufmann, the ZOA president from June 1940 to September 1941 and a Brandeis loyalist, to be a pale figure. Many others shared this impression, including some Brandeisians. Ben-Gurion met with Kaufmann two days after arriving in the United States and jotted down a tepid "not bad" in his diary to describe him. He summed up Kaufmann's policy as a desire to draw rich Jews to Zionism. Almost two months elapsed after that first conversation before Kaufmann, whether because of faulty administration or because he had little respect for Ben-Gurion, invited the Palestinian leader to the meetings of the ZOA Executive Committee. By the time the invitation arrived, at the end of November, Ben-Gurion was unable to accept, although he took pains to express his wish to cooperate with that body.[38]

Ben-Gurion was disappointed, to a certain degree, with Solomon Goldman, the previous ZOA president and the first person to have been recommended to him by Brandeis. The Jewish Agency Executive chairman, it will be recalled, had enjoyed a full and open working relationship with Goldman for the two preceding years. When Ben-Gurion delivered his first address before the Emergency Committee, Goldman did not come from Chicago, even though he had been cabled an invitation. (Kaufmann did not come either.) Ben-Gurion went to Chicago, saw Goldman, and spent a good deal of time discussing political matters with him. It seems that they came to a modicum of agreement on the subject of a Jewish army. Although a detailed account of their discussion is lacking, one can assume that Goldman explained his boycott of Emergency Committee meetings on the grounds of Lipsky's polar views and the animosity obtaining between the two men. Lipsky, who in effect had begun to conduct Emergency Committee meetings before Goldman withdrew as ZOA representative, had incurred the enmity of the Brandeisians.[39]

In mid-October Ben-Gurion met in Washington with the prestigious triad close to the Roosevelt administration — Brandeis, Frankfurter,

---

38   *Diary*, October 6 and November 26, 1940, BGIA #30. Ben-Gurion to E. Kaufmann, November 25, 1940, BGIA #73.

39   *Diary*, October 7 and 27, 1940, BGIA #30. Brandeis was bitter about the composition of the Emergency Committee (Brandeis to R. Szold, July 5, 1940, in Brandeis, *Letters*, vol. 5, pp. 643–644).

and Ben Cohen. He first spoke to Frankfurter, who apparently agreed with his program. His meeting with Brandeis had a similar result: "The old man said little. He expressed his regret that he was not my age now and totally agreed with the plan, asking that I visit him after the elections." In his laconic style Brandeis wrote Robert Szold, his representative in Zionist matters, asking him to note that "Ben-Gurion was most reasonable in his talk with me." Ben Cohen more openly espoused an approach that the other two advisers hinted at — depending on the Roosevelt administration to promote Zionist interests. Ben-Gurion recorded that "the situation in the State Department is not promising [Ben Cohen admitted, going on to say] but for the present nothing can be done. B. C. [Ben Cohen] is not fearful of the administration's throwing up roadblocks in our path, but he too feels that nothing can be done before the elections." Regrettably Ben-Gurion's diary and letters do not convey his immediate reactions to what occurred during this Washington visit. Ben-Gurion might have been influenced by a cable he received from London telling of an unpublicized decision of the British government to establish a Jewish fighting force slated to be dispatched shortly to the Near East. In the end — in September 1944 — this force, to be known as the Jewish Brigade, was established.[40]

From October 6 to 10 Ben-Gurion had a series of meetings with three men who were to prove of critical help to him on the arduous road to the Jewish state — Henry Montor, Emanuel Neumann, and Abba Hillel Silver, the most prominent member of the group.

On October 6 Ben-Gurion held a lengthy meeting with Montor, who, it will be recalled, regarded the Palestinian leader as the appropriate person to turn to for advice on molding public opinion and for airing his critique of the Zionist leadership in London. "This morning Montor arrived and reviewed the internal situation in the ZOA," Ben-Gurion recorded in his diary. The first segment of the report consisted of a scathing attack on the ZOA president: "He knows nothing, neither about Zionism nor Palestine; he has no understanding of politics; and he

40   *Diary*, October 25, 1940, BGIA #30; Brandeis to R. Szold, in Brandeis, *Letters*, vol. 5, p. 647.

has no links with the administration." He won his post, Montor explained, by having been handpicked by Solomon Goldman "as an act of revenge upon Lipsky.... In addition to Goldman, the Brandeisians, too, supported Kaufmann." Lipsky, also, came in for vituperative attack by Montor: "He surrounds himself with incompetents and non-entities." Seeing the ZOA's two major groupings disqualified, Ben-Gurion drew the logical conclusion: "The only man Montor did not complain about was Silver. Apparently he would like to see him as head of the organization."[41]

Two days later Ben-Gurion sat down to a lengthy meeting with Montor's "candidate," Abba Hiller Silver. This encounter took place on the evening of the very day that saw Silver shaken by the State Department's bludgeoning of American Red Cross aid to Jewish refugees. In a bitter, fighting mood, the American Zionist leader was ripe for radical action. "From his lips," wrote Ben-Gurion in his diary, "I got quite another picture of American Zionism." The other picture Ben-Gurion refers to was that tendered him the same morning by Meyer Weisgal, who painted "a black portrait of the Zionist decline in America," declaring that "the only man who can set things right is Weizmann." Silver, on the other hand, maintained that the internal conflicts within the ZOA in no way proved the weakness of Zionism in the United States; quite the contrary:

> The power of Palestine is great and growing greater. The people are not adopting the political ideology [of the Zionist movement] nor are they joining the official Zionist organization; but the Palestinian idea, the interest in Palestine and the readiness to work for Palestine are spreading throughout the masses. Even groups that were cold and removed are drawing close. The United [Jewish] Appeal has paved a road to hitherto inaccessible and distant circles. The principal speakers of the fund are Zionists, so audiences that never meant to hear a Zionist speech from the United [Jewish] Appeal have now heard of Palestine. The younger generation as well — we do not have a European-style *"intelligentzia"* here — are being swept up by the Zionists. The principal figures in the fund are, for the most part, young people

41   *Diary*, October 6, 1940, BGIA #30.

who have finished college. Their opposition to Zionism has diluted. Anti-Zionist circles are few and weak.[42]

Encouraged, Ben-Gurion asked series of ever more practical questions. When the time arrived, would American Jewry respond to a call for Zionist political action? Silver said they would. Would they answer the call for a Jewish army? (Ben-Gurion, having attributed cowardice to Silver only the day before, phrased his question cautiously, emphasizing that he spoke of a call to be preceded by the agreement of America and Britain.) Here, too, Silver's reply was a ringing yes: "He is confident that no one will be opposed, if they are called upon to volunteer for a Jewish legion or army, not just join Britain's armed forces. There was no opposition in the last war nor will there be now." Next Ben-Gurion raised the problem of the availability of young officers who could take command of such an enterprise. Silver answered that there were officers in the army, navy, and air force and even suggested how to contact them. In the end Ben-Gurion told Silver that he did not intend starting anything so long as no clear and formal agreement had been reached in London and so long as the elections had not taken place in America but that he did intend to move ahead at once with the aerial training program. Here, too, Ben-Gurion was met with a positive response and a guarantee of help.

Ben-Gurion held his third meeting, with Emanuel Neumann, on October 10, thus rounding out his contacts with Silver's group. Ben-Gurion had bitter feelings against Neumann for having set up the Tekumah (renaissance) in Palestine, an organization to which Ben-Gurion ascribed the "ambition of seizing power in Palestine and in the Zionist movement — an update of Revisionism." Nevertheless, Ben-Gurion had more than one reason for welcoming Neumann to a tête-à-tête. Neumann carried weight in the ZOA; moreover, at forty-seven he was relatively young and seemed to express new currents of thought among the Jewish masses. He held an interesting position in the ZOA, being close to the Brandeisians and Silver both. Ben-Gurion was restrained during the meeting, most of which was given over to

---

42   Ibid., October 8, 1940; this and the entry for October 7 are the sources for the ensuing discussion.

Neumann's description of prominent new individuals and groups within American Jewry's growing Yishuv-conscious camp.[43]

As was the case with his contacts with the ZOA, until the elections Ben-Gurion's meetings with Hadassah — the Women's Zionist Organization of America and the ZOA's sister organization — were confined to information gathering and deepening of relationships in preparation for future action. The largest of American Zionist groups, Hadassah, had been expanding yearly since 1933. In 1939 the organization had 66,000 members, and in 1940, the year of Ben-Gurion's visit, close to 74,000 (the ZOA's membership stood at about 43,000 during those years, with a slight drop in membership between 1939 and 1940, see Appendix III).

Ben-Gurion's relations with Hadassah were especially rich. Traditionally, the organization had tried to steer clear of any party affiliation or political involvement. Only from 1937 on can Hadassah be seen — and then only partially — as a political organization. Its first political steps were tentative and moderate. Hadassah was the least activist of the major participants in the Emergency Committee and therefore, at first glance, the Zionist organization most removed from the political course of Ben-Gurion. Nonetheless, several factors led to the forging of strong and fruitful bonds between the two. First, Hadassah was situated historically within the Brandeis camp and in certain ways was the most Brandeisian of all its constituents. A deep respect for the justice; a pronounced low regard for, even animosity toward, Lipsky; and wariness of Chaim Weizmann characterized the Women's Zionist Organization of America. It was Hadassah primarily that in 1930 caused the demise of the Lipsky regime and Robert Szold's rise to the chairmanship as "the gentleman representing the authority of Justice Brandeis." Hadassah's distrust of Louis Lipsky outlasted the 1930s. Toward the close of 1940 it led a stubborn battle against his candidacy for the chairmanship of the Emergency Committee, going so far as to resign from that body temporarily at the outset of 1941. Hadassah generally supported Robert Szold and Solomon Goldman, welcoming the tone they set in the Emergency Committee. In this fashion

---

43   Ibid., October 10, 1940.

Hadassah, despite its political moderation, came to be associated with a camp that included much more militant circles. That in turn led to its greater openness to the influence of David Ben-Gurion.[44]

More links bound the women's organization to the Jewish Agency Executive chairman. He, more than any other Zionist leader, was identified with the emergent Zionist enterprise in Palestine, and Hadassah emphasized practical work in the Yishuv. Moreover, Ben-Gurion exhibited certain traits that sat well with the Hadassah mentality — efficiency, enterprise, practicality, and a good sense of organization. According to Rose Halprin, a president of Hadassah in the 1930s and destined to serve again in that capacity with the declaration of Israel's statehood: "For one thing... he [Ben-Gurion] was an organization attuned man [sic]. He understood what organization was, and I don't think there's another organization in the [Jewish] world as well put together, with as high standards, organizationally, as we are." Many Hadassahites also saw in Ben-Gurion intellectual probity, originality, and strength. (In essence some of these were the traits or values that drew Hadassah to the side of Louis Brandeis and his American allies in their struggle against Chaim Weizmann.) Mutual respect characterized the relationship between Hadassah and Ben-Gurion: he came to see the women's organization as efficient, practical, and dedicated, and its leaders as frank and courageous.[45]

On October 22 Ben-Gurion met with the National Board of Hadassah. He briefly put forward the need for a Jewish army, then devoted most of his remarks to his position on Jewish-Arab relations. Many in Hadassah

---

44   On the politicization of Hadassah, see the proceedings of the national board meetings of that organization, December 10 and 17, 1940, and January 1, 1941, HA; Urofsky, *American Zionism*, pp. 342–360; minutes of the meetings of the Emergency Committee, October 10, 1940, to February 19, 1941. It was primarily Dov Joseph who, through his intermediary capacity and suggestions during his stay in the United States (January–March 1941), brought Hadassah back into the framework of the Emergency Committee.

45   Tamar de Sola Pool interviewed by Y. Donyets, New York, April 25, 1977, BGIA; Judith Epstein interviewed by idem, New York, February 28, 1977, BGIA. Rose Halprin, interviewed by idem, March 9, April 7, 1977, New York, BGIA. See also Ben-Gurion's reports, on returning to Palestine, at meetings of the Jewish Agency Executive, the Mapai Central Committee, and the Zionist Executive, and at a session with journalists in Jerusalem during February 1941, BGIA #150.

felt that the leadership of the Palestinian Jewish Agency was not doing enough to improve Jewish-Arab relations, and the organization was quite persistent in pushing the Emergency Committee to act on this issue. Hadassah's founder, Henrietta Szold, and Rose Jacobs were advocates of constituting Palestine as a binational state. In 1940 Jacobs organized a separate committee in Palestine for Hadassah projects, with the sponsorship of major figures in Berit Shalom (covenant of peace), committee chaired by Szold. The main political aim of Berit Shalom was to promote the cause of binationalism.[46]

In his remarks Ben-Gurion pointed out how logical the Arabs were from their point of view in opposing Jewish *aliyah* and that, in effect, there was no Arab representative who would make peace with the notion. He warned that insofar as *aliyah* to Palestine was Zionism's lifeblood, deluding oneself on the question of Jewish-Arab relations was dangerous. Generally speaking, the reaction of the Hadassah leadership was critical. First Rose Jacobs, recently returned from Palestine, called the visitor to task; her remarks were followed by the more restrained critique of Rose Halprin; then harsh remarks were made by Irma Lindheim, a president in the 1920s and a member of the left-wing kibbutz Mishmar haEmek since 1933, and by Bertha Schoolman, then Hadassah national secretary. All these speakers proposed Jewish initiatives in examining relations and forging better understanding between the two peoples. Only two questions sympathetic to Ben-Gurion's approach were tendered, one by Marian Greenberg and one by Judith Epstein, the latter having served as Hadassah's president in the two years preceding World War II. Hadassah president Tamar de Sola Pool ended the deliberations with a critical summary statement.

Ostensibly, nothing productive had taken place at this meeting, politically speaking, from Ben-Gurion's point of view. However, one can assume that he was satisfied. First of all, a second round of questions showed that his remarks had left their imprint on his listeners. Second, the level of the deliberations and the openness created an intimate

---

46 "Hadassah National Board Meeting, October 22, 1940, Verbatim Account of Remarks by David Ben-Gurion," HA; this account is the source for the ensuing discussion; minutes of the meeting of the Emergency Committee, January 9, 1940, ZAL; Susan L. Hattis, *The Bi-National Idea in Palestine during Mandatory Times* (Tel Aviv, 1970), pp. 171ff.

atmosphere. The leadership insisted on Ben-Gurion's participation in the upcoming Hadassah national convention, and their guest agreed.

The Twenty-Sixth National Convention of Hadassah was held in Cincinnati from October 28 to November 3, 1940. No far-reaching political decisions were made, the prevailing feeling being that the Zionist camp was obligated to come to the aid of Britain under extant conditions. Another thread that ran through the convention was the belief that the Arabs, too, had an interest in supporting Britain and that thereby conditions were created that could lead to closer relations between the two nations in Palestine.[47]

Ben-Gurion's involvement in the convention proceeded by stages. His first speech was ideational, even a bit abstract. Given the atmosphere of the pending presidential election, Ben-Gurion was even more cautious than he had been in his earlier appearance (October 22) before the Hadassah National Board. ("I was prudent enough to speak of Zionism in a general vein without touching on political topics," he later reported to the Jewish Agency Executive.) His auditors, disappointed, insisted on Ben-Gurion's addressing himself to concrete issues, especially Jewish-Arab relations.[48]

Ben-Gurion assented, reporting later: "My reply [on the Arab issue] did not satisfy a large number of delegates; indeed many were up in arms. I was attacked by former Hadassah president Irma Lindheim and the current president, Mrs. de Sola Pool." The report in the *Hadassah Newsletter* hinted at the tension between the speaker and his audience: "Mr. Ben-Gurion... delivered a provocative and challenging presentation of the problems inherent in the attempt to establish good Arab-Jewish relations. This [presentation] was met with an intense interest and an informed understanding that made a deep impression on Mr. Ben-Gurion himself." According to the article, the issue-centered debate was conducted responsibly and with mutual respect. Against this background came stage three.

The meeting was adjourned, but the argumentation in the hall and at the podium continued. The president [de Sola Pool] said to me,

---

47   *Hadassah Newsletter* 21, no. 3 (December 1940–January 1941):3–4.
48   See n. 45.

"Why should we continue this debate among ourselves? We ought to reconvene the meeting and argue openly." This was at 2:00 A.M. They pounded on the table and the convention session was reopened. Elderly men and women sat in the hall, but no one stirred from his seat. I was dumbfounded. I fell in love with this convention, I felt the need to explain the matter more fully. I went into the Arab conundrum at length. I told of all the attempts made by the [Zionist] Executive over the last seven years for Arab-Jewish understanding, and what the Arab reaction was. I saw before me an audience that had the drive to renew a convention session at two o'clock in the morning to go into a serious Zionist issue. My detailed explanation did its work. True, they did not accept my opinion, but the issue was explained to them. They understood, they met with the fact that I, no less than they, sought Jewish-Arab agreement for the sake of good, neighborly relations, but that matters were not so simple. Again there were questions, but not in the same tone. Again Mrs. Lindheim and Mrs. de Sola Pool spoke against me. While not agreeing with my stance, they admitted that the question was complex and that we had made serious attempts to find a solution to it. This went on until five in the morning... . I left the convention full of admiration for these women, so deeply involved in our affairs and ready to absorb a Zionist analysis through the night without stirring from their seats.[49]

According to the memoirs of Tamar de Sola Pool, who was similarly moved, this meeting was not a turning point in Ben-Gurion's relations with Hadassah but a continuation and deepening of what had begun previously. Judith Epstein, who in her memoirs returned time and again to that all-night session in Cincinnati, felt that the meeting did indeed represent a turning point. At the session's close, she recalled, a stirred Ben-Gurion kissed Etta Rosensohn, secretary of the organization for many years and its president from 1952 to 1953; and that historic kiss marked the start of the closest ties between Ben-Gurion and the Women's Zionist Organization.[50]

49 Minutes of the meeting of the Jewish Agency Executive, February 16, 1941, BGIA; *Hadassah Newsletter* 21, no. 3 (December 1940–January 1941):3.
50 See interviews in n. 45; these are the sources for the ensuing discussion.

Rose Halprin, although aware of Ben-Gurion's close affinity with Rosensohn, nonetheless tended in her memoirs to view the entire issue more dispassionately and from a clear political perspective. To her mind, the events of this convention did not signal a meaningful turning point in Hadassah's political involvement. She herself, then chairperson of the organization's Political Affairs Committee, vigorously opposed Jacobs's position; and other Hadassah leaders, together with her, utterly rejected the Berit Shalom notions. Halprin observed that Ben-Gurion even lent his weight in that meeting to the ongoing struggle of her faction. A kernel of truth resides in this last-mentioned assessment. Rose Halprin, Rebecca Shulman (a veteran activist, and president of the organization from 1953 to 1956), Judith Epstein, and others adopted what they held to be a more realistic view of Jewish-Arab relations and of the importance of developing the military strength of the Yishuv. On the other hand, they did not constitute at that time a well-defined, militant opposition.

In sum, David Ben-Gurion's meetings with Hadassah contributed to fostering a more realistic approach on the women's part — from his point of view — and furthered the process of the organization's Zionist radicalization. At the same time excellent personal relationships were forged that were to continue.

During his stay in the United States Ben-Gurion maintained a close working relationship with Mapai's sister party, Poalei Zion–Ze'irei Zion. Since 1933 the party had grown considerably, doubling its membership from 5,000 in 1933 to 10,000 in 1940. Although this was a small organization compared with Hadassah and the ZOA, there were other groups connected with Poalei Zion — Pioneer Women (whose membership approached that of Poalei Zion in 1940) and Farband (a fraternal order) — that together with it, composed an element not to be overlooked. These three groups formed a federation of sorts in which Poalei Zion was accorded the deciding voice on political matters. Poalei Zion was also the dominant force within the League for Labor Palestine, a Histadrut body founded in 1935, most of whose members were drawn from the ranks of entrepreneurs and professionals. Moreover, Poalei Zion was among the founders of the General Histadrut Campaign (popularly and briefly called Geverkshaften), and its affiliates, a successful organization founded in the 1920s. Finally, Poalei Zion's youth movement, HaBonim, together with the Histadrut-associated HeḤalutz, was aimed at pioneering *aliyah* and welcomed undertaking defense and military assignments.[51]

Despite the history and general orientation of Poalei Zion and its associated organizations, the party did not constitute a dynamic force within American Zionism during the first years of World War II. The party's publications — the weekly *Yidisher Kemfer* and the monthly *Jewish Frontier* — of those years show that it lacked initiative and did not inspiringly address burning issues. Moreover, the leaders of Poalei Zion were neither well known nor influential on the American Zionist scene. Yosef Yizre'eli, HeḤalutz emissary to the United States during World War II, concluded that the party, though ostensibly at the center of the various groupings just mentioned, was actually the weakest element of them all. Ben-Gurion came to the same conclusion, holding the party to be conservative and flacid.[52]

One week after his arrival in America Ben-Gurion addressed the Central Committee of Poalei Zion on the issues of raising a Jewish army and activating American Jewry politically. Several auditors expressed their concern over the first point and their skepticism on the second. In his reply, Ben-Gurion clarified that a precondition to raising a Jewish fighting force in America would be the agreement of both England and the United States. However, he emphasized that to obtain such an agreement, American Jewry, numbering five million, had to realize its potential. Given the situation of European Jewry, Ben-Gurion maintained, American Jewry was the only Jewish community capable of effective political action. Clear-sightedness and aggressive leadership, he said, could change history. He brought this same message to the convention of the General Histadrut Campaign and to various local groups.[53]

51 Halperin, *American Zionism*, pp. 159–162, 173–175; Baruch Zuckerman, *Memoirs* [Zikhroynes], vol. 2 (New York, 1963), pp. 285–323; Sima Altman et al., eds., *Pioneers from America: 75 Years of Hehalutz, 1905–1980* (Tel Aviv, 1981), esp. pp. 83–111; David Breslau, ed., *Arise and Build: The Story of American Habonim* (New York, 1961), esp. pp. 26–65.

52 Yizre'eli, *On a Security Mission*, p. 26; minutes of the meeting of the Mapai Central Committee, February 19, 1941, BGIA.

53 Minutes of the meeting of the Poalei Zion Central Committee (in Yiddish), October 10, 1940, BGIA; *Diary*, October 10, 1940, BGIA #30.

Ben-Gurion was ambivalent toward Poalei Zion from the very start of his American visit. On the one hand, the party provided him a vehicle for sounding out his ideas as well as a malleable audience. On the other hand, he may well have borne a grudge against the organization from his stay in the States during World War I and looked on it as a marginal element, a museum piece of sorts. The party organs did provide him with a platform for a sizable article (on October 11 in the Yiddish weekly and in November in the English monthly) that called for the establishment of a Jewish army. Yet, at an early stage the Jewish Agency Executive chairman apparently concluded from his evaluation of Poalei Zion's listlessness and lackluster leadership that "at this point the party is not the conduit for the establishment of a Jewish army."[54]

Ben-Gurion's diary and reports on his return to Palestine make no mention of the Mizrachi, Religious Zionist Organization of America, a lacuna clarified by a later account. "I found a common language with the Mizrachi people at once on all Zionist matters," he noted. Mizrachi was then the third-largest Zionist organization, following Hadassah and the ZOA, numbering 37,000 members (women's organization included). Rabbi Meyer Berlin (later Bar-Ilan) then served as the organization's honorary president. Though living in Palestine at the time, he still imbued the organization with his activist spirit. The second honorary president was Gedalia Bublick, a journalist and author who wrote frequently for the daily *Morgen-Zhurnal*, a daily highly regarded by Ben-Gurion. The American clear leader of Mizrachi was Leon Gellman, who had served as vice president from 1930 to 1935 and as president from 1935 to 1959. Bublick and Gellman generally represented Mizrachi on the Emergency Committee during Ben-Gurion's stay in America and in most instances supported his proposals and actions.[55]

As noted, Ben-Gurion's primary practical goal in setting out for America was to further the establishment of a Jewish fighting force.

---

54   David Ben-Gurion, "A Yiddishe Armei," *Yidisher Kemfer* 19, no. 367 (October 11, 1940):1–3; David Ben-Gurion, "A Jewish Army," *Jewish Frontier* 7, no. 11 (November 1940):7–9; minutes of the meeting of the Mapai Central Committee, February 19, 1941, BGIA; Phillip Cruso, interviewed by Y. Donyets, New York, January 26, 1977, BGIA.
55   *Diary*, October 5, 1940, BGIA #30. These conclusions are based on the protocols of the Emergency Committee, 1939–1941, ZAL; *Diary*, October 6, 1940, BGIA #30.

During his first month in the United States he invested considerable energy in the long-range promotion of volunteerism and some concrete steps to meet the defense needs of the Yishuv. In a special meeting he instructed Histadrut emissaries from Palestine to start drawing volunteers from the Zionist youth movements — Masada, Avukah, HaShomer haTza'ir, HaBonim, Young Judea, and, finally, Poalei Zion and Farband. When told of the lack of Jewish Agency funds for agricultural settlement training and for aerial training, he stated flatly: "Under all circumstances, I insist — even if we cannot get down to raising a Jewish army at once — on establishing settlement training groups and an organization for air training; I am committed to getting the necessary funds."[56]

Ben-Gurion was particularly adamant about air training, a matter with which he had dealt during his previous trip to the United States in January 1939. The appropriate sum was allocated and put to use. In mid-November Ben-Gurion obtained the full backing of the Emergency Committee for "civil air training" on the HeHalutz farm. After a month had passed he cabled Berl Locker in London that the first group of pioneers was to start receiving instruction within a week. An article titled "Halutzim on the Wing" in the February 1941 issue of *New Palestine* related that the young people who had begun flight training during Hanukkah of 1940 in the training farm Cream Ridge were already flying solo. This was a landmark in the military history of the Zionist movement.[57]

Ben-Gurion had explained his diplomatic stance on the question of the Jewish army to Nahum Goldmann a few days after his arrival in the United States: "If London's answer proves positive and if here, after the elections (no issue can be raised before the elections) the American government will not object to Jews enlisting in the army and fighting

---

56   *Diary*, October 6, 1940, BGIA #30; Yizre'eli, *On a Security Mission*, pp. 36–37.

57   On Ben-Gurion's initiatives and cooperation with Yizre'eli on the aerial training project, see also W. B. Ziff to Ben-Gurion, November 20 and 24, 1940 BGIA #73; Ben-Gurion to W. B. Ziff, November 25, 1940, ibid.; Ziff to Ben-Gurion, November 26, 1940, ibid.; minutes of the meeting of the Emergency Committee, November 11, 1940, ZAL. No one voted against the decision; only Bertha Schoolman abstained (Ben-Gurion to B. Locker [cable], December 20, 1940, BGIA #73; *New Palestine* 21, no. 19 [February 21, 1941]:11–12).

with England — then I will remain here for that purpose, whether the Zionist leaders give their imprimatur or not." Phrasing the matter more delicately in light of American Zionist fears of illegal activity, he explained to Baruch Zuckerman: "I will not stay [in America] to work nor will I begin any activity until two conditions are met: (1) an affirmative response from London on the Jewish army; (2) non-opposition of the American government to any kind of enlistment activity. If these two conditions are met I will devote myself to setting up the unit with the help of all parties and factions, or without them, or despite them." However, on October 25 it became clear to Ben-Gurion that the British government was opposed to setting up the Jewish force that the Zionist movement had sought. Despite this, Ben-Gurion did remain in the United States for an additional two months. Doubtless, he wished to devote himself to building up American Zionism, in the light of postelection developments, not only for the purpose of recruiting soldiers and funds but also to establish a base for long-range political action.[58]

The American elections and Roosevelt's victory over Willkie deepened Ben-Gurion's faith in American democracy and in the political potential of American Jewry. A few days after the election he wrote:

> It is difficult to describe the bacchanalia of reckless propaganda, demagoguery, and waste that Willkie had at his disposal. Almost all — excluding 20 percent — of the capitalist press (which is to say, all the newspapers in America), all the media, publicity and propaganda, thousands and tens of thousands of paid speakers, the radio, the wires, means of transportation, the airplanes, tens of millions of dollars, all manner of coercion by employers, bank presidents, heads of insurance companies, and the like — tried for weeks to muddy Roosevelt's name in the public eye, and lavished endless praise and encomia on Willkie, the one and only saviour

---

58 B. Locker to Ben-Gurion and Ben Gurion to Locker, October 25, 1940, BGIA #30;
    For background see Yoav Gelber, *Jewish Palestinian Volunteering in the British Army during the Second World War: Volunteering and Its Role in Zionist Policy* [Toldot haHitnadvut: haHitnadvut uMekomah baMediniyut haTziyonit vehaYishuvit, 1939–1942], vol. 1 (Jerusalem, 1979), pp. 106–122.

and redeemer... . His propaganda machine reminded me of Hitler's before he came to power... .
Never before had so much money been spent on an election as had been spent this time by Willkie and his supporters. It is estimated that Willkie supporters spent about one hundred million dollars.[59]

Despite all efforts of the Willkie camp and despite the impression fostered by Republican leaders on the eve of the election that a reversal in Willkie's favor was in the offing, the Democratic candidate won, Ben-Gurion wrote in his diary, observing:

> I believe that these elections are England's first great victory in this war and the most grievous blow delivered to fascism in the world — and in America. Once again democracy's banner flies high, proving the power of a free people. The results of the elections show that a bought press cannot deceive the people... . The nation did not panic, was not blinded, was not hoodwinked. I know of no more encouraging grounds for faith in a nation and freedom and free elections than what has just been demonstrated in America.[60]

Roosevelt's victory was fresh proof for Ben-Gurion of the political power of American Jewry. During the last stages of the election, as Willkie drew close to Roosevelt in public opinion polls, the president became very dependent on the Jewish vote. The Jews, for their part, leaned overwhelmingly toward the candidate whom they perceived to stand for democracy and justice at home, and a readiness to defend these values abroad — that is, by helping the suffering Jewish people. In the end, more than 90 percent of American Jewry voted for Franklin Delano Roosevelt, and that was of critical importance: Roosevelt won by one-half the margin he had enjoyed in the elections of 1936. In his report to the Zionist Executive, Ben-Gurion maintained that the Jews had played a major role in the Roosevelt victory. Although he warned against exaggerated claims, he suggested that New York Jewry and the American Labor party, founded and led by Jewish trade union leaders, assured Roosevelt his majority. In his speech to the Mapai Council in March 1941 Ben-Gurion noted that although the Jews of America

---

59   *Diary*, November 9, 1940, BGIA #30.
60   Ibid.

comprised only 5 million of 130 million, "they could influence public life, the press, the working masses, intellectual life... . Under certain conditions it [Jewish power] can be the decisive factor."[61]

America presidential elections were a milestone on Ben-Gurion's political path in yet another way. Following the elections, Franklin Roosevelt, in word and deed (albeit quietly during the first few weeks), deepened American involvement on the side of the Allied powers. Open-eyed political analysts could see that America, in the not distant future, would join the war against the forces of world fascism. Furthermore, after the elections the American public became much more aware of the vigorous defense-oriented thrust that had characterized the American economy since 1939. Surging forward on the wave of vast resources and innovative technology, the gross national product shot from 104 in 1939 to 137 in 1941; and the expenditures of the federal government, devoted mostly to defense, rose from $5 billion in 1939 to $17 billion in 1941. Ben-Gurion realized that the prospects for American involvement in the war were increasing daily (these prospects seemed greater still following Roosevelt's "arsenal-of-democracy" speech of December 29, which will be discussed later) and that in all likelihood America would have a decisive voice both in the war's conduct and in attendant political developments.[62]

61   Lawrence H. Fuchs, *The Political Behavior of American Jews* (Glencoe, Ill., 1956), pp. 71–79; the quotation is from the minutes of the meeting of the Mapai Council, March 5, 1941, BGIA.

62   Robert Dallek, *Franklin D. Roosevelt and American Foreign Policy, 1932–1945* (New York, 1979), pp. 252–256; Lester V. Chandler, *America's Greatest Depression, 1929–1941* (New York, 1979), pp. 128–133; Ben-Gurion's report in the minutes of the meeting of the Zionist Executive, February 24, 1941; Ben-Gurion's remarks at a press conference in Jerusalem, February 26, 1941, BGIA #150; David Ben-Gurion, "Jewry and the War," *Palestine and the Middle East* 13, no. 2 (February 1941):21–22.

CHAPTER SIX

A JEWISH COMMONWEALTH

November 1940 brought to the shores of Palestine a drama that was to have far-reaching effects on the Yishuv, the American Jewish community, and the career of David Ben-Gurion.

On November 1 the *Pacific* sailed into Haifa bay to be followed two days later by the *Milos*, the two boats carrying a total of nearly 2,000 refugees. No sooner had the vessels entered the port than British soldiers and police transferred the immigrants to a ramshackle passenger ship, the *Patria*: the arrivals were to be banished to the island of Mauritius in the Indian Ocean, east of Madagascar, until the conclusion of the war. This step marked a stark shift in British policy. In the past the authorities had imprisoned immigrants temporarily in Atlit (near Haifa), then freed them, subtracting their numbers from the sum of the certificates allotted under White Paper regulations. On November 11 the Yishuv's Assembly of Delegates met in special session to consider the threat of expulsion hovering over the immigrants' heads. On November 20 the British authorities officially announced the expulsion, sparking a general strike in Palestine. Four days later the *Atlantic* arrived with about 1,730 more immigrants, some of whom were transferred immediately to the expulsion ship *Patria*. The Yishuv was gripped with outrage at the new policy and its brutal enforcement. On November 25, with the authorization of the Jewish Agency Executive, the Haganah set off a bomb in the *Patria*'s hold intending to put the ship out of service temporarily. The boat, however, was far frailer than the Haganah knew. Moments after the explosion it sank and with it more than 200 passengers. The Mandatory government allowed the survivors to remain in the country but did not budge from its intention to deport the *Atlantic* immigrants. The expulsion was carried out on December 9, savagely, with no organized reaction on the part of the Yishuv. After seventeen days the *Atlantic*'s passengers reached Mauritius, where they were

137

housed and maintained under wretched conditions until August 1945.[1] Against the backdrop of these events the moderate-activist debate within Mapai burst forth afresh. On December 15, 1940, and January 9, 1941, the deliberations took on a new dimension, especially with the address of Berl Katznelson at the second session. Katznelson maintained that, given the destruction of European Jewry and the new British brutality, more was required than argumentation over immediate responses to the authorities' actions. No longer would it suffice, he held, to demand that Britain nullify the White Paper and fulfill its prior obligations (he had put forward this line of thought at the convention of the World Union of Poalei Zion, to which Mapai belonged, in Ayanot in mid-December 1940). No longer was it possible to disregard Zionism's ultimate goal. The Yishuv, he declared, had to "raise the banner of the solution of the Jewish question, *of the Jewish state*," and to that end launch a two-pronged campaign in America to strengthen the independence of the Zionist movement and "Zionize" the Jewish community. To effect the first goal, he called for the autonomy of Zionist fund-raising; as to the second, he proposed that "we must do what our friends did twenty years ago: infuse the Jewish masses in America with the Zionist faith. This might be much more difficult now, since over the years they have become more aware of difficulties." No decisions were reached on the root issues raised by Katznelson; at a meeting convened but a few days later, the Mapai Central Committee deferred summoning the party's Political Committee until David Ben-Gurion's return from America.[2]

Katznelson's call to bring American Jewry into the Zionist fold fell on receptive ears in Mapai. Some Mapai emissaries in America though — the moderates George Landauer and Eliezer Kaplan — were pessimistic. They described American Jewry as fear ridden and Zionism as paralyzed, with no future to speak of. Their colleagues in Palestine, however, were by no means prepared to accept this prognosis. Even so cautious a party member as Yosef Sprinzak could not accept his like-

---

1   Slutsky, *Haganah History*, vol. 3, pp. 152–158; Sharett, *Political Diary*, vol. 5, pp. 151–156.

2   Minutes of the meetings of the Mapai Central Committee, January 9 and 15, and February 9, 1941, BGIA; Shapira, *Berl*, pp. 289–291.

minded colleagues' prophecy of doom. In a meeting of the Mapai Central Committee in August he declared: "Kaplan has brought back a bleak report from America, one that can plunge our efforts to defeat... . We cannot remain indifferent to this 'declaration,' for much of our Zionist effort now hangs upon the actions of American Zionism... . Every day that passes without a herculean effort on our part to change the face of American Zionism is a tragedy for Zionism."[3]

Other participants joined in the bitter critique of Kaplan's approach. Golda Meir ended the deliberations with a call to blend theory with action. "The Geverkshaften fund can serve as a typical example.... Success came only because we miraculously managed to fuse both elements: by demanding concrete activity in Palestine we were able to educate a large body of people, affording them a Zionist education of sorts." In the continuation of her remarks, she lambasted the liaison with the United Jewish Appeal. "The heads of the UJA," she asserted, "consistently oppose our Palestinian emissaries; we hear it year after year. It's much more convenient for them... to have a 'respectable' English-speaking American Jew go to this city or that and hold forth on aid to 'suffering brethren,' than have Zionist emissaries go to speak of Zionism.... I pray for the moment," she concluded, "that we find the courage to sponsor a separate Zionist fund in America, for I see that as the realistic means for Zionist education." In sum, the tone of that Mapai Central Committee meeting was set not by the pessimistic report of Eliezer Kaplan but by his critics, and particularly Golda Meir. More convinced than ever of American Zionist potential, the party saw the need for Ben-Gurion to stay on in the United States. Only after Dov Joseph's departure to America was ensured did Mapai send the Jewish Agency Executive chairman a telegram asking that he return — after meeting with Joseph Stateside.[4]

---

3 "G. Landauer Report on America," minutes of the meeting of the Histadrut Executive Committee, May 9, 1940, HECA; "Report of [Committee] Member E. Kaplan on his visit to America," minutes of the meeting of the Mapai Central Committee, August 22, 1940, BGIA.

4 Minutes of the meeting of the Mapai Central Committee, August 22, 1940, BGIA; E. Kaplan and M. Sharett telegram to Ben-Gurion, January 8, 1941, BGIA #73.

Not until November 12 was Ben-Gurion informed firsthand of the arrival of the *Pacific* and the *Milos* in Palestine, and the very next day he learned of the planned expulsion to Mauritius. He cabled Berl Locker in London at once, suggesting a direct appeal to Churchill, and simultaneously "got hold of Wise, who telephoned the British embassy in Washington on the spot.... He [Wise] told him [the assistant director of the embassy] of the affair, warned him of the impression that would be made in America, and called upon him to contact London immediately." Subsequently, the leadership of the Emergency Committee met, authorized Wise's step, and decided to ask William Green, president of the American Federation of Labor, to cable Ernest Bevin, a Labour party leader and minister of labor in the Churchill government. The committee decided as well to ask Maurice L. Perlzweig, a British Zionist of stature then visiting the United States, to cable some British members of Parliament.[5]

All the preceding actions bespoke unanimity. Soon, however, the *Patria* incident revealed, like litmus paper, differing and contrasting approaches. On the evening of November 19 Ben-Gurion received a cable from Weizmann stating that Lord Lloyd believed that the two ships were only the first of a convoy leaving Rumania under German sponsorship and were part of a calculated plan to foist Jews upon Britain, stir up ill will between Englishmen and Jews, and infiltrate secret agents into Palestine. The World Zionist Organization president then instructed Ben-Gurion in no uncertain terms to prevent any rise of feeling that could complicate matters. Ben-Gurion sent off a long cable insisting that he had accurate information as to who the ship's passengers were — bona fide refugees expected by the Yishuv (the American press had been informed of this); and he demanded "most vigorously that they be allowed to disembark at once." Three days later the British government was to issue its official edict of expulsion. "The edict is perhaps worse than the expulsion itself," Ben-Gurion wrote in his diary, noting that "the most contemptible section... states that even after the war these refugees will not be allowed to enter Palestine." He

5   *Diary*, November 12 and 13, 1940, BGIA #30; minutes of the meeting of the Emergency Committee Executive, November 14, 1940, ZAL. On Ben-Gurion's reaction to the expulsion of the illegal immigrants and related issues, cf. Penkower, "Ben-Gurion, Silver, and the 1941 UPA," pp. 70–76.

prepared a counterstatement for the press, anticipating the authorization of the Emergency Committee.[6]

On November 22, however, at the Emergency Committee meeting, Ben-Gurion's proposal met with opposition. "[Israel] Goldstein objected because it might hurt the UJA... others were concerned that American papers would not publish a statement without a covering story." Henry Montor rescued Ben-Gurion's initiative by suggesting that the declaration be issued as an announcement to the press during the visit of an Emergency Committee delegation to the British embassy — thus providing the story element. Two additonal decisions, however, diluted Ben-Gurion's original intent. First, a condensed draft of the declaration was to be prepared by Tamar de Sola Pool of Hadassah. Second, the Hadassah leader watered down the already modest proposal to organize several protest gatherings in America's largest cities. She sponsored a resolution, carried by the meeting, calling for the use of Zionist conferences planned anyway in two to three of the largest cities to give expression also to the feelings stirred up in the wake of the expulsion. It was clear who was the winner and who the loser in this first round of internal struggle.[7]

Immediately following this confrontation, additional forces grouped to oppose Ben-Gurion's plan. Rabbi Isadore Breslau informed Emanuel Neumann that the Washington triad of Brandeis, Frankfurter, and Ben Cohen was against any public statement. Solomon Goldman as well, who himself supported publishing the declaration, personally brought Neumann the opinion of Brandeis, with whom he had met; Goldman also cited the cable that Weizmann had sent Ben-Gurion as an element to be taken into consideration. Solomon Goldman, together with ZOA president Edmund Kaufmann, both known as Brandeisians, managed to find reasons not to be numbered in the delegation to the British embassy. This group shrank in stages to Wise, de Sola Pool, Breslau, and Neumann. Before leaving for the embassy, Wise conferred with Neumann on how to reconcile the dictate of the Emergency Committee

6 Chaim Weizmann to Lourie for Ben-Gurion, November 11, 1940, ZAL, Szold Collection, VII/2; Ben-Gurion to Chaim Weizmann, November 19, 1940, BGIA #73; *Diary*, November 22, 1940, BGIA #30.
7 *Diary*, November 22, 1940, BGIA #30; minutes of the meeting of the Emergency Committee, November 22, 1940, ZAL.

— to submit the declaration to the press — with the pressure of Brandeis's opinion. Their decision was to publish the declaration, but only after calling on the embassy. Following the November 26 visit, de Sola Pool voiced her total opposition to any public statement whatsoever. She raised several objections: the opposition of Brandeis, Frankfurter, and Cohen; Goldman's agreement with their position; the sinking of the *Patria* on the preceding day; Weizmann's cable to Ben-Gurion, calling for caution and moderation; and the likelihood that the British government or the British embassy would publish a revised proclamation. To ensure some measure of publicity, Neumann suggested delivering a brief message to the press on the protest call, but de Sola Pool and Wise opposed (only these three remained to discuss the matter following the visit). Wise was supported later as well by most members of the ZOA Executive Committee, which gathered that evening in Washington and before whom he raised the issue informally.

The episode had yet another epilogue. On the morning after, Neumann, who had remained in the capital, telephoned Brandeis informing him of the delegation's negative decision. Brandeis, Neumann related, expressed satisfaction. "He [Brandeis] felt the sinking of the *Patria*, 'whether an act of God or an act of man,' had disposed of the matter for the time being." He suggested that before any public action be taken, those involved think through the need to avoid discomfiting the American government, embroiled as it was in foreign policy quandaries. Generally speaking, Brandeis averred, the most effective Jewish response was that provided by action on the scene, in Palestine. That sort of thing would make a stronger impact on American public opinion. Neumann went on to ask what Brandeis counseled in the event that Britain went on to expel the refugees: should public response still be avoided? Brandeis answered that it was too early to consider such an eventuality, and it seemed likely that it would never take place.[8]

Three days after the Emergency Committee delegation visited the British embassy, its executive met to consider the affair. Ben-Gurion participated in the meeting, as did Emanuel Neumann, by special invitation. No sooner had Neumann delivered a detailed report on the

8   E. Neumann, "Note on the Visit of the Delegation of the Emergency Committee, Washington, Tuesday, November 26, 1940, in Connection with the Attempted Deportation of Jewish Refugees from Palestine," TA, UPA/ECZA 10–3–12.

events than Schoolman and de Sola Pool, the representatives of Hadassah, took Ben-Gurion to task, albeit restrainedly. The major clash, however, was between Ben-Gurion and Stephen Wise. The protocol of the meeting exuded tension: "He [Ben-Gurion] was not concerned with this particular case, but with the principle behind it, and he could not accept the idea that no action should be taken by American Zionists to protest when victims of inhuman persecution were being deported as these refugees were being deported, because such action might be displeasing to the British or American governments or peoples." Stephen Wise raised his strong objection. He ventured that the conversation at the British embassy had made a positive impression on him, hinting thereby at the logic of cooperating with the British and of approaching them through diplomatic channels. Then he launched an explicit attack on Ben-Gurion's position: "It was difficult to see [Wise said] how Mr. Ben-Gurion could on one day say that everything must be done to assist Britain to win the war, and the next day to issue statements which might create further difficulties for Britain." Wise won the day: the proposal to distribute the declaration to the press was crushed. Instead, the committee decided to send a letter to the British embassy detailing, in essence, what had been discussed. A subcommittee of three was set up to draft the letter — Wise, de Sola Pool, and Neumann, with the clear intention that the first two would set the tone of the message.[9]

December, however, altered the American political scene, especially in regard to Zionism. On the one hand, American anti-Semitism had not diminished; on the other hand, during that month President Roosevelt took ever-clearer steps drawing America closer to England, thereby undercutting the isolationist and anti-Semitic camp and encouraging the liberal forces. At a December 18 press conference he broached the idea of lending England military equipment and three weeks later proposed the matter formally to the Congress; ultimately this resulted in the Lend-Lease Bill. It was now clear to all that the president had skirted the neutrality laws to further Anglo-American cooperation. On December 20 Roosevelt announced the formation of a new body, the Office of Production Management, whose function was to be the gearing of civilian production to the war needs of the anti-Nazi camp. Prominent

9   Minutes of the meeting of the Emergency Committee, November 29, 1940, ZAL.

among this four-man team was CIO (Congress of Industrial Organizations) leader Sidney Hillman, a Jew and a Zionist sympathizer.[10]

On November 20 Hungary joined the Rome-Berlin-Tokyo axis, to be followed three days later by Rumania, and on December 24 Slovakia joined ranks with the fascist forces. The plight of the Jewish communities of all these countries turned desperate, both legally and actually: they were exposed to terror and murder. Toward the close of November a certain self-deception was still evident among the Jews of America regarding the situation of their brothers in Europe; but chilling reports published in December 1940 drastically dispelled the clouds of illusion.[11]

Concomitantly, the *Patria* tragedy awoke the American public to events on the shores of Palestine, swelling sympathy for the victims of the Nazi maelstrom. The expulsion of the *Atlantic's* ill-fated refugees (December 9 to 26) showed that a radically new policy had been introduced, and the attendant callousness and brutality of the Mandatary enraged broad segments of the Jewish community. The sinking of the immigrant ship *Salvador* off the coast of Turkey in mid-December sparked spontaneous demonstrations of support in America. On several occasions protests organized by Jewish Communists attracted not only the man in the street but recognized Zionist groups as well. The British embassy in Washington was often forced to adopt an apologetic stance in the face of critical public opinion. Under these circumstances, rank-and-file Zionists were in ferment. Many activists sought avenues for protest and dynamic leadership, but in vain. The Zionist establishment found itself in the grip of a major crisis.[12]

---

10   Dallek, *Roosevelt and American Foreign Policy*, pp. 255–256; Langer and Gleason, *Undeclared War*, pp. 243–245. Sidney Hillman (1887–1964) was a staunch supporter of Zionist efforts in Palestine and took a special interest in the accomplishments of the labor movement. He was active in Histadrut fund-raising in the United States and from 1929 onward served as a non-Zionist member of the expanded Jewish Agency Council. On the day following the declaration, a German spokesman condemned the Roosevelt initiative, labeling it "moral aggression" (ibid., p. 254).

11   *New Palestine* 31, no. 7 (November 20, 1940):4, no. 8 (December 6, 1940):4, 5, no. 9 (December 13, 1940):5.

12   Shpiro, "The Role of the Emergency Committee," pp. 176–193. According to Julius Haber, it was only the founding of the American Palestine Committee, in March

Having failed to convince the Emergency Committee to turn to the public, Ben-Gurion took matters into his own hands. He began his major address at the annual convention of the Geverkshaften in New York, November 22–24, with the expulsion episode. Evoking his own banishment from Palestine during World War I at the hands of Jemal Pasha (the Ottoman governor of Greater Syria, which included Palestine), and drawing an analogy between his personal experience and the high commissioner's expulsion of the thousands of Jewish arrivals, he quoted the Turkish decree "that he never return," translating the same into Yiddish for his listeners. "I told him then, 'I shall return!' and I kept my word." At Ben-Gurion's urging, the convention passed a special resolution on the refugees, castigating British policy even while calling for understanding of all progressive forces in Britain and solidarity with them.[13]

While Ben-Gurion was forging ahead, a significant development was taking place in what can be called Silver's circle. On the very day that the Emergency Committee voted not to issue a press release (November 20) Neumann wrote Silver a letter expressing his dissatisfaction with the handling of the entire affair. Silver's reply revealed that he had crossed over wholeheartedly to anti-British militancy, to the inclusion of marshaling American public opinion. Since his historic meeting with Ben-Gurion on October 8, he had met with additional frustration at the hands of the American Red Cross and had come to grasp more fully both the mentality and stubbornness of the Near East Section of the State Department and the limits of Zionist quiet diplomacy. Now, at the

1941, that gave some outlet to the frustration and rage of American Jewry from November 1940 onward (Julius Haber, *The Odyssey of an American Zionist: Fifty Years of Zionist History* [New York, 1956], serves as a useful summary, rather than a scholarly inquiry, albeit certain sections contain important source material; esp. pp. 7–13). I. L. Kenen characterizes the period of late 1940 to early 1943 similarly in a letter to the author, July 14, 1980. See also reports of Ben-Gurion, minutes of the meeting of the Jewish Agency Executive, February 16, 1941, BGIA; minutes of the meeting of the Mapai Central Committee, February 19, 1941, BGIA.

13 "David Ben-Gurion Address at the Opening of the 16th Convention of the Geverkshaften Campaign," (in Yiddish), November 23, 1940, BGIA #150; "Resolution on the 1771 Refugees" [Resolutzia Wegen die 1771 Flikhtlinge], *Yidisher Kemfer* 19, no. 374 (November 29, 1940):22; 19, no. 376 (December 13, 1940):2–3.

outset of December, he was even prepared to take on the prestigious Washington-based Brandeis "high command."[14]

Silver began his letter to Neumann by describing British Jewry's vehement reaction to the expulsion of the refugees — a far cry from the restraint of "Brandeis and Frankfurter and members of the ZOA Executive" (thereby alluding to Stephen Wise). Most of the rest of the letter comprised a statement of principles and presaged the open struggle of Silver and Neumann to strengthen their position.

> Our desire to help Great Britain in this war is maneuvering us into a policy distinctly harmful to Zionism. We are asked not only to withhold criticism of outrageous acts on the part of the Palestine government, but actually, as Butler's letter to Wise suggests, to become apologists for the Palestine government and to make its position "understood among the Jews of America." In the meantime England intends to pursue her policy of appeasing the Arabs even more aggressively than she did before the war. We are also being asked to withhold criticism of Great Britain's policy toward Palestine so as not to embarrass the administration in Washington. In this way we practically acknowledge not only that the United States government will do nothing to help us in affairs touching Palestine; but also tie our hands and silence our voice in the name of *American* patriotism. This is an intolerable situation into which we are being moved. Every people speaks up for its own rights in these desperate times, and for its own needs. The Jews alone, the most hard-pressed of all, must speak up only in behalf — of Great Britain.[15]

Silver's primary target was Wise, which the latter learned only indirectly, from the copy of the letter sent him by Neumann. While the Wise-Silver

---

14   E. Neumann to A. H. Silver, November 29, 1940, TA, UA 10-3-26; A. H. Silver to E. Neumann, December 2, 1940, TA, UPA 10-3-26; A. H. Silver to H. Montor, October 14, 1940, CZA A 243/132; H. Montor to S. Wise, October 15, 1940, CZA A 243/132. For a deliberation on the Red Cross, see the minutes of the meetings of the Emergency Committee, October 29, November 15, 1940, ZAL; A. H. Silver to Davis, November 30, 1940, ZAL, Szold Collection IX/29; A. H. Silver to E. Neumann, December 2, 1940, TA, UPA 10-3-26.

15   A. H. Silver to E. Neumann, December 2, 1940, TA, UPA 10-3-26.

animosity rose to new heights, Neumann kept his supporters updated and ready for action. He especially maintained close and constant contact with Robert Szold.[16]

Solomon Goldman was rather distressed by the Emergency Committee's decision not to release a statement to the press protesting the expulsion. While he had accepted Brandeis's dictate and consequently avoided joining the delegation to the British embassy, he found himself unable to deny his own position, which he had been striving to advance for more than two years. On the very day of the Emergency Committee's negative decision, he wrote Stephen Wise, faulting the committee for not having laid the groundwork for criticism of the British Colonial Office and the high commissioner. One could not take on Halifax, Eden, or Lloyd in America, he maintained, without first convincing the press and involving churches and clubs — this outreach being an allusion to his own sweeping program, which had not been set in motion. Only by such means, Goldman wrote, was there any chance of winning public opinion and influencing the administration. One sentence of his programmatic missive, a copy of which Goldman sent to six top figures in the Zionist movement, irked Wise especially: "We cannot at this late hour undo hastily the mischief wrought by the exchange of letters between Dr. Weizmann and Mr. Chamberlain fifteen months ago." Goldman was apparently referring to a letter Weizmann had written Chamberlain, the then British prime minister, on the eve of World War II, in accordance with the decision of the Twenty-First Zionist Congress, expressing the Zionist movement's total support of Britain in its war against Hitler.[17]

Wise replied at length, setting down his political credo. First, he defended Weizmann's letter. Although Weizmann decidedly knew at the time that England was about to enforce the White Paper, he contended that "even from a Zionist perspective this would be a petty evil compared with the defeat of England." Wise recalled, as well, March 1939, when Zionist representatives received final word of the White Paper policy and

---

16 E. Neumann to S. Wise, December 2, 1940, CZA 243/126. See, for example, E. Neumann to R. Szold, December 1, 1940, ZAL, Szold Collection VII/2.

17 S. Goldman to S. Wise, November 29, 1940, CZA 243/126; C. Weizmann to N. Chamberlain, August 29, 1939, in Weizmann, *Letters and Papers*, vol. 19, p. 145.

had pressured Lipsky and himself to return to America and "start a great fight" against England. "I said at this time, to the dismay of the [militant Zionist] group, that I would do nothing of the kind... that I could not bring myself to forget Hitler and Nazism... when at any time we might be compelled to give our unmeasured and unequivocal support to Britain." He was mentioning this, Wise wrote, because that was still his opinion. "I still feel deeply as ever that to act as if we had two enemies, Hitler and England, would be suicidal folly on our part." Wise leveled his diatribe straight at Silver, quoting Silver's letter of December 2 to Neumann. He concluded his critique of Silver by declaring with typical flourish: "To add the weight of a feather to the crushing burdens now borne by England is to sin against the Holy Spirit [sic]."[18]

Wise leveled another section of his letter at Ben-Gurion. The latter had initiated an unofficial meeting of Zionist leaders for that very afternoon. Preparing himself for confrontation, Wise wrote: "If England fall we are fallen. If England win we have a chance, whether the implementation of the White Paper come or not. And whether Ben-Gurion will agree with us or not at today's meeting, we ought to take the position very firmly that, of course, we have made our comment (and I made it as strongly as I could at the embassy), we still wish England to understand that we are with her, not because we must be, but because we Jews choose to be; that we would not, if we could, live in a world from which democracy has perished."[19]

Following his critique of Ben-Gurion, Wise rose to the defense of Weizmann, with whose policies he had come to identify more and more over the years. "We must stand together in this matter," he insisted, "but we shall not move forward if we deepen strife within our own ranks by such insistence as your own upon the unwisdom of Dr. Weizmann's unequivocal and unconditional commitment to Britain fifteen months ago, or if any of us imagine that the way to strengthen the Zionist position in America is to indulge in sharp and bitter criticism of England.... Let none of us weaken the force of our united support of Britain by any diversion in any direction whatsoever."[20]

The gathering in preparation for which Wise wrote took place in the

18   S. Wise to S. Goldman, December 5, 1940, CZA 243/126.
19   Ibid.
20   Ibid.

afternoon in New York's Winthrop Hotel. Besides Ben-Gurion (and Arthur Lourie, secretary of the Emergency Committee), the meeting was attended by Israel Goldstein (president of the American Jewish National Fund), Nahum Goldmann, Louis Lipsky, Robert Szold, Tamar de Sola Pool, Abba Hillel Silver, and Stephen Wise. (Solomon Goldman, who had been en route to New York from Chicago, explained that he had been caught by a snowstorm in Cleveland. The absence of Kaufmann, president of the ZOA, probably needed no explanation.)[21]

David Ben-Gurion opened his remarks with an immediate call for a fresh, clear-cut policy. The world depended largely on America's stance, he maintained, and more than that, the "fate of the Jewish people depended on the stance of American Jewry; and said Jewry could be led by the Zionist movement." He proposed a sweeping program to the assembled leaders — working toward the establishment of a Jewish state to absorb the millions uprooted from Europe and, while the war went on, taking the difficult steps needed to set up a Jewish army and prepare Jewish fighting nuclei in America. These goals, he declared, had to be furthered through a broad campaign to educate and mold public opinion, both Christian and Jewish. Regarding the proper stance vis-à-vis England, Ben-Gurion acknowledged that the situation of the Zionists was complex. "As a people we are fighting Hitler and are anxious to help Britain in the prosecution of the war; but there is, on the other hand, an England implementing the White Paper. And while we must give England our whole-hearted support, we cannot support her where she is unjust, and we have the right to criticize like any Englishman. If we forget the White Paper, we renounce Zionism; if we forget the war, we renounce everything."

The attitude toward England, was the focal issue of this historic deliberation. Contrary to Stephen Wise's expectations, the two figures who dominated the proceedings were Ben-Gurion and Abba Hiller Silver.

Silver, who swiftly won recognition, demanded greater latitude for American Zionists in their relations with the World Zionist Organization, the better "to fight on a maximum Zionist program." He

---

21 "Report of a Meeting with Mr. Ben-Gurion held at the Winthrop Hotel, New York City, on December 5, 1940, at 2 P.M.," BGIA #150. This is the source for the ensuing discussion.

denigrated pressures emanating from the World Zionist Organization — that is, Weizmann — that "had caused a muting of the voice with regard, for example, to the Jewish Legion." Silver gave full backing to Ben-Gurion's view on the need to educate the public to Palestine's ability to absorb masses of Jews and so solve the refugee problem. "But when an effort was made to bring this home to the American public it was badly done," he maintained. Silver's listeners understood full well that he was attacking the public relations efforts of the Emergency Committee and that, in his opinion, Neumann was the man suited to do the job properly. Nahum Goldmann, the next speaker, came out for "a full-blooded Zionist program" and for the need to rouse the public, but he stopped short of offering a concrete political agenda. Silver reacted at once: "The British apparently took us for granted to such an extent that the embassy had in effect actually asked us to excuse their dirty actions to our own people."

Israel Goldstein began to speak of the possibility of bringing some of the non-Zionists into the picture, but Silver was not in a mood to let others expatiate. He knew from personal experience, he argued, that unanimity of thought within American Jewry was an impossibility. Hence he called for disregard of the non-Zionists, whose ranks were thin anyway outside of New York. At that moment, he claimed, American Zionists were ready to push forward vigorously in support of Palestine. They had to be given the leeway to do so.

After Silver had laid down his challenge, Stephen Wise took the floor. He summed up his approach briefly: "Dr. Wise warned," the protocols read, "that there was going to be a recrudescence of anti-nationalism among the anti-Zionist forces, and now was the time to bring our case home to our people in a big way, but the underlying objective was the defeat of Hitler." Repeating almost verbatim what he had written to Solomon Goldman, Wise asserted that "anything that might in any way affect sentiment in this country to Britain's disadvantage, that might add a featherweight to Britain's burden, must be avoided."

Once more Silver was recognized and challenged Wise frontally, laying out a position that effectively mirrored Ben-Gurion's. The protocol reports:

> Dr. Silver suggested that Dr. Wise was talking himself into a position disastrous to Zionism. Mr. Ben-Gurion said that Dr.

Wise's position was also wrong from the British point of view, for if the moral basis of her fight went wrong, so, too, would Britain's strength. He stressed again that if Britain were defeated we were lost, but if Britain won, we would not yet have won. He wanted as much as Dr. Wise to defeat Hitler, but for Britain to commit such acts as that in Haifa was for her to harm herself. If the British thought that the Jews were powerless from their point of view they were no doubt right, having the greater objective before them, to sacrifice us. But they must be made to realize that we were a factor and only thus can we save the honor and the future of the Jewish people. Dr. Silver added that it was not merely that the British government had taken up the attitude she had toward us, but that attitude was also followed by the American government. The Red Cross was an example. A section of the State Department had accepted the British point of view and discounted our own reaction.

Robert Szold espoused a position midway between that of Ben-Gurion and Silver and that of Wise. Interestingly, two leaders who generally supported Wise — Lipsky and de Sola Pool — said nothing on this occasion. Under these circumstances David Ben-Gurion was able to sum up the proceedings forcefully.

All agreed, he maintained, that there was need for a sweeping propaganda effort among Jews and non-Jews. He suggested a Zionist conference that would include all Zionist groups whatsoever to articulate the Zionist goal clearly to the American public. Ben-Gurion insisted that young Jews be given aeronautical and naval training. He claimed that, regarding Britain, the principle he had espoused had been accepted by everyone, even if "there was not such clarity on the application of that principle." When the Jewish Agency Executive chairman proposed that such leaders as Ussishkin, Berl Katznelson, and Sharett be invited to the United States, his listeners grasped more clearly how central the United States was to his Zionist calculations. In his concluding sentences Ben-Gurion blasted American Jewish inaction in the face of the expulsion of the refugees. "There was a feeling in Palestine that they were abandoned by American Zionism. To some extent that feeling was unjustified, but people here must realize as one example, that if they in Palestine had found it necessary in the middle of a war to undertake a general strike in connection with Haifa refugees, it was difficult for them to interpret the American decision against even the publication of a statement."

The pressures of Ben-Gurion and the more militant ZOA leaders, together with growing Jewish agitation and developments within America and on the international scene, all moved the Emergency Committee, if slowly, in the direction of public and radical action. On December 13 the committee's executive decided to issue a brief statement to the press and, in the spirit of Ben-Gurion's suggestion at the informal December 5 meeting, officially raised the issue of an encompassing conference of all Zionist bodies in America. The next full meeting of the committee, a few days later, saw a heated debate over the appropriate reaction to the expulsion. Nahum Goldmann proposed a Zionist conference and was seconded in this by David Wertheim of Poalei Zion. Phillip Cruso, also of Poalei Zion, proposed a mass protest meeting. The Hadassah representative suggested that official reaction be confined to a protest to the British embassy. Wise and Lipsky, the latter chairing the meeting, managed a compromise: no mass protest was to take place, but a delegation would be sent to the British embassy and a conference would be convened of the executive committees of the four largest Zionist bodies — the ZOA, Hadassah, Poalei Zion, and Mizrachi — together with the Youth Council. By the next meeting of the Emergency Committee Executive, America was being deluged with graphic and verifiable reports of the expulsion of the *Atlantic* refugees. It was decided that the Zionist convocation would take place three days later and that Neumann and Lourie would prepare a background report.[22]

Although the decision had been a compromise, it clearly reflected outrage with Britain's anti-Zionist policies, as well as increased militant strength, witnessed by the growing prominence of Emanuel Neumann. One month earlier Neumann had been invited to attend Emergency Committee meetings regularly "in an advisory capacity pending reorganization." At the December 19 meeting, in which he had participated, he had been given the responsibility of heading the Emergency Committee's "Office of Public Relations." Finally,

22 Minutes of the meetings of the Emergency Committee Executive, December 13, 18, and 19, 1940, ZAL.

Neumann was designated as one of three speakers slated to address the December 22 convocation, along with Ben-Gurion and Wise, thus guaranteeing the dominance of the militant Zionist camp.[23]

The meeting took place as scheduled, with the British government being raked over the coals for having expelled the refugees, "in spite of the obvious problems involved in a vigorous stand against such action [by Jews and non-Jews] at this time." Ben-Gurion spoke first, setting a belligerent tone. After reporting on the visit of the delegation to the British embassy, he devoted most of his remarks to counter Brandeis's opinion. Confronting the latter's, and Wise's, position that the British war effort dared not be hampered, Ben-Gurion stressed the Zionist right and duty to act like Englishmen, fully aware of British interests. Zionists had to assume, as did many Englishmen, that rendering aid to refugees from Nazism strengthened the British war effort. Ben-Gurion recorded: "Morris Rothenberg followed me to the podium. I expected him to support Goldstein's (i.e., Brandeis's) opinion, and I was flabbergasted when he came out behind Ben-Gurion's position one hundred percent. Speaker after speaker took up arms against what had happened [the lack of public Zionist reaction]. Only Abe Goldberg and L. Fishman were afraid that any action would harm the war effort."[24]

If, in the end, the resolution that passed included several expressions of concern over hampering England's war effort, the document was, from start to finish, a condemnation of British anti-Zionist policy. Criticism was leveled at the expulsion and at the entire White Paper as well. The convention vigorously called on England to halt expulsions and abandon its policy of appeasement in the Near East on humanitarian grounds, honoring an oppressed people's right for refuge, and out of British self-interest as well.

The significance of the declaration extended beyond its content. The very fact of its publication in the face of high-level opposition and a recent pattern of inaction represented a turning point. Even the women of Hadassah did not oppose publication, though they would have

23   Minutes of the meetings of the Emergency Committee Executive, November 5 and December 19, 1940, ZAL; *New Palestine* 30, no. 11 (December 27, 1940):7.

24   *New Palestine* 30, no. 11 (December 27, 1980):7. Minutes of the meeting of the Jewish Agency Executive, February 16, 1941, BGIA; this is the source for the ensuing discussion.

preferred milder wording. Significantly, *New Palestine* printed the full text of the statement, together with a report of the convention proceedings alongside. News organs as well joined the campaign to describe and lambast the expulsion. The editors of the *Yidisher Kemfer* published a lengthy and impassioned article that same date under the (Yiddish) headline, "The Deportation of the 1584" and the editors of the Poalei Zion's monthly, in its first issue following the convention, acted similarly. American Zionism, it may be concluded, had begun to emerge from a period of flaccidity and confusion.[25]

Moving American Jewry to rise up against the White Paper was only one aspect of Ben-Gurion's policy following the U.S. presidential election; the other was the elucidation and entrenchment of Zionism's political goal — Jewish sovereignty in Palestine at the war's end. A review of the Zionist press in America from 1930 to 1941 reveals that the term "Jewish state" or any like phrase patently expressing Jewish sovereignty was all but anathema. The popular expressions were "national home" or "homeland." The aspiration for a state came to be regarded as quasi-immoral by many Zionists, who preferred to focus on spiritual Zionism or philanthropic endeavor. Now some might maintain that this finding renders a simplistic picture, given America's diverse Zionist reality. Moreover, one can point to Rabbi Leon I. Feuer, "Silver's man," who at the close of 1940 was busy preparing *Why a Jewish State* published in 1942. Still, when one examines public pronouncements of American Zionists — which is only appropriate following the St. James Conference, where both Weizmann and Ben-Gurion raised the option of Hebrew statehood — one finds them vague, if not mealy-mouthed.[26]

As mentioned in Chapter 4, in the weeks that followed the outbreak of

---

25   Minutes of the meeting of the Hadassah National Board, December 24, 1940, HA; *New Palestine* 31, no. 11 (December 27, 1940):3, 7; *Yidisher Kemfer* 19, no. 378 (December 27, 1940):2; *Jewish Frontier* 8, no. 1 (January 1941):3.

26   Halperin, *American Zionism*, p. 210. "In 1940 and 1941 I was working on a book entitled, 'Why a Jewish State.' They [the copies] were used as propaganda material by AZEC [the American Zionist Emergency Council] and Zionist organizations generally, here [United States] and in Great Britain," L. Feuer to the author, July 21, 1980 (and see Leon I. Feuer, *Why a Jewish State* [New York, 1942], pp. 9–13).

World War II Ben-Gurion had held that the goal of Jewish statehood must dictate Zionist policy. Before the presidential election his remarks were sporadic and did not constitute a solid and well-articulated program. Not so thereafter. Ben-Gurion strove persistently, at first through contacts with the central Zionist bodies in America, to make Jewish sovereignty the clear Zionist strategy as the end of the war approached.

In the postelection period the Jewish Agency Executive chairman mounted his campaign for the formation of a Jewish army also as an instrument for the attainment of Jewish independence. In meetings that he held after November 5, 1940, he emphasized the need for mobilizing a "Jewish force in the course of the war, to ensure our status [in Palestine] immediately following the war." In a document that Ben-Gurion presented to the Emergency Committee on November 14, he proposed setting up in Palestine, at the war's end, "a regime which would enable the absorption of a maximum number of Jews from Europe in the shortest possible time." To arrive at this complete reversal of the White Paper policy, a new constellation of forces had to be created. "Without that it was idle to suppose that the British government would, of its own accord, risk a quarrel with the Arab world; or that the American government would take up our cause against the wishes of Britain." The Jewish army was to be a central instrument for attaining independence in Palestine. "The creation of a Jewish army to aid Britain, and its existence as an instrument for changing the status of Palestine at the end of the war in our favor, must, therefore, be the main aim of Zionist policy at present," he maintained.[27]

About two months passed before the Emergency Committee took any action on the question of such a Jewish force. After hearing from the London Zionist executive of progress in negotiations on a Jewish fighting unit, the committee decided, on January 17, 1941, to approach Sumner Welles, an American assistant secretary of state, and urge that "the U.S. encourage the British government to establish a Jewish military unit in the framework of the British army." After some debate, the Emergency Committee declined to petition the U.S. government

27   "Note of Mr. Ben Gurion's statement to the Emergency Committee for Zionist Affairs, Thursday, November 14 [1940], New York City," BGIA #156.

directly that Jewish American citizens be allowed to join the Jewish army, but left it to Sumner Welles to raise the issue.[28]

The Emergency Committee's decision showed how far removed its members were from Ben-Gurion's idea of the Jewish army as a tool for the attainment of Jewish independence in Palestine (as will be recalled, it was only with great difficulty that Ben-Gurion had succeeded in moving the Emergency Committee to take a public, anti-British stance on the expulsion of the illegal immigrants). No longer prepared to regard this body led by Lipsky and Wise as the major vehicle for furthering his postelection strategy, the Yishuv leader began to focus his energies on the committee's constituent bodies.

The first time that Ben-Gurion raised the issue of a Jewish sovereignty-oriented program during his American visit was at the November 26, 1940, meeting of the National Board of Hadassah, to which he had been invited following his presentation at the Cincinnati conference. As will be recalled Ben-Gurion and the women's Zionist organization, despite political differences, held each other in warm regard. Hence he was able to get to essentials in a friendly but forthright manner: "I am here again. I want to tell you — and this is not a politeness — I am glad to be here. I am afraid I am going to disturb you again. It is an unpleasant job, but it has to be done."[29]

He reminded his listeners how at their prior meeting he had spoken out against succumbing to illusions. Now, he said, he would try to point out in a positive manner what had to be done. Three developments, he explained, required a new program of action: the Mandatary's changed policy, the state of the world conflict, and the special danger looming over European Jewry. A twofold policy was needed, Ben-Gurion declared — a Jewish state and a Jewish army. The Yishuv leader devoted most of his remarks to justifying an all-out effort for the former goal. There had been no logic to demand such a state during World War I, he

28   Minutes of the meeting of the Emergency Committee Executive, January 17, 1941, ZAL.

29   "Verbatim Account of Mr. Ben-Gurion's Remarks at the National Board Meeting of Hadassah, November 26, 1940," BGIA #150; this is the source for the ensuing discussion.

explained, because there had not been enough Jews in Palestine at the time and "you cannot have a state just by declaring a state." The Mandate had failed, he held; it would not be revived. Nor could the British be depended on, even the most pro-Zionist among them, to set up a Jewish state. They would not risk military confrontation with the Arabs. There was always the possibility of an Arab state being declared; then, however, the vast majority of the Yishuv would take up arms to defend what had become for them, in the deepest sense, their homeland. Western Palestine was capable of taking in 5 million European Jewish refugees, the Jewish Agency Executive chairman argued, and a Jewish state was the indispensable vehicle for effecting their settlement and absorption.

Ben-Gurion maintained that the incorporation of a Jewish army in the war effort would lead Britain to disregard the White Paper, and the army's existence would contribute significantly to the creation of a Jewish state. If American Jewry would press for the establishment of such a force, he said, there was a good chance that the American government would agree. This dual goal, he concluded, a Jewish army and a Jewish state, comprised the whole content of Zionism "for the present hour."

Whereas most of Ben-Gurion's remarks had centered on gaining Jewish sovereignty in Palestine following the war's end, most of his auditors' reactions focused on the Jewish army. In response to one question, Ben-Gurion sketched a possible scenario: "If America will have to give more help to Britain, the whole scene in America will change — the psychology, too, will change. I assume there will be a change in America. If this assumption is right, given English and American consent, I am sure many Jews here will respond, even people who are non-Zionists." Bertha Schoolman, who chaired the meeting, apparently spoke for most of those present when she thanked Ben-Gurion "for a thought-provoking speech" but also expressed reservations. Still, the meeting was characterized by deep concern and a thirst for information; moreover, Judith Epstein and some others indicated through their questions a good deal of support for Ben-Gurion's platform. Ben-Gurion concluded in his diary: "Questions were raised — and so were challenges. A Jewish army does not clash with American interests (I explained that the agreement of the American government would be prerequisite, as would be [working] only within the framework of the law) but would likely harm the status of American Jewry and foment internal conflict. The women were impressed. For the moment I find no better Zionist forum."[30]

The great importance that Ben-Gurion attributed to Hadassah is attested additionally by the fact that, until the last days of his stay on the eastern seaboard, he pressured the organization, whose members bore no great love for Lipsky and his methods, to keep itself on the Emergency Committee. Finally, before leaving America, Ben-Gurion wrote a long letter to Tamar de Sola Pool, president of Hadassah, in which he expressed his high esteem for the organization: "Though we argued and disagreed and did not always see eye to eye," he said, "I have found in the Hadassah women a Zionist awareness beyond my expectations, though not perhaps to the extent to which I might desire." He ventured that the organization held great potential and concluded with a challenge: "This is a moment pregnant with significance and every historic hour has its vision. Only to the daring, the courageous and enterprising is it given to achieve great deeds. And now the time has come for great and far-reaching Zionist achievement. My blessings to you — may you live up to the demands of the present time."

In her warm reply the Hadassah president disregarded the political issues raised by the Jewish Agency Executive chairman but informed him that the letter had been read aloud at the National Board meeting and that copies had been sent to active Hadassah members throughout the country. She took to task the leadership of the American Zionist movement, referring to the Emergency Committee under the guidance of Wise and Lipsky — this being one point on which Ben-Gurion's position clearly coalesced with Hadassah's — and expressed her hope for continued close relations.[31]

30   Minutes of the meeting of the Hadassah National Board, November 26, 1940, HA; *Diary*, November 26, 1940, BGIA #30. See also Ben-Gurion's reports on his return to Palestine, minutes of the meeting of the Jewish Agency Executive, February 16, 1941, and minutes of the meeting of the Mapai Central Committee, February 19, 1941, BGIA.

31   Minutes of the meeting of the Hadassah National Board, January 14, 1941, HA; Ben-Gurion to Tamar de Sola Pool, January 16, 1941, BGIA #73; Tamar de Solar Pool to Ben-Gurion, February 20, 1941, BGIA #73; minutes of the meeting of Hadassah National Board, January 21, 1941, HA.

When Ben-Gurion returned to Palestine he held a press conference in which he expressed his enthusiasm for the Women's Zionist Organization of America:

> The most significant and encouraging thing I met with this time in America is the Hadassah movement, a large and growing women's organization, and a women's Zionist organization — by American Zionist standards. There is high dedication — eighty thousand women doing their job, keeping in touch with each other, really well organized, not just a machine.... They spend their time in worthwhile efforts for the Jewish people, for Palestine, systematic work, much dedication, much warmth.... This is a Zionist phenomenon of the utmost significance, bringing credit to American Jewry and winning the respect of the non-Jews.[32]

For all his high regard and affection for Hadassah, Ben-Gurion openly continued his attempts at the political education of the organization. Thus in the aforementioned farewell letter to the president of Hadassah he continued to hammer home his program for the war's end. Exploiting Roosevelt's dramatic postelection call to the American people to abandon "business as usual," the Yishuv leader urged American involvement in the global conflict:

> Roosevelt anticipated a historic need when he urged a cessation of "business as usual," despite the fact that "business" in America on the whole was not bad at all. If America can adopt such a policy, how much more so does it apply to Zionism in America!
>
> All previous considerations, all former relationships, all the current concepts, all the usual procedures — no longer hold. There can no longer be continued inertia. There should be well-planned, zealous endeavor, both politically and organizationally. There should be a comprehensive program, permeated by a strong determination and directed to meet the needs of the immediate future. There should be readiness and renewed awareness, both in thought and in deed. There should be a program of broad scope and outlook. There should be a serious and maximal effort to

---

32 Ben-Gurion, remarks at a press conference, Jerusalem, February 26, 1941, BGIA #160.

reach, during the war and immediately thereafter, a fundamental and complete solution to the Jewish problem by the transfer of millions of Jews to Palestine and the establishment of Palestine as a Jewish Commonwealth, an equal member in the family of free commonwealths which will be set up after this war.[33]

To a certain extent David Ben-Gurion's relations with Poalei Zion were the reverse of those that obtained between him and Hadassah. While he liked and respected Hadassah, he hardly identified with Poalei Zion and, as noted earlier, was disdainful of its conservatism and insularity. There was a wide ideological gap on the question of Jewish Palestine sovereignty that separated him from Hadassah, whereas, Poalei Zion, Mapai's sister party, tended to accept Ben-Gurion's ideological authority and echoed his demand for a Jewish common-wealth, being first among all Zionist bodies in the United States to do so.

Ben-Gurion's address at the Sixteenth National Convention of the Geverkshaften on November 23, 1940, demonstrated his shift to political goals following the U.S. presidential election. Not even mentioning on this occasion the issue of the Jewish army, he launched an impassioned attack on Britain's policy of expelling refugees. While praising Britain's courageous stand against Hitler, he devoted most of his remarks to his opening critique: Europe had become the site of the destruction of the Jewish people; Jews would no longer wish to remain there at the war's close. Where, then, would the millions of displaced persons go? Elaborating on the Yishuv's economic growth and settlement record, he claimed that western Palestine alone could absorb 5 million newcomers. There were but two supreme goals to work for, he concluded, "a victorious England and a Jewish Palestine."[34]

At the December 12 meeting of Poalei Zion's Central Committee Ben-Gurion spelled out his goal for a Jewish state at the war's end. He opened his address with one of his oft-repeated themes — a comparison of the status of Zionism in World War I with its present situation, highlighting the differences. He focused on the situation of the American Poalei Zion.

33   Ben-Gurion to Tamar de Sola Pool, January 16, 1941, BGIA #73.
34   "David Ben-Gurion Address" (see n. 13, above).

He pointed out various sociological factors that, in his opinion, led to the party's decline following World War I but added that a subjective factor had to be considered. The American party, Ben-Gurion claimed, no longer had a sense of public mission and, in its absence, had lost creativity and influence. Similarly, he added, the Emergency Committee lacked cohesion and a central challenge. A dual platform was called for, he claimed, with both wartime and peacetime goals. The peace platform was tripartite: (1) the granting of full equality for Jews in all countries; (2) the status of Palestine, a subject he chose to explicate later; and (3) opposition to the least suggestion of Jewish dispersal. Any attempt at territorial solutions outside of Palestine had to be unmasked as illusory or deceptive.[35]

The future of Palestine, the speaker continued, hinged on two things: first, its capacity to bring in and absorb the Jewish millions from blood-drenched Europe, a task whose dimensions he detailed even as he acknowledged the tremendous cost involved. More than technical readiness would be required, he said. Determination and love were crucial, for which "one needs a mother," a Jewish state. The second prerequisite was the state's sovereignty, and he listed three possibilities: full sovereignty, autonomy within the framework of the British empire, or autonomy within a Middle Eastern federation. What counted most, he emphasized, was that the Jewish leadership really run the country's affairs and control immigration. He summed up his thoughts thus:

> I hold that the founding of a Jewish state must be our Zionist platform in America now. This means, first of all, serious political propaganda, not for a state per se, but that Palestine and only Palestine can absorb millions of Jews after the war, with a Jewish state being the indispensable means for bringing millions of Jews to Palestine. This must be the focal point of American Jewry's Zionist effort. This is the peace program: a struggle for equal rights, a struggle for all the Jews who cannot remain in Europe nor wish to do so — Palestine, a Jewish state.

35 Minutes of the meeting of Poalei Zion Central Committee, Winthrop Hotel, New York City, on December 12, 1940, BGIA #159; this is the source for the ensuing discussion.

In his war platform Ben-Gurion emphasized the importance of Jewish independence in aiding England. In America, he argued, political action should back such a demand, for although Jews were a very small percentage of the American population, they could be a decisive factor under certain circumstances. Given the play of forces obtaining in America, he claimed, Poalei Zion fell far short of what it could do in eliciting the potential of American Jewry.

Ben-Gurion set the need for a Jewish army at the center of his war platform. Jewry's goal had to be the crushing of Hitler, not necessarily helping Britain. Poalei Zion had to reach out to the masses, the Yishuv leader maintained, as it had done during World War I. Ben-Gurion completed his remarks on the war platform by emphasizing the need to fight the White Paper, taking care at the same time not to paint Britain so black as to jeopardize American aid to that country.

He devoted the last part of his remarks to the Emergency Committee. Scoring the committee for its lack of focus, Ben-Gurion called on his listeners to demand of that group the implementation of his proposals — systematically educating the Jewish and general public toward establishing Palestine as a Jewish state or commonwealth at the end of the war. (Non-Zionists, he added, should not be allowed to join the committee until they accepted this position.)

Ben-Gurion continued to expound his views under the unusual circumstances of the December 24 meeting of Poalei Zion's Central Committee. At that time, the American Jewish Congress had decided to purchase British debitory notes, at the instigation of Stephen Wise — then president (1936–1949), a past president (1925–1929), and among the organization's founders. (The American Jewish Committee was leaning in the same direction: like Wise, its members were pursuing the matter at the State Department and the British embassy.) A debate on this subject, which had opened the Poalei Zion meeting, was interrupted to allow for Ben-Gurion's presentation. In his prefatory remarks, however, Ben-Gurion, honed in precisely on the debitory note issue. He repudiated the American Jewish effort to help bankroll Britain, not only because the sums involved were insubstantial but also, more fundamentally, because the project vitiated independent Jewish action. Such initiatives, he claimed, damaged the Zionist cause, hampering relations with the embassy and State Department both. Following the deliberation on Ben-Gurion's program, the Central Committee voted to oppose the American Jewish Congress position and to bring the issue before the Emergency Committee.[36]

The Poalei Zion deliberations were stamped in no small measure by a sharp confrontation between Ben-Gurion and Aryeh Tartakower, a World Jewish Congress activist living in America for the duration of the war. While supporting the Poalei Zion stance on the debitory notes, he nonetheless sought to soften that opposition. During the deliberations over Ben-Gurion's proposals he twice voiced reservations over the harsh repudiation of alternative territorial solutions. He also took exception to Ben-Gurion's differentiation of Jewish obligations as American citizens and as Jews. (Ben-Gurion had opened his remarks with the assertion that although American Jews had to fulfill all their civic responsibilities, their Jewishness imposed special obligations on them vis-à-vis England.) "The distinction between Jews as American citizens and Jews as Jews," Tartakower remonstrated, "is not valid. Above all we are bound to England." Political stances such as these led Ben-Gurion to speak disparagingly of the American Jewish Congress at a later date.[37]

The document that Ben-Gurion brought with him to the Central Committee covered four topics: (1) a peace plan, (2) a war platform, (3) the White Paper and the war, and (4) the Emergency Committee. In essence, his proposals were the same as those he had raised before that body on December 12, if more concrete on this occasion. Twice in the first section (the peace proposal) he raised the demand of Jewish sovereignty at the war's end as the appropriate Zionist wartime strategy: once to explain that only Jewish governmental action in Palestine could cope with Jewish immigration and absorption and once as a clear-cut demand for "establishing a Jewish state in Palestine to absorb, as rapidly

---

36 Minutes of the meeting of the Poalei Zion Central Committee, December 24, 1940, ILPA, section 3, 101/40. On December 23, 1940, the Inter-Faith Committee for Aid to the Democracies was founded. Louis Segal, the representative of Poalei Zion, demanded independent Jewish and Zionist action, but his was a minority opinion in a convention dominated by Stephen Wise. See the protocol of the "Emergency Conference, American Jewish Aid to Great Britain, summoned by the American Jewish Congress, New York, December 29, 1940" [118 pp.], IGA, 3002, 3003.

37 Minutes of the meeting of the Poalei Zion Executive Committee, December 24, 1940, ILPA section 3, 101/40; minutes of the meeting of the Mapai Central Committee, February 19, 1941, BGIA.

as possible, the Jewish masses from Europe and other lands of the dispersion marked by Jewish suffering."[38]

The deliberations revolved about this platform. In one way or another most participants accepted Ben-Gurion's position on the question of aid (debitory notes) to Britain. Some even called on the Palestinian leader to remain in the United States to impose his policy on the Emergency Committee. Isaac Hamlin, national secretary of the Histadrut Fund from its founding until his *aliyah* in 1956, threw all his weight behind Ben-Gurion, with apparent results. Some few speakers expressed concern lest the demand for a state lead to the partition of western Palestine, and one of the participants even suggested that restoring the Mandate to Britain would solve Jewry's problems after the war. The sentiment of the meeting was stated clearly by David Wertheim, the Poalei Zion representative to the Emergency Committee, who rejected the notion of non-Zionists joining the committee because a clear-cut platform on a Jewish state was the need of the hour. The deliberations were summed up by Ben-Gurion himself, and the platform was accepted without a formal vote. In addition, a formal resolution repudiated the path chosen by the American Jewish Congress to aid Britain and called on the Emergency Committee to adopt the Poalei Zion position.

Significant as it was, the Poalei Zion decision to work toward the establishment of a Jewish state at the war's end was not a landmark in the history of American Zionism. The resolution was all but ignored within the party, which, in any event, was peripheral to Zionist political life in the United States. The significance of these decisions lay in their serving as guidelines to party representatives of umbrella organizations (such as the Emergency Committee and the United Palestine Appeal) and in affecting developments in Mapai in Palestine. Ben-Gurion returned home, announcing that Mapai's sister party in America had adopted a platform calling for the establishment of a Jewish commonwealth at the war's end. Moreover, Ben-Gurion prefaced his report to the Mapai Central Committee on his stay in England and the

---

38   "Ben-Gurion Notes For a War Program" (in Yiddish), December 31, 1940 (the date of the publication of the program after its ratification), LA, Section 3, 12 (73), File 1085 (this document includes the four topics discussed in the text); minutes of the meeting of the Poalei Zion Central Committee, December 24, 1940, ILPA, section 3, 101/40. These are the sources for the ensuing discussion.

United States with an account of the Poalei Zion decision. He even cited the platform in detail as far as his memory allowed.[39]

Of much greater significance were Ben-Gurion's activities within the orbit of the ZOA, the politically oriented and second largest of all Zionist bodies in America, which contained within its ranks most of the country's prominent Zionist figures. It was the ZOA, more than any other Zionist group, that determined the path of American Zionism.

On December 5, 1940, it will be recalled, Ben-Gurion initiated a meeting with the ZOA leadership (Hadassah president Tamar de Sola Pool attended in an observer capacity), calling on them to protest publicly the expulsion of the "illegal" immigrants. At this same meeting Ben-Gurion fully articulated his political program for the first time. The Mandate, he declared, was defunct and could not be resurrected. After the war a new international forum would arise, but not one modeled on the Geneva pattern. What mattered most was that the British would no longer be dealing with Jewish immigrants and their settlement in Palestine. Hence it devolved upon the Zionist movement to move toward the creation of those political conditions that would ensure the absorption of millions of Jews in the homeland. Again Ben-Gurion hammered home his themes of possible modes of autonomy and the urgent need for educating the Jewish and non-Jewish public on the proper and eminently possible role of Palestine in the years ahead.[40]

The meeting did not proceed to debate Zionism's goal at the war's end; that had not been Ben-Gurion's immediate objective. However, the gathering did produce significant results beyond the decision to protest the expulsion of the refugees: Stephen Wise was put on the defensive; Silver's credit rose; and Ben-Gurion, after having laid out a sweeping political program, was accorded more respect than ever before.

Ben-Gurion's second appearance before the ZOA leadership, in November–December 1940, was under more formal circumstances, against a backdrop of continuing radicalization of American Zionists. These processes found expression, among other things, in the effort to refurbish the United Palestine Appeal (UPA) within the framework of

39   Minutes of the meeting of the Mapai Central Committee, February 19, 1941, BGIA.
40   "Meeting at Winthrop" (see n. 21).

the United Jewish Appeal (UJA). When the UJA had been founded in 1939 in the wake of *Kristallnacht*, many viewed the fund's central task to be the tendering of aid to Jewish victims in Europe and to refugees reaching America. In the spirit of this approach, the 1940 allocations were divided as follows: to the Joint Distribution Committee, which principally looked after refugees in Europe — 49 percent; to the National Refugee Service, a fund helping new arrivals in America — 28 percent; and to the UPA — 23 percent.[41]

In 1940 growing segments of the Jewish community felt the need to change the proportion of the allocations, for three reasons: (1) it was very difficult to get any monies or supplies through to Europe; (2) very few Jews were reaching America; and (3) Palestine had become a major haven for Jewish refugees. Consequently, during the summer of 1940, many influential voices in the Jewish community, particularly in the Zionist camp, were calling for an increased UPA allotment within the UJA. Leading this campaign were UPA chairman Abba Hillel Silver and executive director Henry Montor. As they came to realize that the non-Zionist philanthropic leadership adamantly opposed any change in the allocation percentages, Silver and Montor began to raise the possibility of an independent Palestine fund. After conferring with the Palestinian Zionist leadership, Silver mustered support from all quarters. Even the cautious and moderate Eliezer Kaplan, head of the Jewish Agency's Finance Department, was prepared to back such an independent effort. By November, and again at the outset of December, the Jewish Agency leadership approved exploratory discussions between the UPA leadership and the ZOA about an independent fund.

Ben-Gurion held to the position he had come to during his visit of January 1939 — namely, that Zionist activity in America divorced from fund-raising could never be vital. Thus he favored independent UPA activity but avoided any radical initiative on this issue. Finally, by December 25, an official statement proclaimed the existence of two different funds. On January 5, 1941, the ZOA National Administrative Council assembled in a belligerent mood; Silver's bold step in

---

41　*New Palestine* 31, no. 11 (December 27, 1940):5–6, 10; Raphael, *History of the United Jewish Appeal*, pp. 13–19; Halperin, *American Zionism*, pp. 195–204. These are the sources for the ensuing discussion.

confronting the public with a separate campaign contributed much to this mood. Following Henry Montor's detailed progress report the assemblage gave its full backing to his and Silver's steps. Some even called for more extreme measures to win financial autonomy for Zionism. It was in this atmosphere that Ben-Gurion delivered his prominent political address on Zionism in America.

The better to appreciate the import of Ben-Gurion's remarks, we must recall one more event that took place between the official announcement of separate funds and the meeting of the ZOA National Administrative Council. On December 29, 1940, Roosevelt had issued an almost revolutionary statement: "We must be the great arsenal of democracy. For us this is an emergency as serious as war itself. We must apply ourselves to our task with the same resolution, the same sense of urgency, the same spirit of patriotism and sacrifice as we would show were we at war." These strong and transparent statements brought the United States much closer to the side of fortress England and, in practical terms, laid the groundwork for the passage of the Lend-Lease Bill, which was being drafted at the time by the U.S. Treasury. Most of the American public welcomed Roosevelt's challenge enthusiastically.[42]

Roosevelt's dramatic call straightened the backs of American Jewry, and especially its Zionist component. *New Palestine*, the major organ of the ZOA, reacted immediately with a lengthy editorial stating that fear of internal anti-Semitism was a thing of the past. In addition, the Zionist weekly praised a raid on Nazi party headquarters in a midwestern city, telling its readers that "the Justice Department was reported considering the possibility of a nation-wide drive on all Nazi agents who had failed to register with the government." The article called for strict judicial action against the Nazi party in America and, following Roosevelt's lead, for the baring of pro-Nazi figures in high places. Here indeed was a new spirit among the Zionists of America.[43]

Ben-Gurion felt that Roosevelt's plea to the American public on December 29 had radically altered the political map in the United States. Reporting to the Mapai Central Committee, he wrote: "Many feared that Roosevelt would buckle — especially when weeks passed [following

42   Dallek, *Roosevelt and American Foreign Policy*, pp. 256–257.
43   *New Palestine* 31, no. 12, (January 3, 1941):3–4.

his election] and he still kept silent. ... So there was great fear until finally he came out with an address in which he said that England must be supported. ... These words had tremendous impact. The mood in America has changed. It is likely that Willkie helped this a great deal... by publicly coming out... after Roosevelt's election, in his support." Ben-Gurion's conclusion was: "I have been in America three months, but during these three months a truly revolutionary change has taken place in the country's mood." One week after the president's historic public address and two days after the appearance of the aforementioned issue of *New Palestine*, Ben-Gurion, who by that time had already attained considerable status in the public eye, delivered his major political address to the ZOA.[44]

The heart of the speech, this time delivered to the leading Zionist political body in America, was identical with the main points that he had raised before the Poalei Zion Central Committee on December 12 and 24, 1940, and that appeared in his program (accepted at the last of those meetings). Ben-Gurion called for "first, help even during the war, in the rebuilding of Palestine. ... Secondly, vigilance against the application of the White Paper, as true, devoted friends of England. Thirdly, the mobilization of American Jewry and American public opinion for the creation of a Jewish Commonwealth in Palestine, after the war." Ben-Gurion emphasized more strongly than ever before the Yishuv's readiness for sovereignty. Beyond the Yishuv's economic achievements in absorption, settlement, and development, Ben-Gurion asserted, lay a political and psychological reality: the Jews of Palestine "regarded themselves potentially as a state, as a nation." Here was a community that taxed itself and was functioning well in all essential areas. Indeed, Yishuv initiatives and competence often confounded the colonial clerks unused to anything other than subservience. "I have noted," he observed wryly, "that this Zionist zeal at times seems exaggerated even to members of the Zionist movement outside of Palestine."[45]

44   All quotations are from Ben-Gurion's report at the Mapai Central Committee meeting: minutes, February 19, 1941, BGIA.

45   Minutes of the ZOA National Administrative Council meeting, January 5, 1941, at the Benjamin Franklin Hotel, Philadelphia, ZAL, ZOA XIV/1; this is the source for the ensuing discussion.

Ben-Gurion struck a new chord in depicting America's role in determining the fate of Palestine. His certainty sprang, first, from the visibly imminent participation of the United States in the war. He had long assumed that if America were to enter the conflict it would determine its outcome.

This was the first political address in which Ben-Gurion used the term "commonwealth" throughout rather than "state," as he had previously to describe the goal of Jewish sovereignty in Palestine.

> We must provide for the establishment of Palestine as a Commonwealth after the war. It is not a new thing; it is not a new invention. This is what America said in the last war; this is what Wilson wanted; and I know that the present America, which certainly is not worse than the America of Wilson — this democratic America which asserted itself in the last elections, and which spoke last week through President Roosevelt — will understand us.

Ben-Gurion had so phrased his remarks as to invite American involvement in the attainment of Jewish sovereignty in Palestine; the use of the term "commonwealth" was one clear indication of this intention. From this point onward (or, one might claim, beginning with Roosevelt's December 29 speech) Ben-Gurion would use the term increasingly in his major appearances and in his recommendations for official Zionist resolutions. He later explained his adoption of "commonwealth" in America rather than "state," Weizmann's preferred term in England. "Inasmuch as the former term was a recognized term in the American lexicon wherever Palestine was concerned, it was valuable — and deserved to be treated respectfully. Wilson... used the term 'commonwealth' in his declaration [in support of the Balfour Declaration]."

In anticipating a new regime in Palestine to rise on the ruins of the White Paper, Ben-Gurion took care to bring the United States into the picture, this being one more example of his, by now full, shift from an English-oriented to an Anglo-American policy (with the accent on "American"): "There must be a good Mandate. Not only a Mandate by England, but a Mandate by America. There must be a new order."

The American motif in Ben-Gurion's address included as well his praise for Roosevelt, who, he declared, was "expressing the real spirit of

American democracy and Jewish democracy, which are one." The aspiration for a Jewish commonwealth, he told his listeners, embodied American principles — democracy, freedom, and justice — and therefore Zionists had a right to expect America's support. Ben-Gurion concluded his remarks with the same forward-looking message as that conveyed by Roosevelt to the American people, and with a like inspirational tone (see Appendix IV).

Ben-Gurion's November 5 presentation soon found a broad Zionist readership. The editor of *New Palestine*, Carl Alpert, who two months before had replaced Samuel Kaplan, a Louis Lipsky protégé, informed the chairman of the Jewish Agency, "I consider it [the address] a most statesmanlike presentation of the direction that Zionist policy should take." So it was that the January 17 issue of the leading American Zionist journal prominently displayed the address (only lightly edited). That same issue contained an editorial, facing the Ben-Gurion speech, titled "The Ideal," preparing ZOA readers for the approaching Washington convention of the independent UPA. The editorial expressed the certainty that the convention would remain true to the Zionist legacy of Herzl, Nordau, Weizmann, Sokolow, and Brandeis, a legacy dictating that the distress of Europe's victims not be solved through charity, with its concomitant dependence. The concluding section showed how Ben-Gurion had put his stamp on the political direction of American Zionism. The journal declared:

> This point of view cannot be too often repeated, for it is the very basis of the ideological conflict which underlies the dissipation of the united drive this year. Zionists maintain that the problem of Jewish homelessness can be solved only by the creation of a Jewish Commonwealth, as so eloquently presented by Mr. David Ben-Gurion elsewhere in this issue. To that end every Zionist must subscribe, and to the realization of that ideal the United Palestine Appeal is dedicated.[46]

---

46   C. Alpert to Ben-Gurion, January 10, 1941, BGIA #73; Ben-Gurion, "Zionist Policy Today," *New Palestine* 31, no. 14 (January 17, 1941):7–8; editorial, p. 6. This issue of *New Palestine* came out on the very day that Ben-Gurion left for Palestine.

For all the radicalization that American Zionism had undergone and for all the influence of David Ben-Gurion, the political landscape of the ZOA and the Emergency Committee remained varied on the eve of the UPA convention.

Still keeping at a certain distance, Stephen Wise continued to broadcast his stand in the pages of *Opinion*. The December 1940 issue of the monthly contained the editorial "Do All for Britain," written against the backdrop of the entry of Hungary, Rumania, and Slovakia into the fascist sphere and fear of systematic and barbaric anti-Semitism in those countries. For Wise, this was yet another opportunity to remind his readers that England was the sole barrier between barbarism and civilization, and that American Jews had to support Britain unflaggingly. If they so acted, he claimed, the day would come when England and America would remember with gratitude and pride that the Jews had stood in the forefront of the struggle for freedom and human dignity. The alliance with England was of paramount importance; Jewish independence in the struggle against Nazism was by no means crucial. This was the cornerstone of Stephen Wise's international policy. The January 1941 issue of *Opinion* was devoted largely to the theme of "Do All for Britain." In Wise's flowery and emotional style, the editorial informed the readership of the American Jewish Congress's decision to found a movement called "American Jewish Aid to Britain." Details on this decision were presented in a news article titled "Britain Forever." Among other things, readers learned that this new movement was proposing that every American Jew "do something each and every day for Britain."[47]

Of the Brandeisian elite, Felix Frankfurter and Ben Cohen took positions close to those expressed in the *Opinion* editorial. No less than Wise, one may safely assume, they felt that political Zionism should move forward on the confined path of diplomatic activity in America, taking extreme care not to offer any possible injury to England.

Brandeis, despite his advanced age (eighty-four in 1941, the last year of his life), was keenly aware of what was going on around him and retained a certain flexibility in his positions. One must also remember the deep mutual respect obtaining between Brandeis and Ben-Gurion;

47 *Opinion* 11, no. 2 (December 1940):3–4, no. 3 (January 1941):3–4.

during this period of conflict between the two (November–December 1940) on the issue of relations with Britain, they continued to maintain a warm and meaningful rapport. Thus Dov Joseph, who met with Brandeis for in-depth discussions immediately after Ben-Gurion's return to Palestine, relates:

> I had four long talks with Brandeis himself. Ben-Gurion had given me a first-hand report of his conversations with Brandeis during his stay in America and had informed me that he [Brandeis] had warmed to our work considerably. Perhaps he has been impressed by what we have accomplished in Palestine. He advised me to write Frankfurter at once about [Sir Harold] MacMichael [High Commissioner for Palestine]; he thought that Frankfurter could be of great help in this [influencing MacMichael's policies]. He took great interest in the issue of the Jewish army as well. My impression is that at this juncture he would support an activist, responsible Zionist effort more than he has thus far.[48]

In his memoirs, Yosef Yizre'eli tells of three "singular" meetings with Brandeis. His impression from the first meeting was that the justice was none too enthusiastic about "our programs". His view of the last meeting, which took place at the outset of 1941, was quite different:

> He [Brandeis] had the highest regard for the work we had done with the youth, and despite the official positions of some Zionist leaders, looked upon this effort as essential. Beyond that, he encouraged us in our efforts to broaden the framework of [the youth movement] HeHalutz in preparation for the establishment of the *plugot* [groups trained for pioneering work and self-defense]. He held that following the world war we would have no option other than fighting, in order to establish an independent Jewish commonwealth in Palestine; and if the *plugot* from America could contribute to that struggle, nothing could be more important.[49]

In early 1941 Wise was probably able to count on the support of one member of the Brandeis circle — Edmund Kaufmann, president of the

---

48   Minutes of the meeting of the Mapai Central Committee, April 14, 1941, BGIA.
49   Yizre'eli, *On a Security Mission,* pp. 35–36.

ZOA — not because Kaufmann had worked out a particularly pro-Wise position, but mainly because he was lacking in interest and was anything but a dynamic leader. Kaufmann attended few Zionist meetings but spent most of his time relaxing in Florida — to the chagrin of Solomon Goldman, who had invested much effort in championing Kaufmann over the Lipsky group.

Despite the growing Zionist radicalization of American Jewry and Ben-Gurion's fine relationship with Hadassah, that organization continued to follow its traditional bent on political issues at the outset of 1941. It avoided any politicization of public opinion, subjugated Zionist policy to Britain's war against fascism, sought compromises with the Arabs to ensure the success of the Zionist endeavor, and eschewed any call to American Jews to enlist in a Jewish army or work for Jewish sovereignty in Palestine. At the same time, however, it would seem that the strength of the traditionalist camp within the organization was declining, even though the Hadassah representatives to the Emergency Committee continued to demand a reorganization of that body (a motion raised well before they met Ben-Gurion) so as to include non-Zionists. However, the motion was defeated at the December 25 meeting of the Emergency Committee. On the Arab question, Hadassah ostensibly retained its traditional stance; but here, too, a change took place. Increasingly, influential members distanced themselves from the acts and pronouncements of Rose Jacobs, an enthusiast of the pro-binationalism the League for Jewish-Arab Understanding, and Hadassah began to incline gradually toward positions generally accepted in the Zionist movement. Last and most important, the organization accepted *de facto* the more militant position pressed on the UPA by Silver.[50]

On January 7, 1941, the National Board of Hadassah took up the UPA demand for 50 percent of the funds raised together with the American Jewish Joint Distribution Committee. The Hadassah

---

50   Minutes of the meeting of the Hadassah National Board, January 7, 1941, HA; minutes of the meeting of the Emergency Committee, November 14 and December January 25, 1940, ZAL. R. Szold to Brandeis, December 12, 1940, on Mrs. Jacobs's activities, and Brandeis to R. Szold, December 23, 1940, on his talk with Tamar de Sola Pool, ZAL, Szold Collection IX/29; minutes of the meeting of the Hadassah National Board, January 7, 14 and 28, 1941, HA. These are the sources for the ensuing discussion.

leadership, who raised funds for their own organization outside the framework of the UPA (resembling in this the Jewish National Fund), felt uncomfortable supporting this demand and voted for a sixty-forty ratio (i.e., only 40 percent for the UPA). Judith Epstein, one of the two Hadassah representatives to negotiate with the UPA, took pains thereafter to give a clearer signal of support from Hadassah to the Zionist fund. On January 8 representatives of Hadassah met with Abba Hillel Silver to hear officially of the UPA decision to raise monies separately in 1941.

At the next National Board meeting of Hadassah, on January 14, a motion by Epstein to support, in principle, Silver's position was passed; that was done in opposition to the leadership of the Council of Jewish Federations and Welfare Funds, under the presidency of Sidney Hollander. On January 23, two days after the opening of the UPA convention, a delegation of Hadassah leaders, together with the Executive Committee of the ZOA, held a meeting of solidarity deciding, at the suggestion of Solomon Goldman, to put the services of the ZOA at the disposal of an independent UPA. Hadassah's National Board appointed a distinguished delegation to the UPA convention, including, among others, Judith Epstein and the president of the organization, Tamar de Sola Pool.

From mid-December onward the militant camp within the American Zionist movement moved forward with greater vigor than the moderates. Silver became an increasingly focal figure, in which process he continued to sharpen his positions. On more than one occasion, and especially during three Sunday sermons of January 1941, he saturated his Cleveland congregants with political statements. On January 5 he highlighted America's emergence from isolationism as the most significant event of 1940 and focused on the topic of the Jewish refugees. These unfortunates, he declared, were making their way by sea and by land circuitously to Palestine, their sole refuge, and that immigration, legal or "illegal," had to be given full support. Possibly this sermon constituted a catharsis of sorts for Silver, who at the Twenty-First Zionist Congress had opposed illegal *aliyah*. For his listeners, at any rate, his remarks were a call for a firmer and prouder Jewish policy.[51]

---

51   Synagogue sermons of A. H. Silver, TA: "Taking Stock," January 5, 1941; "The Immortal Story of the English," January 12, 1941; "What Kind of a Peace Do We Want?" January 19, 1941. These are the sources for the ensuing discussion.

One cannot conclude from this that Silver consciously attempted to plant the seeds of anti-British feeling among his auditors. He told his congregants on January 12 that he had great respect for the British spirit, which he saw linked to American culture and basic Jewish values. However, his conclusion on the next Sunday was that the British empire should be disassembled following the war, and its component peoples, including the Jews of Palestine, should be given the freedom to develop independently. To attain this goal, he said, there was a need to struggle now, during the course of the war, for those values of liberty by whose light the Jews, too, would develop their nationhood. America, he concluded, had to become involved without delay in the struggle for a peace that would ensure individual liberty and the freedom of small nations.

During December 1940 and January 1941 Silver and his circle gained power as a result of Emanuel Neumann's enlarged responsibilities in the Emergency Committee, where he had served in an advisory capacity from the start of November. As pressure for action swelled within the Zionist rank and file, Nahum Goldmann confronted the committee with an issue that had been raised before — public relations. At the following meeting on December 30, attended by Silver as well, the committee decided to set up a public relations department immediately. The meeting also took up the issue of the approaching UPA conference. Emanuel Neumann offered suggestions for exploiting the opportunity to dramatize Jewish participation in the defense of Palestine and the Near East. It was clear to all components of the Emergency Committee that the Zionist Bureau in Washington headed by Rabbi Isadore Breslau was not meeting the needs of the hour. On January 9 Neumann was officially appointed head of the public relations department, at which time the committee decided to disband the Washington bureau, subsuming Breslau's activities under Neumann's.[52]

Neumann won his new post with the prior agreement of Ben-Gurion, with whom he was then working to enlist the support of Eddie Cantor

---

52   Minutes of the meeting of the Emergency Committee, December 18, 20, 25, and 30, 1940, ZAL.

and Paul Muni for the Zionist effort. Needless to say, Neumann's approach, mobilizing public opinion on the broadest scale possible to pressure the U.S. administration, won the enthusiastic support of the Yishuv leader.

We have seen the depths of Ben-Gurion's faith in American democracy in the wake of Roosevelt's electoral triumph; and we have seen how he would not accept the constraints of diplomatic initiatives to battle the refugee expulsion decree. In his report to the Jewish Agency Executive on his return to Palestine, Ben-Gurion pointed out how difficult it was to influence the president via high-level personal contacts:

> I have come to the conclusion that the way to win the American government is to win the people, win public opinion; and the American people can be won. ... We must mobilize the American people, the press, members of Congress (the Senate and the House of Representatives), the churches, the labor leaders, the intellectuals; and when they are with us — the government will be with us, and Roosevelt will help us. The road to Roosevelt is via the American people.[53]

With his ally Neumann holding a key post on the Emergency Committee and with Ben-Gurion still in the United States, Silver plunged into preparations for the conference of the now independent UPA. On January 3 he published a lengthy article in *New Palestine* to prepare the ZOA membership for this pivotal event. Five days later the UPA Administrative Committee met, with Ben-Gurion participating. Much of the proceedings were devoted to the attendant problems of the fund's new independent status. Rabbi Irving Miller of New York, a Silver ally since the winter of 1940–1941, played a prominent role in the sessions. (Years later he was to serve as president of both the ZOA and the Presidents' Conference.) In his remarks to the Administrative Committee, Ben-Gurion strongly advocated an independent fund. He restated the positions he had espoused at his meetings with Hadassah in November, Poalei Zion in December 1940, and the ZOA National

---

53   On December 28, 1940, N. Goldmann wrote to E. Kaplan informing him that Ben-Gurion agreed Neumann "should be used" (CZA S 25/2376); quote, minutes of the meeting of the Jewish Agency Executive, February 16, 1941, BGIA.

Administrative Council in early January 1941. Once again he proclaimed the struggle for a sovereign Jewish commonwealth in Palestine as the movement's central goal: "There is but one solution to the Jewish problem — establishing Palestine as a Jewish commonwealth that will draw millions of Jews to settle there, in their own land, as free and productive citizens."[54]

Ben-Gurion's remarks were brief, reiterating his standard themes of growing American involvement in the war and the shared values of Jewish civilization and American democracy. Again he took care to use the term "commonwealth" throughout, with an eye to this term's connotation of an American-leaning policy.[55]

Three days later (January 11, 1941) Ben-Gurion attended a meeting of the Poalei Zion Central Committee, in which he pushed that organization in the direction of Silver's new effort: "Not one member [of Poalei Zion] was present at the UPA meeting this week. That is suicide." He demanded that the party send two or three representatives to the UPA, just as it did to the Emergency Committee. A debate ensued, with several speakers expressing concern lest participation in the UPA would adversely affect Histadrut fund-raising. Ben-Gurion again took the floor to say that "there is no contradiction between the UPA and the Geverkshaften fund. ... We will fulfill our Zionist role through the UPA, and our workers' role through the Geverkshaften fund." The Central Committee decided that, in principle, Poalei Zion would become more active in the UPA, and it appointed a special committee to address the issue.[56]

Ben-Gurion left the Poalei Zion leadership with his traditional challenge: to proselytize for the ideals of Zionism, and particularly labor Zionism, among young people and the intelligentsia. Under the conditions obtaining in America, he reiterated, theoretical Zionism alone would not suffice: only a movement rooted in fiscal activity and in

54 *New Palestine* 31, no. 11 (December 27, 1940):3–6, 13; minutes of the meeting of the Administrative Committee of the United Palestine Appeal, January 8, 1941, BGIA #150.
55 Minutes of the meeting of the Administrative Committee of the UPA, January 8, 1941, BGIA #150.
56 Minutes of the meeting of the Poalei Zion Central Committee, January 11, 1941, LA, section 3, 101/41.

the realization of social ideals had a chance to succeed. This was the task that had to be taken up in anticipation of the major, international role awaiting America — and, of course, American Jewry as well — in the postwar period.[57]

On January 16 David Ben-Gurion arrived in San Francisco for a flight to Palestine and there met with Dov Joseph, who had returned to the United States as an emissary to the American Zionist movement. Having arrived in San Francisco but one day before Ben-Gurion, Joseph managed to find his compatriot and later noted, "Eventually I ran him to earth and we talked from 9 A.M. to 6 P.M. without pause. Then from his report of things here it is evident my mission here will be most useful and that they are all glad I have come." For his part, Ben-Gurion reported on this meeting to the Jewish Agency Executive on his return to Palestine:

> I would not have left the United States confident that the decisions and promises would be carried out had it not been for Dr. Joseph's arrival in America. We dare not leave America without [placing there] someone from Palestine who knows the situation thoroughly. ... I met him [Joseph] in San Francisco ... and I had a long and detailed talk with him on the situation and on internal relationships within American Zionism, about the program, about political and personal difficulties, and how to deal with each and every one of the Zionist leaders, and how to see to it that the political line laid down with such great effort would be adhered to.[58]

Dov Joseph's political diary contains no entry for the date of the meeting with Ben-Gurion, but there can be no doubt as to the nature of the "political line finally set down after great effort" that the Jewish Agency Executive chairman passed on to the representative of the Political Department. Relatedly, on the very next day, January 17, while waiting at the St. Francis Hotel for his flight, Ben-Gurion framed "the Zionist Agenda for the Present Hour" for Nahum Goldmann, the world

---

57   Ibid.
58   Dov Joseph to Goldie Joseph, January 21, 1941, YIBZA, Dov Joseph file, 5/4/4/21; Ben-Gurion to Arthur Lourie, January 16, 1941, BGIA #73. The quote is from the minutes of the meeting of the Jewish Agency Executive, February 16, 1941, BGIA.

Zionist movement's representative to the Emergency Committee. In structure and content this program resembled that presented to Poalei Zion in December, except that it had become tauter and clearer (the full text appears in Appendix V). Its first component was the "peace platform," comprising three paragraphs: the first treated of full Jewish rights wherever Jews lived; the second called for "the designation of the Land of Israel as a Jewish commonwealth for the purpose of organizing mass *aliyah*, on a governmental scale, of millions of Jews from Europe and other countries, and their absorption..."; and the third paragraph cited three possibilities for the status of the Jewish commonwealth: a dominion in the British empire, a fully independent entity, or a member of a Jewish-Arab federation (Nahum Goldmann himself, the recipient of this summary letter, favored only Jewish autonomy in the framework of a Jewish-Arab federation).

The second section, the "war platform," opened with two paragraphs dealing with principles: the first declared the full commitment of the Jewish people to the war, at England's side; the second called for the participation of "a Jewish army, as an ally of the English army, under the same conditions that obtain for all allied armies." The next paragraphs detailed the roles of the army — first and foremost "the defense of Palestine" — and the force's constitution and structure.

Ben-Gurion's affinity with American Jewry found expression in the third and fourth sections. In the third section, treating of the war and the White Paper, we read: "The Jewish people's opposition to the White Paper ceases not for a moment, and American Jewry shall rise up against any attempt on the part of the Mandatory administration to effectuate the White Paper during the war and deny the rights of the Jewish people in their homeland." Ben-Gurion devoted a special paragraph in this section to the desired campaign to thwart the White Paper: it would be "conducted publicly and with the mobilization of maximal help of American public opinion." The last section, encompassing half of Ben-Gurion's letter, was given over to the Zionist Emergency Committee. Again the Jewish Agency Executive chairman stressed what he considered to be the requisite political style: "to explain to American public opinion, to the heads of the church, leaders of literature and the press, leaders in the Congress and the Senate, governors and American federal officials" the Jewish problem and the Zionist solution. Only this solution, Ben-Gurion reiterated, would make possible "the transfer of millions and their entrenchment on the land and in the economy" and would "designate Palestine as a Jewish commonwealth."

At the conclusion of his detailed program of January 17 Ben-Gurion reacted to Dov Joseph's report on conditions in Palestine. He was worried, he wrote, about "the economic situation in Palestine, necessitating greater and swifter aid." Here the Yishuv leader might have been signaling Joseph not to stake out an extreme position in the campaign for an independent Zionist fund. This directive, if indeed it was given, would have been of a piece with Ben-Gurion's relatively cautious approach in comparison with that of Eliyahu Golomb on the autonomy of a fund for Palestine. In his second comment he expressed his worry over "the MacMichael regime, *which is not far removed from a Nazi regime*, and which calls for a vigorous response in America" [italics added].

An interesting event was on the agenda, prior to soliciting "a vigorous reaction in the United States" — the Twenty-Sixth Conference of the Zionist Organization of Canada, scheduled to begin on January 19, 1941. Canadian born and educated, Dov Joseph maintained close contact with that country's Zionist movement. Joseph, who had flown to Montreal to take part in the convention, emphasized there the Yishuv's resolve, its demands for free immigration and a Jewish army, and the need for a Jewish commonwealth as the radical solution to the Jewish problem.[59]

The Canadian convention's resolutions partly mirrored the spirit of Dov Joseph's remarks. They included an unequivocal demand for the nullification of the White Paper and a call for the establishment of a Jewish army. The demand for political independence, however, was British oriented as it called for "the establishment of Palestine as a Jewish Commonwealth within the British Commonwealth of Nations in order that it shall be able speedily to absorb the masses of Jewry from Europe and from all countries where Jews are in distress." These resolutions at the background, Dov Joseph went on to the United States.[60]

59   Minutes of the meeting of the Jewish Agency Executive, May 13, 1941, BGIA; YIBZA, Dov Joseph files; *The Canadian Zionist*, February 12, 1941, 1–19.
60   Ibid.

Joseph was quite familiar with American Zionism. He had visited the United States, had taken great interest in the American Jewish community, and was well acquainted with the growing radicalization of the Jewish populace. Top American Zionist leaders, including Silver's supporters, saw him as a principled, yet practical, activist. When in December 1940 Henry Montor learned of Joseph's imminent arrival, he quickly wrote to Abba Hillel Silver, recommending that Joseph speak at the coming UPA convention. Silver accepted Montor's suggestion, and Joseph brought a report from Palestine to the independent UPA convention. Before appearing at the Washington gathering, however, Joseph performed various missions that laid the groundwork for that historic gathering.[61]

On January 21 the Palestinian emissary arrived in New York and in the course of two long meetings (the first that day and the second two days later) gave the Emergency Committee a detailed account of events in Palestine, particularly the political atmosphere, and suggested the required Zionist political strategy in America. On January 23 he met with the presidium of the Emergency Committee as well, which decided to assign him, Emanuel Neumann, and Nahum Goldmann to prepare a draft of the UPA conference resolutions, to be assisted by the resolutions passed by the Zionist Organization of Canada convention.[62]

The following day, the eve of the opening of UPA conference, Dov Joseph met with the ZOA Executive Committee in Washington. Most of the meeting was devoted to the conference, of course, and decisions were reached on the coordination of efforts between the ZOA and the UPA. Joseph stated that there was room for a common Jewish fund only on the basis of a fifty-fifty allocation. In any event it was not the fiscal issue that was being tested, he asserted: "We have been struggling for the last forty years, and we are within reach of our goal. We cannot afford to sacrifice a bigger thing than money and that is, the Zionist basis of our life in this country [the U.S.A.]."[63]

On the very day that Joseph was meeting with the ZOA Executive Committee, a *New Palestine* issue came out, assertive in tone and

61   H. Montor to A. H. Silver, December 30, 1940, TA, UPA 10–3–24.
62   Minutes of the meeting of the Emergency Committee, January 1 and 23, 1941, ZAL.
63   Minutes of the meeting of the ZOA Executive, January 24, 1941, ZAL, ZOA VIa/1.

brimming with optimism. The weekly reminded its readers of the decision of the ZOA leadership to increase membership to 150,000. Though years would pass before the ZOA would realize that goal, its confidence and ambition were justified: the organization's membership increased significantly that year over the preceding one, and the trend remained constant up to the proclamation of the State of Israel. The issue also ran an editorial presenting Dov Joseph as a symbol of the Yishuv's courage. While acknowledging the embarrassing failures of American Zionism the article pointed up past successes and expressed a resolve to fight shoulder to shoulder with the Yishuv, as comrades in arms. Given the circumstances, this editorial statement was not empty rhetoric but approached a genuine commitment to a well-defined line of action.[64]

The main speaker at the conference was, of course, Abba Hillel Silver. Taking non-Zionist Jewish philanthropy to task, he maintained that the Zionist solution was, in effect, the most humanitarian solution to the Jewish problem and that there could be no Zionist solution at that hour except through a return to the basic goal of Jewish sovereignty. As a brilliant speaker, Silver brought home his argument with a series of rhetorical questions; and as a rising leader sensitive to nomenclature, he used the term "commonwealth" to describe the desired sovereignty:

> What are all our efforts for? What are we aiming at? We have no new aims. We accept no substitute aims. Ours is the historic and millenially unsurrendered and uncompromised aim of rebuilding Israel's national life in Israel's historic national home. Our aim is a Jewish Commonwealth. Such a Jewish Commonwealth was the clear intent of both the letter and the spirit of the Balfour Declaration. Two decades of legal hair-splitting and sundry White Papers have not succeeded in whittling down the clear, full-orbed intent of that historic document or in giving moral sanction to any deviation from it.[65]

---

64   *New Palestine* 31, no. 15 (January 24, 1941):6, 15; Halperin, *American Zionism*, p. 327.

65   *New Palestine* 31, no. 16 (January 31, 1941):7–8, 25–27 (quotation on p. 27). This is the source for the ensuing discussion.

In the last section of his speech, Silver debated, in effect, Stephen Wise's approach. Relations with England, he maintained, had to be reciprocal. The Jewish people were obliged to help England in its war, but England had to fulfill its promises to the Jews. If England did not, then American Jewry had to exploit its political strength. That America had to become England's arsenal and assume an ever-greater role in the war was a matter of life and death for the latter; American Jews therefore — this being hinted at, but clearly enough — could exert very effective pressure on that score.

Dov Joseph's address, complementing Silver's, detailed systematically the Yishuv's contribution to the war effort, industrially and agriculturally, and summed up the Yishuv's vital aspirations: in the military sphere to be regarded by England as an ally, like the Czechs and Poles, and in the political sphere to be granted the right to a Jewish Palestine, to a free national life. Toward the end of his speech he "raised the Jewish problem, whose solution would be sought at the war's end, and called upon the American movement to lay the groundwork for the demand that will issue from us [the Yishuv] to establish Palestine as a Jewish state with the capacity to absorb the masses of the Jewish people from the Diaspora."

Dov Joseph's address, complementing Silver's, detailed systematically the Yishuv's contribution to the war effort, industrially economic and otherwise. Moreover, the clear political message that Palestinian Jewry was resolute in moving forward toward sovereignty was just the message that broad sectors of American Zionists were waiting to hear.

Among the main speakers at the Zionist fund convention were Stephen Wise and Louis Lipsky, both of whom delivered a message that differed from Silver's. Both men, while emphasizing the need to aid Britain, did not raise the issue of guarding Jewish interests in the process. Looking past the war, both avoided use of the term "commonwealth" preferring the Balfour Declaration's "Jewish national home" instead.

At any rate, neither Wise nor Lipsky set the convention's tone, but Silver did. The resolutions passed bore his stamp and were based on the drafts prepared by Joseph, Neumann, and Nahum Goldmann. The first, "Jewish Defense of Palestine," emphasizing the need to defend Palestine with a Jewish force, echoed Joseph's remarks. The second resolution opposed the non-Zionist philanthropic complex — the Council of

Jewish Federations and Welfare Funds (CJFWF), warning against the creation of undemocratic bodies. Inordinate authority would be given to the CJFWF, the resolution warned, enabling it to disregard what most Jews in fact wanted done with their contributions. The third resolution bitterly attacked the White Paper policies, repudiating the land decrees and the closing of Palestine's gates. The fourth resolution tendered unqualified approval of America's new policy of supporting the British war effort. The fifth resolution detailed at length the UPA's readiness to solicit funds independently and the attendant need to educate the Zionist public. The whole concluded with a strong message of support for the Yishuv in its stubborn and fearless struggle for its future and the future of the Jews pounding on its gates.

The resolutions on Palestine gave clearest expression to the convention's aggressive stance and deepened linkage with the Yishuv. These decisions, both in content and at times in their phraseology, mirrored the platform that David Ben-Gurion had presented to the various Zionist bodies since mid-December. They can also be seen as a positive response to Ben-Gurion's speech to the UPA Administrative Committee two weeks previously. The demand to constitute Palestine as a Jewish commonwealth appeared twice: "The Conference declares its belief that in the conditions which will prevail in post-war Europe, Jewry will be faced with the task of finding a home for large masses of Jews from Central and Eastern Europe and that it is their [the Conference's] deep conviction, proved by past experience, that only by large-scale colonization of these Jews in Palestine, with the aim of its reconstitution as a Jewish Commonwealth, can the Jewish problem be permanently solved." Again, the Jewish demands for the postwar period included the call for "the establishment of Palestine as a Jewish Commonwealth" (Appendix VI).

The decisions of the UPA conference had a profound and immediate impact on American Zionism. *New Palestine* devoted a major editorial to the convention titled "Challenge Accepted." A new era in American Zionism had begun, the editorial declared, and closed with a Ben-Gurion–Silver style demand for Jewish sovereignty: "The conference marked the opening of a new era in American Zionism, and the year ahead will indicate whether, by our deeds, we are capable of translating ideal into reality. The deeds? Fulfillment of the quota set for the United Palestine Appeal, and mobilization of a mighty membership in the

Zionist Organization of America." Neither money nor numbers alone would suffice, the editorial claimed, holding both goals necessary "if we are to keep faith with Herzl and with the millions who wait for the establishment of the Jewish Commonwealth."[66]

The UPA convention, with its far-reaching resolutions, was at once a turning point in the history of American Zionism and the climax of Ben-Gurion's political efforts in the United States in the winter of 1940–1941. (The compromise that enabled the UPA later to rejoin the UJA in 1941, did not hinder the ongoing surge of the Zionist movement).

In his accounts following his return to Palestine (in mid-February 1941) Ben-Gurion lavished his exclusive praise on one American Zionist leader — Abba Hillel Silver. In his report to the Jewish Agency Executive he noted: "It was a pleasant surprise for me to see that the man now heading the Zionist fund is the strongest person from a Zionist and Jewish perspective — Rabbi Abba Hiller Silver." In describing the Zionist withdrawal from the UJA he praised Silver for his courage and readiness to fight. Again, in his report to the Mapai Central Committee he lauded Silver for his "exceptional" courage. (At the same time, before leaving the United States Ben-Gurion renewed his connection with Solomon Goldman, who had returned to his Chicago base largely because of the Lipsky-Wise domination of the Emergency Committee.) Like Ben-Gurion, Dov Joseph praised Silver as a brave leader and "a true Zionist." Such pronouncements demonstrated the understanding that had been achieved between Mapai's political activists, led by Ben-Gurion, and that stream of American Zionism headed by Silver in January 1941.[67]

---

66 Ibid., p. 6.
67 Minutes of the meeting of the Jewish Agency Executive, February 16, 1941, BGIA; minutes of the meeting of the Mapai Central Committee, February 19 and April 14, 1941, BGIA.

CHAPTER SEVEN

BILTMORE: THE ROAD TO 1948

In February 1941 David Ben-Gurion reported in detail to the Mapai Central Committee and the Yishuv's Zionist bodies on his trip to England and the United States, highlighting his new emphases: his conviction that the United States would enter the global conflict and play a major role in shaping the postwar world; his faith in the ability of American Jewry to influence American policy through mass action; and the need to reconstruct Palestine, at the war's end, as a sovereign Jewish entity to absorb masses of immigrants.[1]

During the spring and summer the Jewish Agency Executive worked steadily to frame its political platform. At its first session in early March, Ben-Gurion presented "Proposals for a Zionist Plan of Action"; at the last meeting held that month his "Guidelines for Zionist Policy" were placed on the agenda. These "Guidelines" were taken up at the policy meetings of the Jewish Agency Executive before Ben-Gurion's departure from Palestine at the end of July.[2]

Zionism's political mission was defined as creating "such conditions as will allow, at the war's end, the establishment in Palestine of a regime geared to facilitate government-sponsored *aliyah* and settlement of masses of Jews; and to ensure that the representative body of the Jewish people (the Jewish Agency or a Jewish government) will be given the

1   Minutes of the meeting of the Jewish Agency Executive, February 16, 1941; of the Mapai Central Committee, February 19, 1941; and of the Zionist Executive, February 24, 1941 — all in BGIA. One might add to this list Ben-Gurion's press conference in Jerusalem on February 26, 1941, wherein he described his U.S. trip and, in response to questions, laid out the essence of his strategy, BGIA #150.
2   Minutes of the meetings of the Jewish Agency Executive, March 9 and 23, 1941, BGIA; the last-mentioned minutes are the source for the ensuing discussion.

authority and the means to effect the rapid transfer of millions of Jews and settle them in Palestine as an autonomous people." The detailed list of the steps toward Jewish sovereignty reflected the maturity of the new orientation: the Anglo-American world, and not England alone or primarily, was seen as the fitting arena for the decisive political struggle of the Zionist movement. A special section of the program determined that "with Hitler's defeat, the Anglo-Saxon nations, upon the war's conclusion, will be the primary effectors of political decisions; hence Zionist public political education must be aimed primarily at said nations."

Ben-Gurion hoped to obtain the help of the Anglo-American world through patently democratic tactics: "Public political education in these countries must be aimed at winning over public opinion; i.e., convincing the Anglo-Saxon peoples — and through them, their governments — to accept the Zionist solution to the question of the Jewish people and Palestine. We must not limit ourselves to official negotiations, but must concern ourselves as well with the press, the labor movement, churches, and parliamentary and intellectual circles."

The concluding paragraph in the section "Public Political Education" highlighted the potential contribution of the world's English-speaking Jewish communities: "The vehicles for Zionist public political education in the Anglo-Saxon countries are the Jewries of England, America, and the British Dominions; hence all Zionist energies must be directed to ready the Jewries of these lands for this political task, through missions to the youth and the people; the creation of appropriate literature; and the bolstering of the ethical influence of Zionist Palestine."

The "Guidelines for Zionist Policy" (see Appendix VII) reflected a change in direction but were milder on two counts than the political platform for which David Ben-Gurion had struggled in the United States in the winter of 1940–1941. First, the demands for sovereignty were expressed circuitously, whereas in the United States Ben-Gurion had come out vigorously for a state or commonwealth. Second, acknowledgment of America's growing role, and that of American Jewry, was toned down through use of the term "Anglo-Saxon countries" and their Jewries. In addition, Ben-Gurion hardly thundered or pounded tables when appearing before the movement's institutions in support of his proposals: it would appear that he, too, had been drawn into the ambivalent mood that characterized many a meeting of the Jewish Agency Executive during the spring and summer of 1941. In the end neither the Jewish Agency Executive nor the Zionist Executive formally adopted any new decision.

Yitzḥak Gruenbaum, who chaired most meetings of the Jewish Agency Executive at that time, was asked by the Zionist Executive why the Jewish Agency leadership had not come to a decision after so many deliberations. He had an explanation:

> I say that there are no concrete results [political decisions] not because we are divided, but because the conditions are not yet ripe for anyone to say, "Look, such-and-such is possible and such-and-such is not." Nothing is possible at this moment and everything is possible. Consequently we cannot come to any agreement; consequently appointing a committee to work up proposals in anticipation of a peace conference... is not yet possible. What should be worked up? I don't know. A Jewish state? Within what borders? Are we a Jewish state in the British Commonwealth of Nations or a Jewish state outside the commonwealth? Shall we content ourselves with permission for unlimited *aliyah* without sovereignty? I have simply listed the issues.[3]

On three points raised by Gruenbaum — sovereignty, the international context, and borders — Ben-Gurion did have a clear-cut position. On the first two he had expressed himself unequivocally, as we have seen, in his appearances in the United States in the winter of 1940/41 and again in his reports on his return to Palestine. On the border question, too, Ben-Gurion had an unambiguous stand. Borders, he maintained, would be determined by more fundamental considerations. He had adamantly favored partition during the great Zionist debate of 1937 (when Britain proposed the establishment of a Jewish state in a tiny portion of Palestine). In the face of Britain's retreat to the White Paper, Ben-Gurion continued to relate to partition as an option. He had so spoken, for example, at the Mapai conference of April 1939. In the summer, at the Mapai Central Committee, he reemphasized the position that had characterized him through the years: "Every commander must always

---

3   Minutes of the meeting of the Zionist Executive, June 17, 1941, BGIA.

anticipate the possibility of retreat, and every movement must consider varying possibilities. However, even as it would be mistaken to declare at this moment that Zionism's goal is the establishment of a Hebrew state in part of Palestine, so it would be a fatal mistake if the movement fails to realize that such options exist and will not be prepared to deal with them at the right moment."[4]

In the changed and shifting circumstances of 1941 not one of the three problems outlined above could have been placed squarely on the Yishuv's agenda, according to Ben-Gurion's calculation. First, until the end of 1941 the United States was not, officially speaking, a participant in the war; and there was no way for the Palestinian leaders and public to have sensed to what degree the United States had become surreptitiously involved in the global struggle that year. Second, beginning with the German-Italian offensive of March 1941 until the Allied victory at El-Alamein in October–November 1942, the Middle East, militarily speaking, was very much in danger. In Consequence, Ben-Gurion held that the Yishuv leadership could not effectively deliberate on the nature, framework, and boundaries of a sovereign entity.[5]

These circumstances explain why the first meeting of the Fifth Mapai Conference in June 1941 passed without Ben-Gurion's having attempted to impose his views on the delegates. One cannot forget either the stance of the increasingly consolidated Faction B. Without proposing a clear and realistic Zionist international policy, Ben-Gurion had no chance whatsoever of overcoming this faction, with its emphasis on practical accomplishments in defense and settlement. We have already considered the position of the movement's leader, Yitzhak Tabenkin, vis-à-vis the St. James Conference and the White Paper. During the two years that had passed, Tabenkin had adopted an even more extreme stance — further emphasis on practical upbuilding of the land as the keystone of Zionist policy; the firm belief that by founding settlements and a self-defense force a sovereign Jewish state would arise; and the assumption

---

4   Shmuel Dothan, *The Partition of Eretz-Israel in the Mandatory Period: The Jewish Controversy* [Pulmus haHalukah biTekufat haMandat] (Jerusalem, 1979), pp. 38–49, 63–71ff; remarks of Ben-Gurion at the first session of the Mapai Council, April 14–16, 1939, BGIA; minutes of the meeting of the Mapai Central Committee, July 5, 1939, BGIA.

5   Slutsky, *Haganah History*, vol. 3, pp. 95–102.

that the autonomous Zionist entity that would emerge as a result of independent Zionist action would occupy the whole of Palestine. This approach, which repudiated the political focus, began during those years to be wedded to a rigid socialistic doctrine — that the capitalist world was rotten to the root and that fascism was its natural and inevitable fruit. The tainted capitalist bloc in its entirety was contrasted with a vision of a utopian future under the banner of the Soviet Union. This ideology complemented and bolstered the practical, settlement-centered approach of the kibbutz movement under Tabenkin's leadership.[6]

Looking ahead to the Mapai conference, Faction B in April prepared "Guidelines," the first formulation of the faction's ideological-political platform. Although titled "Zionist Policy," the opening section characteristically focused on "practical Zionism," defined as "*an active struggle* to break the White Paper regime through incessant and unbridled 'illegal' immigration, the conquests of land settlement, and a self-defense force. This must be accomplished through guiding the community to readiness for popular warfare; and through the political leadership of the working class in independent, pioneering initiatives." Practical Zionism did not place on its agenda the question of attaining Jewish sovereignty, but looked rather to "international assistance" and the sympathy of "the forces of progress and the future, who will determine the fate of the world." This document (see Appendix VIII), blending practical yet intrepid Zionism with a pronounced socialist vision, carried great weight in the Palestine of 1941. Given that fact, together with America's neutrality and the clear and present danger of the Axis armies, Ben-Gurion had no prospect of convincing his party of

---

6   Ben-Gurion did not call for the establishment of a Jewish state and was restrained in his advocacy of political affiliation with the Anglo-Saxon world. See Ben-Gurion's remarks in the minutes of the opening of the conference, June 12, 1941, BGIA; Tabenkin's speeches in Yizḥak Tabenkin, *Collected Speeches* [Devarim], vol. 2 (Tel Aviv, 1972), pp. 292–352, vol. 3 (Tel Aviv, 1974), pp. 9–49. See also the treatment of Yael Ishai, *Factionalism in the Labor Movement: Faction B in Mapai* [Si'atiut biTenu'at haAvodah: Si'ah Bet beMapai] (Tel Aviv, 1978), pp. 39–57. While the debaters tended to focus on the question of enlisting volunteers, Eliezer Livenstein (Livneh) proposed mobilization toward the single goal of the Jewish state (minutes of the Fifth Mapai Conference, June 12–13, 1941, BGIA). See especially, the chapter of the minutes titled "Summary of the Political Situation."

a political program containing (1) a demand for a state and implicit readiness for partition of the country; and (2) dependence on capitalist America and its Jewry. Hence at the first session of the Fifth Mapai Convention Ben-Gurion softened his controversial points and supported resolutions that were more in the nature of pronouncements than political observations.

The international situation and the issue of security in 1941 might also explain why, during his stay in Palestine that year, Ben-Gurion defined himself more than once as a "Zionist preacher" rather than an active statesman; indeed he was a frequent lecturer and participant in ideological gatherings in various circles throughout the country.

The preceding notwithstanding, Ben-Gurion's appearances in the spring and summer of 1941 were not lacking in political import. In his lectures he repeatedly sounded the dual theme of the unity of Jewish destiny and the Jewish people abroad as comprising the Yishuv's loyal and best ally. He focused on the Jewish communities of the Anglo-Saxon world in particular as the most logical and surest supporters of the Zionist endeavor in Palestine. Moreover, in several "Zionist sermons" he set forth, in effect, his direction for Zionist foreign policy — an example being a speech delivered in March of that year at the Mapai Council and published under the title "Zionist Readiness":

> [The Jewish people] is not all that powerless at this time. It is more powerful now than the Polish people, more powerful than the Czechs. There are as yet eight million free Jews in the world... who can, with their political strength, their moral strength, and their military strength help destroy Hitler. The war will end with a British victory and all arrangements will lie, primarily, in the hands of two nations — one that is itself a nation of nations, the British Commonwealth of Nations, ... On the other hand stands America.... These two will determine [everything] following the victory in this war.[7]

---

7 Quotations here and in the ensuing discussion derive from the minutes of the meeting of the Mapai Council, March 5–8, 1941, BGIA. A censored version appeared in *HaPoel haTza'ir* 12, no. 12 (March 16, 1941):406.

He went on to list the principal advantages in this situation: (1) the opportunity for the Jews to exercise freedom of speech in both nations; (2) the political leverage of Jews in Britain and particularly in America, where such influence might prove decisive under certain circumstances; (3) the centrality of the moral factor in the war effort in both countries, with attendant enhancement of Zionist prospects; (4) the profound trauma of the war having created a readiness to reexamine fundamental issues and consider "bold, sweeping solutions"; and (5) the possibility that large-scale settlement of Palestine would be an acceptable program, given the impressive achievements of the Zionist effort in Palestine.

After sketching the Jewish and international factors that would make for the success of the Zionist effort at the war's close, Ben-Gurion clarified "Zionist readiness in Palestine," to which he had devoted his time and energy during his 1941 Palestine stay. "Zionist readiness in Palestine — [means] that the Yishuv sees itself not as an end in itself, but rather as a component of the Jewish people, and as that component of the people seeking to establish the [national] homeland." Following this generalization he addressed the issue of the Yishuv's affinity to American Jewry, so vital to the future of the Zionist endeavor. Disregarding this, he warned, meant "rolling a stone over the well of Zionism."

On other occasions, too, Ben-Gurion repeated themes he had accented in the United States, as in the meeting of the Zionist Executive at the outset of May, where he went so far as to say that "without [Zionist, political] activism in America I doubt that what we do in London will lead to anything." So striking were Ben-Gurion's remarks on the international question that they elicited a sharp disclaimer from the head of the Jewish Agency's Political Department, Moshe Sharett: "On one point I disagree with Ben-Gurion — on the... evaluation of London and America. It is not that I do not agree that from a certain vantage point America is more important than London; but I cannot accept the flat, and somewhat overly-broad, statement that the center of gravity lies now in America rather than in London... . We ought not conclude that London is not the decisive locus."[8]

8   Minutes of the meeting of the Zionist Executive, May 7, 1941, BGIA.

Sharett's comment expressed a fine distinction in the political sphere. Ben-Gurion came very close to saying that, indeed, *Washington* was "the decisive locus" and that Zionist foreign policy had to mold itself accordingly. He himself decided to leave for America on a political trip (which was to last almost a year). A few of Ben-Gurion's public remarks shed light on his motives.

At a meeting of the Jewish Agency Executive in mid-May, Ben-Gurion put forward the goal of a Jewish state and linked it with the resolution passed by the convention of the UPA: "Have you not heard," he challenged Werner Senator and Arthur Ruppin, "that the Zionists of America and Canada, precisely now, have adopted a political Zionist program demanding 'the establishment of Palestine as a Jewish Commonwealth'? Apparently the program that I am proposing ['Guidelines for Zionist Policy'] is not so alien to the minds and hopes of American Zionists. I authored the formula accepted in America and Canada."[9]

David Ben-Gurion's speeches on the eve of his departure for the United States expressed his political position more and more openly. On the one hand they reflected the fact that the circumstances in the Yishuv and beyond were not conducive to a full exposition of a new political program and a struggle on its behalf; on the other hand, Ben-Gurion did stress the correctness of the program and the need to implement it in the not distant future. Before his departure in July 1941, he hoisted his standard, as it were, at the meeting of the Mapai Central Committee, concluding that "the subject and object of Zionist policy is a state." America, he claimed, offered the appropriate "foothold for a sweeping, positive... program" aimed at such a state because it was unencumbered by past traditions vis-à-vis the Arabs. Moreover, America's State Department, unlike Britain's Foreign Office, was not laden with sweeping ambitions and numerous goals in the Middle East. Efforts had to be invested in ensuring the friendship of the U.S. State Department, the Jewish Agency Executive chairman maintained, even while acknowledging that the department was but a small unit in America, "while England's Foreign Office is almost all of England." At the same time, American deference to British apprehensions had to be recognized.

---

9   Minutes of the meeting of the Jewish Agency Executive, May 16, 1941, BGIA.

Still, Ben-Gurion was optimistic, pointing out that initial Zionist efforts in the United States, in the direction he supported, had been taken and been crowned with success. What was yet required was "Zionist momentum in America. No Jewish-Zionist position has yet emerged. ... In order for American Jewry to attain a Jewish-Zionist stance, the Yishuv must put its shoulder to the wheel in America."[10]

Ben-Gurion's summary called for "a Jewish state as the object of Zionist policy... political efforts to prevent England from committing herself now to any avenue that would block a Jewish state... efforts in America to win Jewish public opinion there to the conversion of Palestine into a Jewish state as the sole solution to the Jewish problem."

Similarly, in his parting words to the Jewish Agency Executive at the end of July, Ben-Gurion emphasized the beacon light of statehood at the end of the war, referring to "that same formula that the Zionist organizations of America and Canada accepted," which, after acceptance, would require careful follow up and implementation. He clarified that during his forthcoming, brief stay in England he would forge "a connection with the American embassy in London." Thereafter, and following talks he would hold in London, he would leave for America. His mission would be to implant the goal of a "Jewish commonwealth" in American Jewry and promote a pro-Zionist foreign policy in America.[11]

That same farewell meeting saw a pregnant exchange between Ben-Gurion and Menaḥem Ussishkin, chairman of the Zionist Executive but not a member of the Jewish Agency Executive. Ussishkin — an avowed militant General Zionist — had not come simply to extend a bon voyage to the Jewish Agency Executive chairman. Having reserved the last slot on the speakers' list, he warned Ben-Gurion not to regard himself as an official representative of the Yishuv during his trip insofar as his political program was concerned. This adjuration related primarily to any programs that would not ensure the Jewish state's strength and, specifically, being possessed of "our borders." He closed his remarks with a stern admonition against the pursuit of any policy that would

10   Minutes of the meeting of the Mapai Central Committee, July 27, 1941, BGIA; this is the source for the next quotation.

11   Minutes of the meeting of the Jewish Agency Executive, July 27, 1941, BGIA.

circumvent the elected, Zionist bodies. Herein Ussishkin forcefully represented the camp which, ever since the 1937 partition debate had feared that pursuit of statehood at too early a stage would lead to partition of the country.[12]

In the previous chapter we encountered Ussishkin's inflexible stand on Zionist foreign policy. The director of the Jewish National Fund (from 1923 until his death in late 1941) envisaged success for the Zionist enterprise through land reclamation and settlement and the Yishuv's ability to stand up to the Mandatory power. Matters of international policy had little room within such an idea. Like the kibbutz leaders of Mapai's Faction B, Ussishkin believed that independent Yishuv effort, and above all the settlement effort, would of necessity lead to the appropriate result — a Jewish state within the maximal boundaries.

Ben-Gurion's reaction to Ussishkin's closing remarks was: "On the assumption that silence does not always means assent, I close this meeting with such silence." The silence, of course, was thunderous. Ben-Gurion went his way, having made clear his position that the "question of the borders" was, to his mind, subservient to a broad political strategy — that contained in his "Guidelines for Zionist Policy."[13]

Ben-Gurion traveled to America via London, where he arrived in August 1941. After a few months in Britain he wrote home: "My presence in London becomes [increasingly] difficult for me. At least last year... London was under attack and I saw her in all her greatness. Even that compensation was lacking this time. All the while I have been [here] there has been only one short siren. ... Were it not that I had to go to America, and considered that trip important, I would not have come here at all." The Jewish Agency chairman concluded:

> Even in Palestine I thought that, at bottom, there was not much to be done here. The conclusions I arrived at... have in no way been disproved, to my regret; to the contrary, they have been

12 Ibid.; Dothan, *Partition of Eretz-Israel*, pp. 38–53ff. For biographical background, see Yosef Klausner, *Menahem Ussishkin: His life and life's Work* [Menaḥem Ussishkin: Toldotav uMifa'al Ḥayyav] (Jerusalem, 1943), pp. 84–103ff. There is as yet no comprehensive scholarly work on Ussishkin.

13 Minutes of the meeting of the Jewish Agency Executive, July 27, 1941, BGIA.

corroborated. London has not ceased being the center of the world — the free world, of course — but at this time she is not the center of *our* prospects. The weight of our enterprise at this hour is in Palestine and in America.[14]

Little wonder that during his stay in Britain Ben-Gurion closely followed overseas Zionist efforts. He gave special attention and encouragement to the radicalization of Hadassah, largest of all American Zionist bodies, capitalizing on three traits he perceived in that organization: devotion to the constructive endeavor in Palestine; a deep humanism finding expression in Youth Aliyah; and openness to change. The Yishuv leader pursued a tripartite program compatible with these three traits. First, he instilled in Hadassah even greater pride in its involvement with the Yishuv's welfare and development; second, he emphasized the democratic and social message of the Zionist effort in Palestine; and, finally, he portrayed the establishment of a Jewish commonwealth on the ancestral soil as a broad-scale humanitarian solution, the only one possible, to Jewry's disaster.[15]

Ben-Gurion, together with militant circles in the ZOA, made a crucial contribution to Hadassah's changed attitude and, specifically, to its adoption of a resolution for the reconstitution of Palestine as a Jewish commonwealth. This resolution was adopted at the Twenty-Seventh National Convention of Hadassah, held October 29 to November 2, 1941, in Pittsburgh. Following the UPA resolution led by Silver in January of that year, this was Ben-Gurion's (and his ZOA allies') second major breakthrough in the radicalization of the American Zionist movement.

Ben-Gurion continued to view this radicalization effort in the context of his growing orientation toward the United States. Some ten days after his arrival in London, he met John G. Winant, the American ambassador, who had assumed his post at the start of 1941 (he continued until 1946). Winant replaced Joseph F. Kennedy, who had tended toward appeasement and hampered Zionist efforts in the British capital.

14   *Diary,* November 10, 1941 [copy of a letter to Berl Katznelson, Moshe Sharett, and Eliahu Golomb], BGIA #31.
15   *Hadassah Newsletter* 32, no. 3 (December 1941–January 1942), esp. pp. 19–21. This and the *Diary* for the fall of 1941 are the sources for the ensuing discussion.

An admirer of Franklin D. Roosevelt, Winant advocated far-reaching progressive social legislation and an internationalist American foreign policy. In their one-and-half-hour discussion, Winant promised Ben-Gurion help in his future political work in the States. On November 6 they met again for a long talk, after which Ben-Gurion cabled Moshe Sharett in Jerusalem: "Conversation lasted two hours twenty minutes was perhaps most useful talk I ever had." On November 11, on the eve of his departure for the United States, Ben-Gurion met the American ambassador for the third time.[16]

Ben-Gurion's course from 1938 to 1941 reached a riper stage during his next visit to the States, lasting from November 24, 1941, to September 18, 1942. His connections with Winant did not temper Roosevelt's compliance with the British White Paper; hence the Yishuv leader invested all the more effort in mass action. Isaiah Berlin, the noted political scientist who then served as the first secretary of the British Embassy in Washington, D.C., relates in his memoirs:

> I had a long and fascinating conversation with Ben-Gurion on a Sunday in December 1941; so long and so fascinating that when we rose from lunch it was well after 5 P.M.; and it was only then that I learnt from the cab driver that the news of Pearl Harbour had been announced some hours before.... He [Ben-Gurion] put no faith in princes, neither in Churchill nor in Roosevelt nor in any Gentile leader or party or country. He believed that the Jews of Palestine would by themselves be able to repel unavoidable Arab attacks, at least for a time; and he put great faith in the support of the Jews of America: the Jewish masses... fired by the image of an independent state, would prove far stouter-hearted and more effective allies than the powerful politicians whom Weizmann might persuade or charm. When Ben-Gurion spoke in this vein, in short, sharp bursts, punctuated by even more intense, absorbed, brooding silences, it was as if the apocalyptic vision by which he was possessed outran his powers of expression. Jewish opinion

---

16 Bernard Bellush, *He Walked Alone: A Biography of John Gilbert Winant* (The Hague and Paris, 1968), chaps. 5–13; *Diary*, November 10 and 11, 1941 BGIA #31; Ben-Gurion to M. Sharett, cable, November 7, 1941, BGIA #75.

must be mobilized everywhere, and particularly in the United States; that alone would help.[17]

In this spirit, and with American involvement in the global conflict strengthening his hand, Ben-Gurion promoted his political strategy indefatigably during those long months.

From May 9 to 11, 1942, a conference of all American Zionists took place at the Biltmore Hotel in New York. In all, 586 delegates took part in the gathering, 519 from America and 67 representatives of other the president of the World Zionist Organization and the chairman of the Jewish Agency Executive in the thick of the world war lend the Jewish Agency Executive in the thick of the world war lent the conference the character of a world Zionist convention.[18]

The conference, designed to effect and demonstrate Zionist unity, was sponsored jointly by Weizmann and Ben-Gurion; nonetheless, from the start it bore the stamp of the latter's strategy, due especially to Neumann and Silver. Neumann, who titled his speech "Winning American Support," laid out his thesis in no uncertain terms: America had become the center of the democratic world and the Zionist movement had to focus its activities there. More than diplomacy was required, he maintained: Zionists had systematically to enlist, broad public support. Neumann actually identified with Ben-Gurion's policy and method; and he held that there was nothing to be gained from a continued Zionist partnership with Britain, whether in London or Palestine, inasmuch as England had clearly failed the Zionist movement. Efforts in America, he declared, would bring to full fruition the struggle in Palestine. He emphasized that America — especially after the Republicans' adoption of the Willkie line — would be anything but isolationist after the war. Neumann went on to voice strong criticism of the leadership of the Emergency Committee (i.e., Wise and Lipsky); he called for a reorganization of that body to form "a combination of a Department of State and a Ministry of Information for the Zionist Movement." He condluded his address by saying, "If we can effectively mobilize our

---

17   Berlin, "Zionist Politics in Wartime Washington," pp. 27–28.
18   "Stenographic Protocol, Extraordinary Zionist Conference, New York, May 1942," ZAL. This is the source for the ensuing discussion. For background see, Melvin I. Urofsky, *We Are One! American Jewry and Israel* (Garden City, N.Y., 1978), pp. 6ff.

forces and talent throughout the country, if we go in now for an all-out effort for winning the battle of America, there is a good prospect that we will win the battle of Palestine."

Silver, who took the rostrum later, emphasized likewise the potential centrality of American Jewry and the vital need for Zionists to enlist that Jewry in exerting pressure on American policy. He seconded Neumann's contention that there was no future for a Britain-linked Zionist policy and all but called for breaking with England, whose empire was on the brink of dissolution in Asia and world-wide. British colonial rule in Palestine, he maintained, had become a hopeless tangle. Between bursts of applause, he declared: "If there is to be a cutting of the Gordian knot, if there is to be a new start for Palestine and for a Jewish Homeland, the hand that will wield the knife that will cut the Gordian knot, I believe, will not be in London, but in Washington." In citing the Irish struggle for freedom as analogous to the Zionist cause, he met with enthusiastic audience response. Silver's critique of Weizmann was cautious but telling: he hoped, he said, that Weizmann would demonstrate the same courage that Londoners were then displaying and that, despite his fatigue, he would rise to the heights of this historic hour.

Robert Szold, also frequently interrupted by applause, called for a politically independent Jewish Palestine and for an independent Zionist policy to achieve that goal. He enlarged on the Yishuv's economic potential and on its high, militant spirit. Unlike Silver and Neumann, especially the latter, Szold emphasized at the same time the need for Zionist unity in the face of the world war. Eventually, as will be shown, the gathering demonstrated that unity, as well as stamping it with an assertive, militant tone.

Lipsky's remarks were somewhat antithetic to those just summarized — if not to Szold's, then clearly to Neumann's and Silver's. He proposed that American Zionists stick to their tried and true principles, avoiding new political pronouncements or innovative propaganda techniques. Such efforts, he maintained in his conservative address, would be disintegrative. Wise, too, expressed opposition to any new Zionist policy, voicing the hope that "after the Victory Peace Conference of the United Nations, these must recognize not the hope but the fact of the Jewish National Home or Commonwealth of Palestine." In his concluding speech Wise praised Weizmann's policy from start to finish; but he was blatantly out of step with the times in announcing, with gusto, that Weizmann, one of the greatest scientists in the world, was now extending his professional assistance to the United States. It is doubtful that many American Zionists in May 1942 felt they could look to any recompense for the possible scientific contributions of the Zionist leader who, some twenty-five years before, had lobbied for the Balfour Declaration.

Weizmann, in his own two speeches, took pains to stress the need not to despair of Britain. He even refrained from citing, in his concluding address, the goal of political sovereignty at the war's end. With the weakening of the prospects for his diplomatic course he now focused on his gradualist approach and held that what mattered most was winning unlimited immigration and the freedom to buy land and build up the country.

In a formal sense, Wise and Weizmann stood out at the conference: Wise opened the proceedings, and he and Weizmann were the last speakers. But the atmosphere of the gathering, and the plans and activities it spawned, went beyond the thinking of these men. Ben-Gurion did much to engender this new atmosphere, through a forceful and upbeat address on the Yishuv's strength and accomplishments. At that point all American Zionists could see that the Jewish Agency Executive chairman was not merely a leader of the Yishuv but a determined statesman as well, one who pursued his program with consistency and zeal. The first and decisive political goal on the Zionist agenda following the war's end, he declared, had to be the establishment of Palestine as a Jewish commonwealth. In articulating this position, he evoked almost word for word the decisions of the January 1941 conference of the UPA: "a clear and unequivocal reaffirmation of the original intention of the Balfour Declaration and the Mandate to re-establish Palestine as a Jewish Commonwealth as made clear by the President of the United States on March 3rd, 1919." In listing those nations whose sympathies Zionism had to struggle to enlist, Ben-Gurion emphasized time and again that the United States was the first that had to be won over.

In the end, while the Biltmore Conference emphasized Zionist unity, its decisions manifestly bore the stamp of the Ben-Gurion–Silver line. Thus the conference adopted Ben-Gurion's phraseology, calling "for the fulfillment of the original purpose of the Balfour Declaration... [which was] as stated by President Wilson, to found there [in Palestine] a Jewish commonwealth." For Ben-Gurion, the adoption of the phrase "Jewish commonwealth" rather than "Jewish state" in the Biltmore platform, and the reference to Wilson, epitomized what he had been about since the winter of 1940–1941. Genuine national sovereignty now seemed to him to be a concrete goal, one that necessitated a practical political strategy set out clearly and with hard-hitting slogans. Consequently, he became even more vociferous in using the term "commonwealth," with its overtones of pulling away from Britain, even more persistent in aspiring toward a flexible and bold Zionist foreign policy, one increasingly linked with the United States. In this light, one can view the final text of the Biltmore platform, with its demand for Jewish sovereignty at the war's end and its use, exclusively, of the term "Jewish commonwealth," as a culmination of the political efforts of Ben-Gurion.[19]

> The Conference declares that the new world order that will follow victory cannot be established on foundations of peace, justice and equality, unless the problem of Jewish homelessness is finally solved.
>
> The Conference demands that the gates of Palestine be opened; that the Jewish Agency be vested with the necessary authority for upbuilding the country, including the development of its unoccupied and uncultivated lands; and that Palestine be established as a Jewish Commonwealth integrated in the structure of the new democratic world.
>
> Then and only then will the age-old wrong to the Jewish people be righted.[20]

The world Jewish press as well as America's newspapers gave extensive coverage to the conference. Several newspapers saw the gathering as a turning point and emphasized Ben-Gurion's role in the process. Of special interest are the penetrating observations of the British foreign services. Even before the opening of the conference British diplomats in the United States voiced their concern that the

---

19   For an appreciation of Silver's role in the Biltmore Conference and subsequent developments, see Raphael, *Silver*, pp. 85ff.

20   *New Palestine* 32, no. 14 (May 15, 1942):6.

Zionists "are going to turn the heat on in the United States." When the British Foreign Ministry in London received a copy of the text of the Biltmore platform they reacted with an internal memo: "These resolutions are evidently stronger than those formed at a similar conference last year [i.e., the January 1941 UPA Conference]. We know that they expound this Zionist programme, but... it is the first time that this programme has been firmly and enthusiastically put forward."[21]

The British reactions included these historic lines: "The Jews now claim to be a nation and demand Palestine as their homeland and a Jewish Army to fight — us [the British], if necessary — for it."[22]

Finally, this quite perceptive memo, exhibiting more than a little anxiety, stated that "the Zionist aim is nothing less than the forcible seizure of Palestine after the war, relying on American influence to keep us [the British] quiet."

At this juncture the British Colonial Office saw Ben-Gurion as a real threat. When, following the conclusion of the Biltmore Conference, the Yishuv leader began to make arrangements for a flight back to Palestine, the British were in a quandary. They were not at all interested in seeing him return to the country, inasmuch as "Ben-Gurion's extreme and partisan nationalism is... much more likely to do harm than good for the war effort in the Middle East." However, to have forced the Jewish Agency Executive chairman to remain in America would have been even more disastrous, since, in the opinion of British foreign policy makers, American Zionists would then have intensified their criticism of England and their direct anti-British pressure. An examination of the exchanges leads to the clear impression that, for the members of the British foreign service, the most convenient solution would have been to have Ben-Gurion make his way back to Palestine from America by sea, and that on the slowest boat possible and imaginable.

At any rate, British fears and calculations did not fall wide of the mark: Ben-Gurion's political strategy now called for readiness to confront Britain. During his prior trip, the Yishuv leader had called for an Anglo-American orientation; now he was fostering an essentially pro-

---

21   Memos of April 2, 1942, PRO, Colonial Office 733/443/75872/14, May 21, 22, 1942, Foreign Office 371/31378.

22   Memos of May 27, 29, June 3, 9, 1942, PRO, Colonial Office 733/45/76033/3. These are the sources for the next quotes and ensuing discussion.

American foreign policy. Although he had not struck Britain off the map of the Zionist movement, he now advocated preparing for, and taking advantage of, the coming ascension of the United States at Britain's expense.

It is no wonder, then, that about one month after the conference Ben-Gurion and Weizmann had a stinging exchange (in Stephen Wise's study) over the direction of Zionist foreign policy. Ben-Gurion accused Weizmann of a rigid and excessive attachment to Britain, whereby the Zionist movement was losing its maneuverability and was likely to fail in its very goals. The movement, he asserted, had to act on the assumption that America "is the decisive power" and had to pour its greatest energies into massive efforts in the United States. Weizmann opposed Ben-Gurion's stance, insisting that "without England we cannot make it." He proposed that the Zionist movement continue with its traditional tack. Only a handful of the American Zionist leadership was present at this harsh debate.[23]

Outwardly, the Zionist movement continued to hold to its traditional diplomatic line; but the Biltmore Conference, whose platform was loudly acclaimed by Ben-Gurion, gradually came to symbolize an innovative, American oriented, militant policy. One might posit that this process began in earnest later that year — in October, when the ZOA and Hadassah adopted the Biltmore resolutions at their conventions.[24]

In the fall of 1942 Ben-Gurion returned to Palestine and immediately began to work for the passage of the Biltmore platform in his party and within the country's Zionist bodies. By that time it was clear, in Palestine, that the Biltmore program meant a possible confrontation with Britain; and Ben-Gurion spoke most forcefully before Mapai bodies and the Zionist movement on the coming competition between America and Britain, with the former destined to emerge as a major factor in the attainment of Jewish sovereignty.[25]

Montgomery's smashing victory at El Alamein in October over the

---

23 Minutes of the Special Meeting held in Dr. Wise's study, NYC, June 28, 1942, Biltmore File, BGIA; cf., Gorni, *Partnership and Conflict*, pp. 124–133; Zweig, *Britain and Palestine*, pp. 152–156.

24 *New Palestine* 33, no. 1 (November 6, 1942):2.

25 See especially minutes of the Jewish Agency Executive, October 4, 6, 1942, and the Zionist Executive meetings, October 15, 1942, BGIA.

German-Italian axis in North Africa, gave fresh impetus to David Ben-Gurion. From October 25 to 29, in the third session of Mapai's fifth conference (in Kefar Vitkin), the party adopted the Biltmore platform; most of the members of the populist Faction B — it opposed the party line on a series of issues, the Biltmore program among them — left the conference before its conclusion. On November 8 the program was adopted (6 in favor, 2 opposed) by the Jewish Agency Executive. Two days later, at the Zionist Executive, a sharp debate erupted when some representatives (mainly of HaShomer haTza'ir) attacked the program as an obstacle to Arab-Jewish cooperation and illusory vis-à-vis British rule over Palestine. The kibbutz leaders of activist Faction B were opposed for different reasons: they typically suspected that a demand for statehood at that juncture would bring about the partition of Palestine. The wording of the Biltmore demand was "that Palestine be established as a Jewish Commonwealth" (rather than calling for "the establishment of a Jewish Commonwealth *in* Palestine"); ostensibly it referred to the whole of Palestine; but the actual thrust of the conference was the attainment of sovereignty rather than the delineation of borders. The Biltmore message, then, was to a degree ambiguous vis-à-vis the prospects of the partition of the country. Against this background representatives of Mapai's Faction B decided not to participate in the voting. A decisive majority of the Zionist Executive (21 in favor, 3 opposed) voted for the proposal of Ben-Gurion, who was vigorously supported by Berl Katznelson. The three who recorded an opposing vote advocated a binational state; in addition one member offered an alternate proposal (close in its spirit to the binational-state proposal), two abstained, and two did not participate. The Biltmore program (also called the Jerusalem program thereafter) thus became the official course of the Zionist movement.[26]

As interpreted by Ben-Gurion, the Biltmore program was eventually the policy that guided the Zionist movement until the establishment of the State of Israel. Moreover, the very vision of Jewish independence fired the imagination of the agonized Jewish people; gradually the

26   Minutes of the meeting of the third session of the Fifth Mapai Conference (October 25–29, 1942), and resolution; minutes of the meetings of the Jewish Agency Executive, November 8, 1942, and the Zionist Executive, November 10, 1942, BGIA.

document became a rallying cry for the non-Zionist Jewish masses as well. An important milestone in this process was the American Jewish Conference, which took place from August 29 to September 2 1943, in New York City on the initiative of Henry Monsky, president of B'nai B'rith — the huge service order. The 502 delegates included 123 who represented 64 national membership organizations and 379 elected by secret ballot at special conferences in eighty cities and sixty regions. At this gathering Silver made an impassioned plea for a Jewish commonwealth, and a pro-commonwealth resolution was indeed adopted. Ben-Gurion quickly cabled his enthusiastic congratulations and support.[27]

Because of this decision the American Jewish Committee, and later the American Jewish Labor Committee, withdrew from the American Jewish Conference; nonetheless in the years 1943 to 1947 that body continued to press for American public and governmental support. However, the Emergency Committee for Zionist Affairs exerted the greatest and most effective mass pressure on the U.S. government and public. In the fall of 1943 this committee was reorganized as the American Zionist Emergency Council (AZEC), with Silver as co-chairman of the council and chairman of its executive committee. AZEC's intensive efforts under the leadership of Silver and Neumann from 1943 to 1949 aroused public opinion and the U.S. Congress, and exercised considerable influence in shaping American foreign policy regarding Palestine.[28]

The first Zionist congress to meet after World War II (in Basel, Switzerland, December 9–24, 1946) marked the nadir of British-Jewish relations. Political activism of the Ben-Gurion–Silver stripe was the dominant trend among congress delegates. The congress recorded its firm opposition to the latest British scheme of a five-year trusteeship over Palestine, "by which the establishment of the Jewish State would be prevented or postponed." It also resolved not to take part in one more British-Arab-Jewish conference on Palestine called by the Mandatory

27 Isaac Neustadt-Noy, "The Unending Task: Efforts to Unite American Jewry from the American Congress to the American Jewish Conference," Ph.D. diss., Brandeis University, Waltham, Mass., 1976, chaps. 4–8.

28 Ganin, *Truman, American Jewry, and Israel*, chap. 3 and passim; I. L. Kenen, *Israel's Defense Line: Her Friends and Foes in Washington* (Buffalo, N.Y., 1981), chaps. 2–5.

power. Chaim Weizmann, who pleaded for Zionist participation in the London discussions as an attempt to reach a settlement with Great Britain, was not reelected to the presidency of the World Zionist Organization; that office remained vacant.[29]

As the Zionist congress took place, U.S. President Harry S. Truman was already set upon a course that concurred eventually with a pro-Zionist solution to the British-Arab-Jewish entanglement. In the spring of 1946 Truman recommended the admission to Palestine of 100,000 Jewish refugees — "displaced persons" (DPs) — and offered ships and funds for the transfer. In October he issued a statement calling for consideration of Zionist aspirations in Palestine, and during the next months he gradually became attuned to the position of supporting the establishment of a Jewish state in part of Palestine. When the British government submitted the Palestine problem to the United Nations in the spring of 1947, American policy on the issue was still ambivalent. In fact, there was much anti-Zionism in the American position, originating in the State Department. At any rate, on October 11 the American delegation endorsed the scheme to partition Palestine. Moreover, the U.S. representatives solicited propartition votes among the U.N. member states and were thus largely instrumental in securing a two-thirds majority on November 29, 1947. Again, in early 1948, there was a reversal of the declared American position, and pressure was even exerted to postpone the declaration of the establishment of Israel. However, the State was formally proclaimed on the scheduled date, May 14, 1948, by David Ben-Gurion. Its provisional government was recognized by President Truman on the same day "as the *de facto* authority of the State of Israel." This recognition was followed on June 22 by an exchange of "special diplomatic representatives" and on February 23, 1949, by the appointment of a full-fledged ambassador, symbolizing *de jure* recognition of Israel. The United States also extended substantial economic aid to the young state.[30]

29   Amitzur Ilan, "The Political and National Struggle over Palestine, 1917–1947" [HaMa'avak haMedini vehaLeumi al Eretz Yisrael, 1917–1947], in Yehoshua Porath and Yaakov Shavit, eds., *The History of Eretz Israel* [HaHistoriah shel Eretz Yisrael], vol. 9 (Jerusalem, 1982), pp. 72–81.

30   Ganin, *Truman, American Jewry, and Israel*, chaps. 5–11; Nadav Safran, *Israel: The Embattled Ally* (Cambridge, Mass., 1981), chaps. 4–5, 8, 27.

These international developments resulted, in large degree, from the political strategy and activity of Ben-Gurion during the decade 1938–1948. The contribution of militant American Zionist leaders was no less significant — such men as Solomon Goldman and especially Abba Hillel Silver and Emanuel Neumann. During those crucial years, much political experience was garnered and modes of effective action were shaped. Thanks to the Zionist movement's persistent efforts to arouse public opinion during those years, the American people grew accustomed to seeing American Jews asserting their rights and interests; the American government was gradually educated to respect and consider Jewish aspirations. The economic assistance of American Jewry and the arms purchases in America were vital to the founding and sustaining of the newborn Jewish state; and great importance was attached to the American Jewish volunteers' share in manning the illegal immigration ships, Israel's fledgling navy, and, most significantly, its air force.[31]

In short, the considered Zionist foreign policy was generally successful. America and America Jewry provided significant assistance; Britain was essentially neutralized; and the Yishuv's hands were freed to defend itself against the Arab attack of 1947–1948.

In conclusion, the Biltmore policy negated other possible scenarios: over reliance on Britain with concomitant loss of maneuverability, particularly inability to press for sovereignty at the war's close; the fostering of Jewish strength in Palestine solely through such practical activities as *aliyah*, settlement, and defense — in the sterile hope of an organic emergence of a Jewish state in Israel's "historic" borders; the expectation that the eastern European nations (Poland and Rumania essentially), motivated by anti-Semitism, would encourage the emigration and settlement of Jews in Palestine; and finally, a scenario dubious in the extreme, reliance on a raw military struggle degenerating into terror and isolation of the Zionist enterprise.

Actually, David Ben-Gurion's policy did share, in its way, a vital element with populist labor Zionism (the second of the aforementioned roads). We should bear in mind that in addition to cultivating a new

---

31   A. Joseph Heckelman, *American Volunteers and Israel's War of Independence* (New York, 1974), esp. parts 2–3.

foreign policy aimed at winning the approval of a dynamic and enlightened world power, he worked to systematically foster democratic Jewish Palestine and its strength in all spheres. This double-tracked course of Ben-Gurion undoubtedly played a crucial role in the creation of the small new state against long odds.

EPILOGUE

What prepared David Ben-Gurion to remake Zionist foreign policy and at such a relatively early date, when the United States was still neutral? Doubtless his American background and his faith in American democracy, and in the influence of public opinion, dealt with throughout this book, can explain much of his political progress from the close of the 1930s. But there is more to it than that.

In their own ways, Weizmann and Jabotinsky, as we have seen, had broad, even global, political vision. However, a close look at their policies and actions shows that toward the outbreak of World War II and during its course they tried to repeat their achievements of World War I. Ben-Gurion, conversely, tended to analyze global developments with an eye to the changed circumstances in Palestine and the world. Certainly his openness to America evidenced a dynamic mentality.[1]

One of the persons interviewed for this study, a veteran Israeli statesman with considerable American experience, holds that Ben-

---

1 As regards Weizmann, this is the considered opinion of Isaiah Berlin as well, who was an intimate of the world Zionist leader (interview with the author, Jerusalem, April 23, 1979). See, in this regard, Sharett's observations on the subject of Weizmann's chemical inventions and the war: Sharett, *Political Diary*, vol. 4, entries for November 15 and 16, 1939, pp. 496–498, 503–505. Jabotinsky might well have lacked Weizmann's pertinacity: such is the opinion of Benjamin Akzin, an intimate of Jabotinsky during critical periods (see the interview, chap. 5, n. 30, above). However, on Jabotinsky's relationship to the Jewish army and war, see Schechtman, *Jabotinsky*, vol. 2, pp. 368–374, 485–491. As regards Ben-Gurion, see Eliahu Elath, interview with the author, Jerusalem, July 17, 1979; Teveth, *David's Zeal*, vol. 1, pp. 6, 357; vol. 2, pp. 5–6 ff. see, for example, Ben-Gurion's speech following the outbreak of the world war, at the meeting of the Yishuv's National Committee (September 17, 1939) as published in "Looking Ahead" [Likrat haBa'ot], *Davar*, September 22, 1939.

209

Gurion had a tremendous drive for power and a keen eye for the sources of power, and that this explains his grasp of the growing role of the United States. This assessment is perceptive. Even at the start of World War II, Ben-Gurion could sense that America was a burgeoning power destined to become involved in the global conflict and determine its outcome. This same awareness of power apparently brought home to him Britain's deepening dependence on the United States.[2]

Paradoxically, it was Ben-Gurion's Palestinianism that in no small measure made for his openness and political flexibility. His power base was in Palestine, and the cornerstone of his Zionist thought was the development of the Yishuv as the vital center of a revived Jewish people. He tended to view the map of world forces from a Palestinian perspective, and such a view was tailor-made to promote flexibility in foreign policy. Thus Ben-Gurion went through his "Turkish period"; and, of course, he had his period of strong cooperation with Britain. Then, in the fall of 1938 he began to be progressively oriented toward the United States. It would seem that the vigorous Palestinian life and the Yishuv's sense of self-reliance went hand in hand with his shifting international orientation.[3]

This aspect of Ben-Gurion's statesmanship contrasted markedly, of course, with Weizmann, whose personal and political path led consistently to one power, Britain. Jabotinsky, too, despite a seeming flexibility on questions of international relations, acted within a rather limited political theater. More than he was a statesman he was, it would seem, a spokesman of Poland's persecuted Jewish millions and a prophet of doom. In the role of spokesman his steps led him, tragically, to the very oppressors of his people — to the rulers of Poland (and Rumania) and repeatedly to Britain, Poland's supporter.[4]

---

2   Eliahu Elath, interview with the author, Jerusalem, July 17, 1979; Teveth, *Ben-Gurion*, pp. 9ff.

3   Teveth, *Ben Gurion*, chaps. 5, 6, 37, 38; Shlomo Avineri, *The Making of Modern Zionism: Intellectual Origins of the Jewish State* (New York, 1981), p. 203.

4   Schechtman, *Jabotinsky*, vol. 2, pp. 334–335; Avineri, *Making of Modern Zionism*, p. 182. See, for example, the discussion of the "petition" in Shavit, "Fire and Water," pp. 231–233. Weizmann's assessment of Jabotinsky during World War I, when the two men were close, is germane. He had offered to put Jabotinsky in charge of Zionist propaganda efforts and was distressed to learn of Jabotinsky's ambition to be a statesman, since "political work was precisely what he was not suited for"

Still another aspect of Ben-Gurion's Zionism led to his "American connection." Zionism was, for Ben-Gurion, a revolution, a radical break with a long exilic past. This outlook underlay his wholehearted focus on Palestine and his stress on the new Hebrew culture being created there (and especially the study and revival of the Bible and its heritage). Paradoxically, some facets of American Diaspora Zionism in a sense paralleled Ben-Gurion's idea. American Zionism was distinguished for its emphasis on practical work in Palestine. It was also noted for its newness and its detachment from the *Yidishkeyt* (Jewish ambience) of the European past. On these two grounds, then, Ben-Gurion could readily relate to the American movement and anticipate substantial fruits for his labors. This peculiar Zionist context, I propose, partly underlay Ben-Gurion's optimistic assessment of American Zionism's political promise and his rapport with leaders of the major trends of the American Zionist movement.[5]

The deep personal and political ties binding Ben-Gurion to Louis D. Brandeis illustrate this thesis. Brandeis had a distinctive ideology vis-à-vis Palestine. He was hardly interested in Jewish cultural history, nor was he drawn to work for Hebrew revival in the Diaspora. He was a Zionist of the American stripe, immersed in the American public arena and prominently so. At the same time he was keenly interested in the pratical accomplishments of the Yishuv and its society and ethos.[6] The same can be said of Robert Szold, with whom Ben-Gurion developed a warm working relationship.

David Ben-Gurion's rapport with Abba Hillel Silver was not altogether different. True, Silver's Zionism was much richer than that of the Brandeis cast. Still, his understanding with the Jewish Agency Executive chairman somewhat paralleled the Ben-Gurion–Brandeis relationship. First, as head of the United Palestine Appeal Silver had intimate acquaintance with the practical efforts and accomplishments of Jewish Palestine. Second, being very Americanized, he was the natural choice to instruct Ben-Gurion on the differences between American Jewry's pro-Yishuv (later, philo-Israel) sentiment and Zionist ideology

(Weizmann, *Trial and Error*, pp. 168–169); cf. Avineri, *Making of Modern Zionism*, pp. 182–186.

5   See n. 3.

6   Allon Gal, *Brandeis of Boston* (Cambridge, Mass., 1980), chaps. 5, 6.

proper. (As early as 1939 he prophetically assured Ben-Gurion that empathy with the Yishuv was on the rise.) Doubtless, Ben-Gurion's interaction with Silver bolstered the Yishuv leader's faith in the validity of American Jewry's pro-Yishuv attitude and in its great political capacity.[7]

Ben-Gurion's Zionism attuned him well to fruitful cooperation with Hadassah, the massive and most stable of all Zionist organizations in America. Here again we confront the seeming paradox of a radical Zionist leader of the Yishuv placing his faith in the highly acculturated and least ideological of all American Zionist organizations. Hadassah had traditionally de-emphasized ideology, concentrating instead on philanthropic efforts — such as medical work in Palestine and, later, youth rescue and rehabilitation. Ben-Gurion, focusing on Hadassah's practical bent and the inchoateness of American Jewry, firmly believed that the organization could be educated politically. Summing up his visits of 1940–1941 and 1941–1942 he sketched a "bureaucracy that exists to take care of appeal business" on the one hand and a "Zionism that has become almost denuded of any concrete activity" on the other. But "This depiction," he noted, "excludes one branch of the Zionist movement, its largest — Hadassah, which is actively engaged in building Palestine. Although its effort was modest at the start, and clearly philanthropic, concrete interest in the work brought it [Hadassah] closer to Palestine."[8]

It is not enough, of course, to explain Ben-Gurion's political path on the grounds of his Yishuv temperament and locus. As we have seen, the Jewish Agency Executive chairman was embroiled in a continuing struggle with elements within his party that were just as rooted as he in Palestine and were prominent representatives of the country's largest kibbutz movement. These and other groups crystallized into Faction B, broke away from Mapai in May 1944 and became the Tenu'ah leAḥdut haAvoda. The leaders in this trend, it will be recalled, leaned ideologically toward the Soviet Union and held that "tangible" accomplishments in Palestine were of supreme importance. Such a

7   See chap. 2, n. 10 and chap. 5, n. 42.
8   Minutes of the meeting of the Jewish Agency Executive, October 15, 1942, BGIA.

stance hardly called for any real breakthrough in foreign policy and certainly ascribed no central role in Zionist politics to capitalist America and its much Americanized Jewish community.

In the case of Ben-Gurion there was a positive relation between his social-political outlook and his foreign policy. We can agree with the observation that Ben-Gurion's "Marxist patina," as a member of Poalei Zion in Poland "was thin, fragile, and evanescent." His brand of democratic socialism obviously allowed for wide leeway in dealing with such issues as the working class and national movements, even in capitalistic regimes. Ben-Gurion's growing orientation toward America and its Jewry went hand in hand with his faith in the possibility of significant change in democratic societies, whatever their economic base. This political logic dictated that America, with its millions of Jews and its political democracy, could offer Zionism every prospect of success, given the emergence of a strong native leadership. In April 1941 Ben-Gurion delivered several lectures on Zionist policy at the Histadrut's ideological seminar. His remarks at these sessions encapsule, in a sense, his political outlook for the years 1938–1948:

> Zionist policy is possible only in... a democracy. In the three major powers where, recently, dictatorships have come to power — Russia, Germany and Italy — no Zionist policy has been possible. In these countries Jews are a negligible factor, hence these countries no longer constitute an address for Zionist statemanship; for where there is no freedom of speech, freedom of thought, freedom of the press, freedom of communication, freedom to come and go — no Zionist policy is operative. This is not to say that a dictator cannot be favorably disposed towards the Jews. This can happen; it *has* happened. We have the case of Ahashuerus, bowled over by an Esther. But Zionist policy rests on mass action, both of Jews and of others.[9]

Zionism, with its moral demands, required democracy, Ben-Gurion argued at that address. The movement, he claimed, was based on there being areas in the world "where one can educate, where one can appeal,

---

9   Teveth, *David's Zeal*, vol. 2, p. 76; Ben-Gurion, "Zionist Policy," lecture at a Histradrut seminar in Rehovot, April 3–4, 1941, BGIA #159.

argue, prove points, call [the powers that be] to task; which is to say, where moral strength... has value, and the government depends upon the people... [and] must answer questions daily and justify itself." Ben-Gurion's further remarks show the wedding of his Zionist politics to his concept of democracy and justice: "It is clear that England and America are moving toward evergreater democracy, more power for the masses, more power for the workers. There, [Zionist] political education is possible."[10]

It seems that as early as the 1910s Ben-Gurion tended toward the approach with which he became identified over the years — that the building up of the Yishuv (and later of Israel) required an alliance with at least one democratic world power. Ben-Gurion assumed that the Yishuv, to attain stability and develop properly, had to be linked with a region that was scientifically and technologically advanced, and that a prerequisite for the emergence of a healthy Jewish regime and society in Palestine was mutual links with democratic cultures. In his concluding speech at the Histadrut seminar Ben-Gurion emphasized that "the concerns of a Zionist state are not to be restricted to the borders of Palestine," because, among other reasons, such a state should relate to "the world family of nations." Zionist policy rests on "the relationship of the Jewish people to mankind, to the world's society of nations." On another occasion during that same period he voiced his opposition to the notion of "a people that dwells apart" (*Numbers* 23:9):

> Many options lie open to the Jews of Palestine: helplessness, surrender, resignation, toadying, kissing the rod. The opposite path is also possible: arrogance, the aping of Arab terror or Nazi methods, a trampling down of the weak, internal and external terror, brutality. Both paths are anathema to Zionism. The Zionist path declares that Jews are a goal unto themselves, like any other nation; that they relate to every other people with respect and understanding rooted in self-respect and faith in equality. That which we do in this land we do always with an eye to history's exacting account, and to our account with our ultimate goal and with surrounding nations, near or far. No nation "dwells apart,"

10   Ben-Gurion, "Zionist Policy" (see preceding note).

even so mighty a nation as England; how much the more so a small nation such as our own. Even when we have a sovereign state within the historic boundaries of *Eretz Yisrael*, we will always be bound to the world around us, with the nations of the Near East, with Europe and America; and we must shape our actions to this historic account.[11]

This study has shown that, in response to British turnabouts, Ben-Gurion worked in the international context toward a new *political* solution. An isolationist-style struggle based on the force of arms, as conducted by the Irgun Zvai Leumi, struck him as ineffective externally and ruinous internally. On the other hand, he viewed diplomatic efforts alone as highly dubious solutions, in that they lacked the leverage of political pressure. One may say that in this respect Ben-Gurion steered a middle course between the path of the IZL and its commander Menaḥem Begin on the one hand and Weizmann on the other.[12]

Ben-Gurion clearly remained an ally of Weizmann, however, holding that diplomacy is the legitimate brother of statesmanship whereas violence is its bastard sibling. Significantly, Ben-Gurion interpreted "force" in a broad way, holding, together with Weizmann, that the overall democratic development of productive Jewish Palestine was the vital component in realizing Zionism. In this vein, for Ben-Gurion the political pressure to be exerted in the American setting had to be associated with basic values he shared with Weizmann. Both men were tied to the same ideational consensus, one that accorded with American ideals. Indeed, Ben-Gurion clearly hoped that American Zionism would blend "Jewish and human aspirations" and by virtue of this "become a cultural, educative force winning hearts and minds."[13]

11 For an initial exploration of the topic, see Avineri, *Making of Modern Zionism*, p. 199; Ben-Gurion, "Zionist Policy," (see n. 9, above); Ben-Gurion, Remarks at a Social Gathering, Tel Aviv, September 8, 1939, BGIA #159.
12 See Ben-Gurion's remarks in June–July 1938 (preceding and following the execution of Shlomoh Ben-Yosef) and in May–June 1939 (preceding and following the White Paper), in the minutes of the meetings of Mapai and national bodies, BGIA. See also chap. 3, n. 43.
13 Gorni, *Partnership and Conflict*, pp. 46–83. *Diary*, January 24, 1939, BGIA #27; and see Appendix I.

Ben-Gurion, Zionist and socialist-democrat, endowed this blend of Zionism and "human aspirations" with a pioneering spirit very acceptable in the United States. American Zionism was not, at root, a response to anti-Semitism or an expression of vigorous nationalist traditions. Social and human yearnings molded by the democratic American ethos hence traditionally played a significant role in American Zionism. The Zionism of Jabotinsky school, on the other hand, was monistic. Sprung from the circumstances of continental Europe (primarily in the period between the two world wars), Revisionism tended to be autocratic, hierarchic, and leader-centered. This orientation delimited the number of accessible avenues for a successful Revisionist foreign policy. Not only was the movement alien to the American spirit, it was also in variance with the nature of mainstream American Zionism. The fact is that Revisionism never struck deep roots in American soil. The reader will recall Jabotinsky lamenting to Berl Katznelson that he (Jabotinsky) would never win the leadership of the Zionist movement because he was not in a position to "play the game" in America. This statement holds the kernel of a social-historic truth. The current represented by Katznelson and Ben-Gurion — allied with the beliefs of Weizmann — rich in the values of democracy and social concern, had every prospect of success with a Jewry living in a free and pluralistic society.[14]

We have seen how, following the outbreak of World War II and especially in the wake of Roosevelt's electoral victory in the autumn of 1940, Ben-Gurion drove home the concept of Jewish sovereignty as the appropriate Zionist strategy when the war would be drawing to a close. A keen grasp of the potential of American support, Jewish and non-

---

14 Allon Gal, "Brandeis' Social-Zionism," *Studies in Zionism*: 8 (Autumn 1987): 191–209. For background, see the introduction to Arthur Hertzberg, *The Zionist Idea* (Jerusalem, 1970), pp. 53–64; Avineri, *Making of Modern Zionism*, pp. 159–178. Jabotinsky fell wide of the mark in his analysis of the events that led to the outbreak of the world war. Until the last moment he believed that there would be no hostilities. He held to that opinion during the long months of the "phony war"; and, even when in America (June 1940), gave credence to rumors of an approaching British-German détente. Jabotinsky's blurring of the distinction between fascism and Anglo-American democracy lay at the root of these faulty appraisements (Cf., Schechtman, *Jabotinsky*, vol. 2, pp. 366–368; Jabotinsky to Michaelman, June 18, 1940, in Ze'ev Jabotinsky, *Letters* [Mikhtavim] (Tel Aviv, [1958], pp. 213–214).

Jewish alike, lent this approach, as contrasted with Weizmann's, special clarity and force. On the other hand, both Ben-Gurion and Weizmann wedded nationalist aspirations with political solutions; for that reason they, unlike less politically minded circles in labor Zionism and in the Zionist movement in general, were open to the compromise of the partition of Palestine, as reflected in their positions throughout 1937–1948. Thus David Ben-Gurion, emerges as an architect of the historic political Zionist tradition in which he was himself deeply immersed.

Indeed, Ben-Gurion's political realism and his venturing on the new foreign policy were both largely derived from the Zionist democratic tradition. Thus, his drive for an American alignment for the Jewish state was associated with the pervading urge to see the future state well integrated into the structure of the democratic world. Democracy for Ben-Gurion proved to be a central means to achieve Jewish independence, and also formed the basis of his vision of the Jewish state.

BEN-GURION'S SUMMARY OF HIS FIRST "STATE" VISIT TO THE U.S.

ON BOARD THE *AQUITANIA*, JANUARY 22, 1939

The weakness of American Zionism is to be sought not simply in inadequate organization but in ideological difficulties as well.

The primary organizational deficiencies are lack of leadership, lack of unity, putting fund-raising front and centerand subjugating organizational frameworks thereto. American Jewry — and, at this moment, the Jewries of most countries — lacks major figures, men of stature spiritually, intellectually, and politically who can bring order to the chaotic settling of immigrants in this sprawling, inchoate land. The Zionist movement, too, lacks such leadership. Brandeis left the movement upon his appointment to the Supreme Court and since then no one comparable, intellectually and morally, has arisen. Frankfurter is a learned jurist, but lacks the ethical personality, the moral weight that Brandeis has; and his life goal has clearly been to reach the bench of the Supreme Court. He came to Zionism by chance. For him the movement is incidental, rather than fundamental....

Precisely because American Jewry has not yet solidified (America as a whole has not yet done so) she requires, more than other Jewish communities, men of stature, leaders who will draw out her tremendous, untapped potential. The Zionist and labor movements, too, suffer this lack. [Baruch] Vladeck was the one man who could have filled the leadership slot in the labor movement; his death left a vacuum that will not be filled soon.

It seems to me, however, that the ideological dilemma of American Zionism is weakening the movement no less than organizational deficiencies.

218

American Jewry cannot regard Palestine — at least at this juncture — as a refuge for itself, as does East European Jewry.

True, there are suffering masses here and severe economic hardships — but neither of these are Jewish. There is a growing anti-Semitic movement, but it does not present a direct threat as of yet. Certainly there is no pressure for emigration.

Up to now American Jews and American Zionists do not see themselves as bearers of the Zionist ideal, that is, as being called upon personally to fulfill the Zionist program (and there have been, and still are, objective reasons for this). At best they regard themselves as a source of support, political and monetary, for others' fulfillment; i.e., the immigration of segments of Jewish communities from other lands.

The boundary line between *Zionist* activity and *philanthropy* — support for suffering Jews — is by no means clear-cut. Hadassah is the most obvious example of the confusion of these two spheres. One is hard-pressed to say whether its motives are more Zionistic or charitable, and Hadassah is not alone in this.

Even in the Histadrut campaign, so clearly a nationalist-social enterprise, philanthropic considerations play a major, perhaps crucial, role. HeHalutz and HaShomer haTza'ir comprise the only example of maximalist and unadulterated Zionism on the scene, but they are barely nascent, as it were — particularly HeHalutz.

Lacking, too, are the human and ideological setting of pre-Hitler Germany. Here we have no rising up against a deluge of physical and spiritual assimilation, as was the case with German Jewry. America is not acquainted with biological or cultural assimilation à la Germany, hence it lacks the basis for deep-seated protest against such a phenomenon. Here the ground is not ripe for that "return to Judaism" that necessitated a supreme intellectual and spiritual effort in Germany, one which would hardly have been possible without so revolutionary an ideology as Zionism. Here there is no flight from Judaism, no self-repudiation, no movement of conversion that could evoke a bitter and opposite popular reaction. Though Jewish life, Jewish consciousness, Jewish communality and solidarity are all quite pallid, yet they embrace this Jewry in its entirety. There is no profound need for rebellion and a change of values.

Americanism and Judaism in America do not contradict each other, at least not as yet; being an American Jew does not involve an obliteration of the Star of David (*HaTzlav haYehudi*) and being a "Jewish" Jew calls for no alienation or withdrawal from Americanism. With the exception of language, what Americanism means is vague — even as Judaism is vague; so that, generally speaking, the two co-exist affably, not only as regards Zionists but as regards all segments of American Jewry....

America's coming generation, the youth and the intellectuals, however, are wrestling with social and political dilemmas — democracy, fascism, capital and labor, the new world and the old; and if Zionism cannot afford these young people an outlook on life and the world, one that will meet the problems springing from this particular soil, one that will blend their Jewish and human aspirations — then American Zionism will not become a cultural, educative force winning hearts and minds. Zionism in America lacks a Zionist–human *philosophy* rooted in Judaism, yet blossoming on American soil.

I am doubtful that this mission can be accomplished by outsiders. As things now stand, Palestine makes demands, practical demands, one after another, and America is called upon to fulfill them. But Palestine does not manage to provide American Zionism with *all* its spiritual and intellectual needs. American Jewry cannot simply be a Zionist object; but it has not yet mustered sufficient intellectual strength to become a subject. It cannot maintain itself simply through giving. It is starving, and crumbs from the outside are not a filling meal. This is certainly the case now when no independent sources of thought have yet shown themselves and an American Zionist outlook has yet to be born — the lack of which, in my opinion, is one of the major reasons for the movement's weakness, particularly among the youth. Only a homemade product will fill the bill; an import will not do.

Source: *Diary*, BGIA # 27.

BEN-GURION'S POLITICAL REACTION TO THE PROMULGATION OF THE LAND REGULATIONS

ADDRESS AT THE MEETING OF THE ZIONIST EXECUTIVE, JERUSALEM, MARCH 14, 1940

Gentlemen, this time I approach the clarification of a political situation with a trepidation whose like I have never known, for that which must be said and that which must not be said are singularly grave. But before I approach the political issue per se, I wish to step back and echo a basic tenet that come what may in Palestine, our effort will continue — continue in town and village, on sea and on land, and in the economic and cultural spheres, independent of any and all political circumstances or considerations; for that is our lifeblood: calling a halt for one moment is inconceivable. However, everything we do is part and parcel of our political struggle. Continuing our efforts is the equivalent of setting up new strategic outposts on the political front.

I am very sorry that I could not arrive in time to hear Ussishkin's remarks. I don't know that I would have been able to stand by everything he said, but I will say this: given the present set of political circumstances, settlement policy cannot be clarified in and of itself. But I shall not even discuss that issue; rather, I only wish to clarify the political road of Zionism in the wake of the promulgation of the Land Transfer Regulations. Now I know that there are a considerable number of Jews in Palestine — good Jews, too, Jews who hold themselves good Zionists as well — who say that after the Land Regulations, even after the White Paper, even after all we have undergone, Palestine cannot be compared to Poland or Germany. After all, here no Jews have been sent to concentration camps, Tel Aviv is a Jewish city, we have a Hebrew University in Jerusalem, we speak Hebrew in this country, our children are free, they feel at home here.

I understand these Jews; but let us not exaggerate. Certainly Palestine, after the promulgation of the Land Regulations, is neither Germany nor Poland, neither part of the Russian occupation nor the German occupation. I understand these Jews, I feel for them, but I do not share their opinion — even if I cannot (indeed no one dare) judge whether the situation in Palestine is better or worse than that in Nazi Germany. We must not judge this situation from the perspective of the hell of German Jewry, Polish Jewry or any other Jewry, but only from a Zionist perspective — for I believe that Zionists still exist. How many I cannot say. I wish to address you strictly on the Zionist aspect of our political path. My analysis is strictly Zionistic, for a general Jewish analysis is also possible, nor can it be denigrated — looking at the situation of Palestinian Jewry [alone]. Palestine is, after all, one of the countries of the world, and it contains Jews. And we must not be contemptuous if someone makes his calculations on the basis of what will happen to him personally: could his prospect of promotion to the bench of a high court be wrecked by his speaking out? Or what might happen to a rich Jew well-connected in high, non-Jewish circles were he to raise his voice on his people's behalf without asking himself what those non-Jews might think of him? Perhaps doors would be closed in his face. We must not despise these and similar assessments; but a Zionist assessment cannot take them into consideration.

A Zionist assessment raises one question and one question only: will this make possible, will this facilitate the transfer of masses of Jews to Palestine and let them strike roots in the land? No other facts or figures, or calculations enter the picture. I say no other calculations, including that of the Jews of Palestine, for Palestinian Jewry can be just like German Jewry or American Jewry. It is not self-evident that the Jews of Palestine enter a Zionist calculation. The Jews of Palestine, too, can yearn [solely] for [their] independence, but by so doing they give no thought to the future.

A Palestinian Jew, too, might think: might I not be damaged through this, might I not lose my post, one I got from this or that official? Aren't I likely to lose everything that this benevolent Government has deigned to give me, mightn't I be put into a vise (and this government — especially this government — has vises to spare)? The regime here is completely unchecked: it is a military regime, censorial, a war regime, a regime that can do as it pleases, not only with property but with life. So that Jew just might ask himself: won't my business or my status or my career be damaged? We must not dismiss such questions cavalierly, even as we cannot dismiss such a question on the part of a German Jew. But this is not a Zionistic assessment. We must ask: does this or does this not facilitate the transfer of large blocs of Jews to Palestine, does it open a path for the masses of our people to come home and strike roots here? ...

We are now one day past the Land Regulations, and we must demonstrate whether or not Palestine is only one of many countries for world Jewry. We cannot say that this edict is comparable in all respects to the Nuremberg Laws. There is no comparison. The Jew in Palestine does not find himself in the same situation as the Jew in Nuremberg, Warsaw, Lvov, Lodz, or any other place. There is a big difference. However, if we examine this edict from a Zionist perspective, we see that no Nuremberg law, no Spanish auto-da-fé, no pogrom in the Ukraine is comparable to this edict. There, Jewish communities were attacked, butchered, wiped out; but here, the blow has fallen on the entire Jewish nation, on the soul of the Jewish nation — all this, of course, from the Zionist perspective alone; here, now, I have no other. Nor is any other conceivable.

What is to be done? I raise the question and offer an answer. But first I must warn against misleading, deceptive, empty answers. One answer being advanced is this: true, this is a terrible calamity for Israel, but there is a war going on. The war will end, a new world order will arise and we, too, will benefit from this new order.

I would like to confess to you that I, your servant, am one of those who all their lives, and in these times more than in my youth, have been afire in anticipation of this new order; for I have seen, in the course of these past twenty years, what this order has said to the world, to the Jewish people, to mankind. I am not only afire, I believe that it will come — not soon, but come it will; in five years' time, ten, fifteen — I don't know. And that is not all that I don't know. There is something else I don't know: I don't know what status the Jewish people will have in this new order. Perhaps there will be a new order; and perhaps the hope of the Jewish people, in its land, will be cut off. I am aware of an historic pattern — "except the Jews." It has happened before, including in our era. Who will guarantee me, whence this confidence that all this will take place at once, that this new regime that arises after the war will not be marred by this tragic "except the Jews"?

Where is the guaranty that this war must give birth to any new order? Where is the guaranty that carnage will necessarily usher in the world's redemption? Perhaps that will happen — but not necessarily. To so believe is to take refuge in groundless hopes and self-deception; this is an attempt to free ourselves from the effort we must undertake.

There can be no solution to our problem, the Zionist problem, that stands in contradiction to the rescue of our people throughout the world. But that this new war will create a new world, one in which a rebuilt Palestine will fall into the open mouth of the Jewish people like roasted pigeons — how can such a thing happen?

Who, from among all the powers taking part in this war, would raise this issue? England, who promulgated the Land Regulations? Stalin's Russia? How will it come about, how will it issue from the war? This is nothing but an empty, misleading, deceptive answer.

There is another answer. Some say: not [immediately] after the war, not [immediately] after peace is established — but the war will have to end and after that there will be a peace conference, and in this peace conference our problem will be raised. We shall prepare a memorandum, the peace conference will take place and we will put our question before it, our demand: give us Palestine. Now this is a serious matter, I know of nothing so serious. I know that here grave matters will be deliberated. And I say, that for me nothing can be more serious than the fate of the Jewish people, its fate and its future. We dare not toss about empty words.

How will this issue appear at the peace conference? There are two theoretical possibilities. Assuming that the war stays within its present bounds, with Germany on the one side and France and England on the other, then I think — I would say, almost believe — that France and England will win. But if Hitler wins — will he give us Palestine? Shall we receive it of his hand if he becomes its owner? Have those who speak of a peace conference given thought to what those two words mean? They intend, of course, that England and France will win. ([Meir] Ya'ari: Maybe England and Germany will reach an accommodation.) That could happen, too, but I am not listing all the possibilities here; I am not analyzing the war, for the moment, but Zionism. If England wins I do not see how Palestine will appear on the agenda of the peace conference. Will the peace conference deal with Scotland? Well, Scotland is a country that belongs to England, and Palestine is no Scotland. But will they deal with Kenya, a country that is like Palestine? Will the peace conference deal with Britain's colonies? If France and England win they will discuss the fate of Germany, Austria, Czechoslovakia — but why should the agenda contain any country under British rule?

There is yet another possibility, one of an [Anglo-German] accommodation. But will Hitler raise the issue of Palestine? This reminds me of that story of the rebbe walking about God's world in a weekday, while everywhere else it was the Sabbath. On the one hand — the ruin of world Jewry; on the other — the ruin of Zionism in Palestine; and then comes the miracle — the placing of the question of Palestine on the table of the peace conference. What is this nonsense!?

Yes, we can assume that the Jewish question will be at the peace conference — if the democratic forces prove the stronger. I assume that there is at least a chance that they will discuss the Jews of Poland, Germany, Austria and, in general, the Jewish question. But why should they deal with the question of Palestine? Why should they deal with Palestine? Palestine belongs to the English, the English made their decisions, we went along and nothing remains to be done. We accept the [present] situation; so what will happen at the peace conference?

Will England, at the peace conference, declare, "What I did is not done, what I promised not promised?" Will the Jewish question be dealt with? Possibly. Will Jewish suffering be dealt with? Possibly. But Zionism will not be dealt with; and I am not interested in any solution to the Jewish question other than Palestine and Zionism, for there is no other solution. And I will fight for this solution. Any other solution, by comparison, is a deception, wherein the Jews have failed many a time before.

And there is a third solution. It is a well-considered answer. Whatever arises, there is this well-considered prescription: a Jewish-Arab agreement. I here declare that I support a Jewish-Arab agreement with all my heart, not only when things are going badly for us, but even when things go well for us. I don't want to get into this problem. I ask: why should the Arabs agree to an agreement now? Because England has just delivered us a blow, and because without such an agreement with the Arabs there is nothing to be done except to bow to reality? Why do the Arabs have to come to an agreement? Will such an agreement nullify the law, nullify the White Paper, will it make possible a massive Jewish immigration? Why should they do it? Perhaps someone knows, but I find it difficult to grasp his logic. Because we have been dealt a lethal blow, the Arabs will make an agreement with us because it is crucial for us and because we have no other way out?!....

War has come. There was great debate at the [Zionist] congress. Some members present here did not take part in the meetings of the Political Committee and that was where the argumentation was. Immediately following the congress a change took place. The war broke out. Political calculations that take no account of changed conditions become theological calculations or chatter. There are no dogmas in political confrontations. Politics is determined by conditions; by one's standing, fixed goal; but every step taken toward that goal is determined by conditions. The war came. It was not all that unexpected. But expecting war, and war itself, are two different things. The war could not be excluded from our calculations; it brought a radical change to our political strategy. Was this a mistake or not? I think it is too early to judge. Without having conferred (by then conferral between London and Jerusalem was not possible), we turned both to Whitehall and here, if with different styles — we all know that no two prophets prophecy alike — Weizmann in London on August 20 and I here on September 3, on the day the war broke out. Weizmann wrote a letter to Chamberlain. Here, where I was almost the only member of the executive, I issued a statement in the name of the executive on the occasion of the outbreak of the war. I said that the White Paper had struck us a grievous blow; that, as before, we would demand our rights; that now there was a war, a war that laid new concerns upon us. And one of the new concerns imposed upon us was this — helping England as much as we can in this war. We assumed then — we did not determine it had to be so — but we assumed that it was possible, not that the war would abrogate the White Paper, but that it would delay its implementation. At our first meeting following the members' return from the congress, the executive joined me in this opinion. We said that we must not delude ourselves into thinking that the war would do away with the White Paper. There was the assumtpion that during the war the White Paper might become a dead letter.

What does the White Paper mean? It has three elements: certainly the immigration provisions will not be changed to our benefit. The legislation will not become a reality during the war. The litmus test will be the Land Regulations. Before the war broke out, the law had been slated to become effective in September. A meeting of the assembly of the League of Nations was to have taken place, and Malcolm MacDonald had planned to attend that session. He felt that he had the assembly in his pocket — and in that he was certainly not mistaken. The Land Regulations would then have been issued in September. But war broke out and six months have passed, and during these six months they have been busy fighting the Germans on land and at sea. Now, Malcolm is not conducting the war; but at any rate he needed the six months to implement the law, which he had had ready a half year before. They themselves hesitated to do this. For our part, we did whatever we could to have the matter deferred. We took action primarily here and in London, to a lesser degree in America; and had we not been able to take any action, the law would have been promulgated six months ago, without delay. And since, in so acting, the British government determined something of major importance — War or no, Zionism will be destroyed; we had no other choice than to say, War or no, Zionism will be defended.

Now I arrive at what is possibly the most difficult point in this political analysis. It is a point demanding utmost responsibility. I do so with the greatest fear. This analysis is grave, most grave. When I come to this point in particular, mountains press in on me and chasms open at my feet. Though the danger and the difficulties be very great, there is no refuge for a Zionist — and no refuge for me as well — in empty phrases and bogus prescriptions. When we are faced with a grave situation, we must look at it open-eyed. We wanted — and I think rightly so (perhaps someone can be found who feels we were mistaken) — a truce to take effect during the course of the war. We told the [British] government: We are with you wholeheartedly, we will do whatever we can to help you, you needn't even tell us that you are abolishing the White Paper; but for this stretch of time, it no longer exists. Had the government accepted our stand, I believe that our path would have been the proper one.

In this war, too, we have two problems — Jewish and Zionist. This is not any war, as, say, between China and Japan, touching us only as newspaper readers. No, this war touches us to the quick.... We said, defer it [the White Paper] until after the war. But the British government says, we have a world war, a war with Hitler, but this need not bother us in destroying the hope of the Jewish people in its land. They do not have to take the war into account in determining governmental policy in

Palestine. There is a war, there isn't war — it's no affair of mine; there is a White Paper — it must be implemented. Even the section on immigration was carried out beyond the provisions of the White Paper. Malcolm MacDonald has overstepped the limits of the White Paper. He did not have the authority to stop the immigration of the refugees. According to the White Paper, he had the authority to halt regular immigration. He acted similarly as regards the Land Regulations. And this has internal logic. They said, there is a war, there is the White Paper, there is a known need in Palestine, there is a certain policy and it shall be carried out, war or no. Our reply: our defense of our rights, war or no. We, too, are not affected by the war in this.

Well, then, I would like to clarify this in a few words. For us this war means one thing and one thing only: our position is fixed, beyond any doubt. In every "gentiles'" war Jews could take either side. Even during the last war there were some Jews who were for the Allied powers and some for Germany. At the present moment our position is predetermined; to my mind the outcome of the war, to a large extent, has been predetermined. If nothing extraordinary happens, if nothing unforeseeable takes place — England's victory is given. We know who we want to win in this war and who we are interested in seeing as the loser. But should the fact of the war prevent us from defending our vital interest in Palestine? No! The interests of the Jews of Palestine are not important to me — not more than the interests of the Jews of Germany or of any other country. The fate of Polands' three million Jews is much closer to my heart than the fate of 500,000 Jews in Palestine. But if we have to defend Zionism, should the war interfere with us or not? I say: as though there were no war in the world. That there is a war is a political fact. Does not this fact in and of itself provide me with ammunition for the defense of the hope of the Jewish people? Yes, I say. I say that the war is likely to interfere with us, but we must find the means — if by being involved in the war we do not have them — that will help us protect the future of the Jewish people.

What is the political significance of the issuance of the law now? Here, too, we must make a political calculation. I know that there are many Jews who can "put themselves in England's shoes." To this day I am a devotee of England, but I don't want to "put myself in England's shoes." She has experts for that, much better ministers than I. She has a government, ambassadors, Parliament, an army, a navy, they sit and ponder the issue day and night. Why should I have to knock my little head against the wall trying to figure out what is good for them and what is not good for them (and there are Englishmen who can knock my head against the wall, too)? This law means the following: that the English are saying, we can do whatever we please, you Jews can't hurt us, or if you try to hurt us we don't give a hat, such damage doesn't bother us at all. The English have every reason for needing to understand their affairs much better than we. I am not saying that Chamberlain is the greatest of statesmen and is doing the very best for England — as an ordinary person I happen to think the opposite, but that's not my business. He isn't going to listen to me. The British government, the British Parliament — where the government has a majority — has said: we are under no obligation to listen to the Jews. We don't give a farthing for what they might do to us.

There was some stir here for a few days — but what, really, will happen? We all know that the representatives of the cinemas turned to us, because they didn't want to shut down. I walked home on the night of the promulgation of the Land Regulations: [the coffeehouse] in Reḥaviah [a Jerusalem Jewish affluent quarter] was open as usual and people were dancing there. Delegations of communal committees opposed illegal activities, they aided this government in this war. It will help not at all if I know best what England should do in this war. No one has asked my advice and I do not have to give it.

Now someone might say, we are not obligated to give advice, yet it is our moral duty. I said that our stance has been determined in advance. Perhaps we are interested in England's winning more than they are. When we come to the war for our future, from this point on we can no longer say, this will hurt the war going on between England and Germany. To this moral question I reply, if this [our opposition] might prove damaging, then they require our opinion about the conduct of the war. If I am called upon to do something or refrain from doing something because of the demands of the war, then I must be inquired of — for the Zionist perspective says one more thing: we act as a people, not as individual Jews, not as a collation of individuals, not as any Jewish community; rather, we act *as the Jewish people.* Is the Jewish people not obligated to make a calculation, where its survival is concerned, as to what this war requires? It must do so on condition that it is a partner in this enterprise. Then it can be obligated to sacrifice lives. Then I can say that we can be called upon to think of their needs; and we will call upon them to think of ours, and we will lay down our lives like the French; but as regards the latter, everything is mutual, they are conferred with. Now we cannot demand that we be given as much weight as the French; but why should we not have as much weight as the Czechs? There are more Jews in the world than Czechs, we have more power than the Czechs in this war. If the one calculation does not exist, neither does the other. Then we exist for ourselves alone. If they have obliterated this political need, if they have declared that you cannot harm us — we have no more moral obligation. The Jewish people does not exist for those who are conducting this war....

I have something else to say in this regard. Inasmuch as this war affects us very much, I hold this law up to the light of the war, the light of the war's needs, and I say that this law is a grievous blow to the fighting strength of the two democracies. It reduces the power of the British navy. No navy is necessary to enforce laws on land — that does not cut into the strength of the French army. Wars, however, are not waged by armies and navies alone, but by moral force as well. Hannibal knew that, Alexander the Great knew it, Napoleon knew it... they all knew it. We see it in our own time, we hear speeches of Chamberlain and Halifax on the war's goals — that they are fighting for the fulfillment of international treaties, for keeping faith in international relations, for freedom for weak nations against oppression, against racist laws. I don't know if Chamberlain and Halifax say these things with sincerity. From the vantage point of politics, that does not interest me. The fact is, they have to say it. Chamberlain and Halifax need to, for that is moral weaponry in the war. They require it for their people, so that their people go off to fight; they need it for the dominions, for India. Gandhi announced that now we are fighting against Hitler. They need it for public opinion, too, in neutral countries, in America. They need it as much as they need an army and a navy. She [Britain] will lose the war if she loses her moral power; or she well might lose the war if Hitler, Stalin or Italy can manage to prove to the British people, or the peoples of South Africa or Australia, India, or America or the neutral countries of Europe, that there is no difference between them: the one breaks faith as much as the other. That would be a grievous blow to England's war capability, possibly a mortal blow — and we are interested in a British victory....this is no idle speculation from the debate... in the Parliament.

I have to say a word or two about this debate. The debate is significant from a Zionist perspective; but it is not a date in Zionist history. True, there were important speeches — those of Baker, Amery and others. These were important speeches and we cannot dismiss them lightly; but they have changed nothing and will change nothing. That has already been said. Malcolm MacDonald knows these speeches by heart now; Chamberlain does not. But they will change nothing. This was not a significant date in Zionist history: it *was* a date in the history of England at war, a very important date. This was the first time since the outbreak of the war that a very significant political battle took place. An idyllic peace had obtained between the [British] parties since the war began. When it was necessary to elect a representative of Labour in by-elections, the other parties would not put up candidates; and the same went for electing members of another party. Now, for the first time, the workers' party [Labour] set out to bring down the Chamberlain government, to create an uproar in the midst of the war. This is an event of first-rank importance for the British empire. A war is going on, it is no light matter to bring down Chamberlain's cabinet, this is not the way things are done in wartime — it is something extraordinary. During the last war a cabinet was brought down only once, with very serious repercussions. Why did they do it?

Because they had to do it; and don't think that it was done so that the Jewish National Fund might be able to buy some more land near Ma'oz [a kibbutz in Bet She'an Valley]. One doesn't raise a hue and cry over such a matter in wartime. What has happened to the opposition — who, until now, were no opposition at all — that they should suddenly bring down the government? Now they do number among them some loyal friends — Zionists, who, out of their loyalty to Zionism, want to help us. But it would be naive to think that they want to do us a favor. That, too — but they saw here a danger, a danger to Britain in the war. They took their stand on that. They said that this was a breach of faith, the abandonment of an international obligation, contempt for the League of Nations, for an international obligation. It was undermining Britain's position. This, for them, was a grave matter.

If we really have a stake in this war, we must view all this as a serious blow to the war effort. Consequently, a war against this law, mustering all our strength to oppose this law and the legislators and enforcers of this law — this is both a Zionist and human obligation.

I have had a few discussions on this subject in the course of these past two weeks. One talk was with an Englishman, a man with an important position; and the second with a Frenchman, who also holds a high post among his compatriots in Palestine. The Englishman listened courteously, almost in a friendly fashion. (Who can read the heart of an Englishman? No one.) The Frenchman not only listened but spoke as well, hardly less than I. The conversation went on for two hours. We argued, he [the Frenchman] tried to demonstrate what I had heard from a number of people. "How much are you buying yearly?" he asked me. I told him that during the last ten years we had purchased about 40,000 dunam. He told me, "The war will go on for another five years, perhaps. So you have your work cut out for you during the war. May you have enough money to settle what you've already got; and it's worthwhile buying what you can. Strengthen yourselves, strengthen your positions."

I didn't want him to put himself into the position of the Jewish people: that's a hard thing to do for a non-Jew. I knew that we did have a common ground — the war. He was as interested in the war as I was. I explained to him the huge danger, at any rate, the harm, that Britain could expect. I told him that I hadn't come to offer advice to the English or the French, but that I assumed that they had to know these things very well. We are a widely scattered people (I told him), perhaps the war will reach here, too. They [the British] are involved with many matters. For us, this is, baldly, a question of physical existence. I told him, just imagine: the Jews in America are free Jews, not subservient to England. Until now, because of their Zionism they have been warm sympathizers with England; and now England has abandoned Zionism, has delivered a blow to the Jewish people.

The Jews of America have various strengths. There are all kinds of people living in America — there are Germans, there are Irish, sworn enemies of England. The Germans of America are more numerous, but the Irish have more influence. There are also pure-blooded Americans who have not yet forgotten what the English did to them. And this America holds as well a community of four to five million [Jews]. Now it is true that that is not much for America; but when we consider the situation, they are concentrated in a few states, mostly in cities; therefore their influence is greater. They can tell themselves: all of Europe can go to hell, what do we care about Hitler, why should we, America, get involved in all this? We still don't know how this war will end — it just began. Perhaps American aid can be a decisive factor. Till now she has not given help, she is keeping a watchful eye on Japan. One cannot know what will happen with Russia and Italy. Can you afford to put such a factor into jeopardy, even if it is not decisive? Can you allow yourselves to do it? Imagine Jews hearing of this! For them it is an insult. They had Palestine, it's their home; so they will then tell the English, "What do we need this for?" In every city, in every town where there are Englishmen, they will have an address, and they will set up pickets: England broke faith with the Jewish people, the English are our enemies in Palestine, England is scheming against the Jewish people. If the Jews do that throughout the cities of America, it would be very dangerous for England.

I told him, "There is another small community in a faraway land, South Africa, and there the situation is most strange. The people living there are divided into two camps — the one supporting the British empire and the other opposed.... Now there is a Jewish community there, and they could swing the balance. If Hertzog and the South African Republicans promise them equal rights, say to them, "You are our brothers, join us, can't you see that England is scheming against you?" — why, then, wouldn't the danger be very great? This matter is not so simple.

"I speak to you as a Jew who came from Russia; I will do all that I can for the Allies. But here [in Palestine] a new generation is arising, who feel that they belong here, just as the French feel in France. And tell me now, please, what you would do if France were suddenly taken from you? If a French citizen were to be told that he is not a citizen with equal rights — what would he do? A new generation of Jews is rising in Palestine and what is most precious to them has been taken from them. Can they forget that? Is this what they have to endure in this war?"

Now the man was not frightened by my remarks, but I am sure that he saw the matter in a new light; he saw what the opposition in the British Parliament had seen. Now isn't that exactly what I have been saying? Doesn't this deliver a blow to England's fighting power?...

I say that Zionist politics does not wish to turn Palestine into an exilic community at Chamberlain's command, but obeys the mandate of Zionism. A Zionist program that seeks to preserve and struggle for the possibility of *aliyah* and settlement of masses of Jews cannot allow that these Land Regulations, the starkest blow that has fallen upon the Jewish people since Roman legions destroyed their land, be enforced. The Jewish people will not remain silent. I don't know the size of this people, for not every Jew is willing to include himself in this people; but the people that exists will not keep silent.

There are three places where the Jewish people must not be silent: in Palestine, in America, and in South Africa. They must not keep silent, and that with three mottoes, which they must take pains to keep on the pages of the world's newspapers. How to do this is a technical matter and I will not speak of that. The three mottoes are: (1) England has broken faith; (2) England has passed a racist law, she is undermining the foundations of the war for democracy; and (3) Palestine is a question of life and death for the Jewish people.

Source: Minutes of the meeting, BGIA.

MEMBERSHIP OF AMERICAN
ZIONIST ORGANIZATIONS 1938–1948*

Year	Zionist Organization of America	Hadassah, Women's Zionist Organization of America
1938	27,600	54,200
1939	43,500	66,000
1940	43,300	73,800
1941	46,000	80,100
1942	50,000	86,300
1948	250,000	243,000

* Numbers have been rounded out.

Source: Halperin, *American Zionism*, p. 327.

BEN-GURION'S POLICY FOLLOWING ROOSEVELT'S "GREAT ARSENAL OF DEMOCRACY"

ADDRESS (SELECTIONS) AT THE ZOA NATIONAL ADMINISTRATIVE COUNCIL MEETING, PHILADELPHIA, JANUARY 5, 1941

Before I begin my remarks, I want to say that, listening to this debate, I felt that Zionism in America is still a living force which has faith in itself. I am certain that if the whole of the Zionist movement will be animated by that spirit which was given expression at this meeting, and if you will work together with all other Zionist groups in America, you will achieve your objective.

Last week, the President of the United States announced to this country and to the world, that America, in order to maintain its security, and in order to preserve the ideals of democracy, freedom and justice for which it stands, must actively help England and her allies in this war. America must become the arsenal of the democracies.

I know no better Zionist message than the message of the President of the United States, especially to American Zionists. More than America, American Jewry is faced with an unusually dangerous situation. For America as a whole, her future security is in danger. For the Jewish people, its actual existence is endangered. It is for American Jewry — since European Jewry, excepting the Jews in England, are practically in one concentration camp, and Palestine Jewry may very soon be in the middle of the fiercest battle in this war — it is for American Jewry to become now the champion of the Jewish people, as much as the whole of America is going to become the champion of democracy, freedom and justice for the whole world. And just as Franklin Delano Roosevelt, and not Charles Lindbergh, not [George?] Marshall, not [Norman] Davis, is expressing the true spirit of the United States, it is you — and not that people — who are expressing the real spirit of American democracy and of Jewish democracy, which are one.

And upon you, even more than upon the whole of America, rests now a great responsibility. There is one sentence in this great speech of the American President which should be the keynote of Zionist activities, thought, and feeling at the present moment. It was a very significant sentence: He said that, although America is not at war, there are many shortsighted and foolish people who believe that the oceans in themselves defend America. It is such a grave situation for the future of America, that we can no longer maintain any more "business as usual." There can be no more "business as usual" for Jews and for Zionists. We are faced with an upheaval of five, seven, eight million fellow Jews in the whole of Europe....

This is the problem facing us. We must prepare ourselves, mentally, economically, psychologically, politically, and financially. Then we must ask ourselves: What are the necessary conditions which will enable us to achieve this task of settling millions of Jews after the war in Palestine? Of course, not under the White Paper. This needs an explanation. The White Paper must be destroyed, just as Hitler must be destroyed, because it is a result of Hitler. It is a result of the appeasement of the former British Government, which brought misfortune not only to us, but to all of England and Europe. The White Paper is a part of Hitler and of his system, and of the surrender to the system of Hitler; Hitler must be destroyed by the Jewish people and by peoples who sincerely and honestly are fighting not merely for their own interest, but also for democracy, freedom and justice. But when the White Paper is destroyed, we must ask ourselves: What should replace it? There must be a good Mandate, not only a Mandate by England, but a Mandate by America. There must be a new order. We must learn a little from our past.

This job of settling Jews in Palestine is the most difficult job in the world. I will tell you now about the difficulties: I want first to tell you a little story: I was once talking about the difficulties in Palestine, afterwards a Jew came up and said to me: "I am a lifelong Zionist. Yesterday evening, for the first time, I heard the truth about Palestine. I am not a Zionist any longer." I am not afraid it will happen here, but you can take it from me — it actually happened.

Palestine is a difficult country, and the Jews, you know, are a difficult people; and they are not a people who have the tradition of building a land, of working the soil, of generating electricity, cutting stones, building roads, mending ships, etc. And I must tell you one reason why we had trouble with the British Administration in Palestine — not because they are so bad — they are not so good, but they are not so bad. There are many people who came to Palestine with a desire to implement the Mandate sincerely. In a few years' time, they all turned against us, for the simple reason that they are used to rule and to manage bigger countries than Palestine. But they did not know what to do in Palestine, where they were faced with unprecedented difficulties. First of all, they were meeting people who did not look up to them. [They] are real democrats [in] England, but a British Colonial official is not used to it. Then, they learned the truth of what they read in the Bible, that the Jews are a stubborn people. When the district Governor said "No," the Jews went to the High Commissioner; and when the Colonial Secretary said "No," they went to Parliament. And there were several times when the Parliament overruled the British officials. This really made the lives of these British officials in Palestine miserable. They have a certain routine, and they plan their work for a year; but on the following month they find that they have to revise their plan — there are more people in new buildings and new roads; so all their plans are topsy turvy, and they don't like it. It is too much for them. I notice sometimes that it is even too much for Zionists.

And although it is difficult, I am convinced that it can be done and must be done; because I cannot conceive that such a difficult job will be done by strangers. Can you expect a stranger to rear a child as a mother does? It is even more difficult to bring up this child in Palestine, even with the best friends — and the British must be our friends. (After all, what Goy is not susceptible to anti-Semitism?) I say it can be done, and if we mean it seriously and we must mean it — there is no more pressing and urgent issue for the Jewish people. It is a part of this great struggle for democracy, freedom and justice in the world.

We must provide for the establishment of Palestine as a Commonwealth after the war. It is not a new thing; it is not a new invention. This is what America said in the last war; this is what Wilson wanted; and I know that the present America, which certainly is not worse than the America of Wilson — this democratic America which asserted itself in the last elections, and which spoke last week through President Roosevelt — will understand us.

What we want is merely to apply the principles for which America is now mobilizing its forces, to spend billions of dollars, and perhaps more than that — in this great struggle for democracy, freedom and justice. These same principles should be applied also to the Jewish people. An opportunity should be given to the Jewish people that they themselves, with their own labor and their own responsibility, ability, love, and devotion — despite the mistakes which they will make — should be enabled to have control in that country, to settle their millions of brothers who will be obliged to go there.

This is the task confronting the Jewish people, and especially, American Jewry; to point out that here we are faced with this problem as a part of this great world problem, and the only solution is to make Palestine ready to receive millions of Jews through the instrumentality of a Jewish Commonwealth in Palestine. This is Zionist policy. This is the central idea which must animate all our work — daily work, as well as preparations for the future. This is our message to the masses of Jews, to the masses of Americans. This is a part of the great ideals for which America is fighting and is ready to fight.

Permit me a few words, perhaps of lesser importance, but which also cannot be overlooked. For the time being, there is the White Paper. The same England which gave the White Paper, threw off the Government which led England to its disaster. In this fight, in this historical disaster — I cannot find adequate words to tell you what I have seen of this great, brave, decent, fine people in England. But their Government is still maintaining this White Paper policy and I do not ask them now to abolish the White Paper. I know that when England is engaged in a struggle for life and death, they cannot do it. But what they can and ought to do, in order to be true to the deep moral and ethical character of their struggle — and America is helping them because of the character of their struggle — is that they should not, during this war, implement this treacherous White Paper. And we as Jews, as human beings, and you, as Americans, must with all our might help England in this great struggle, and "support your Government" strengthen its hands to help England more and more, for this is our struggle. For the first time in my life, when I was in England — and I am not a Polish Jew, nor a British Jew, nor an American Jew, I am merely a Jew — I was proud of what England was doing, and I felt that deep affection for that city in which I was living for two months. I admired that people. In the same spirit as Jews can help

England, so they can resist the implementation of the White Paper — in the same way as any Englishman will resist if his Government should commit an injustice. There is a free Parliament and a free press, and they freely criticize their Government. And we ought to act vis-à-vis England as Englishmen, not more than Englishmen. Beware of being more English than an Englishman, or more American than an American. Resist the application of the White Paper, whenever there is an attempt to apply it, either by deporting Jews or by shutting off immigration. Resist, protest, raise public opinion here and in England, not as enemies, but as true friends who are identified with this great struggle of the British people.

Let us remember these things: preparing ourselves; preparing the Jews of America; preparing public opinion for the only possible solution of this new problem of millions of Jews, by settling them in Palestine and creating a Jewish Commonwealth in Palestine; and resisting the White Paper during the war. Let us mobilize Jewish help as Jews, in this great modern fight of democracy against Hitler. Zionist policy must consist of these three points: First, help even during the war, the rebuilding of Palestine... . What we need is to continue the upbuilding of the country to bring in new people, and this, the Jews of Palestine cannot do themselves. Immigration is terribly difficult now. To get land is terribly difficult. But we must do it, because this is the foundation of the future. In a measure, we will strengthen our position, not only maintain it, but also strengthen our position in four dimensions. We are working in those four dimensions in Palestine. We will be able, after the war, to achieve our main purpose.

Secondly, vigilance against the application of the White Paper, as true, devoted friends of England.

Thirdly, the mobilization of American Jewry and American public opinion for the creation of a Jewish Commonwealth in Palestine, after the war.

These are, the main points of our Zionist policy. I want, in conclusion, to say that, more than that we need unity — not a deadening, sterile unity, as the American people refused to have (they did not make unity with Mr. Lindbergh and Mr. Vandenberg, and with all of that crowd). We need, first of all, unity in the Zionist ranks. We need courage. Let us once and for all learn from others. Be American and learn from your great leader; have far-sightedness; look ahead and inspire the Jewish people, as your great American leader is inspiring the United States. With such a bold and inspiring program, and with unity in American Zionism, you will lead American Jewry.

Source: Minutes of the meeting, ZAL, ZOA Collection XIV/1

BEN-GURION CONCLUDES HIS 1940–1941 AMERICAN VISIT

LETTER TO NAHUM GOLDMANN, SAN FRANCISCO, JANUARY 17, 1941

My dear Goldmann:

Prior to my departure I will try to set out briefly the Zionist agenda for the moment.

A. The Peace Platform

1. The eradication of all racial, political, religious, national, and linguistic discrimination; and the attainment of full and equal rights for the Jews in all lands of their domicile in the world.

2. *The designation of Palestine as a Jewish commonwealth* for the purpose of organizing mass *aliyah*, on a governmental scale, of millions of Jews from Europe and other countries; and their absorption in agriculture, industry, maritime pursuits, and all other branches of the economy in Palestine.

3. The Jewish commonwealth shall join the British empire as one of the dominions, if England agree; in the absence of such agreement, it shall be completely autonomous. In the event that the Arabs agree to the founding of a Jewish commonwealth on condition that it join an Arab-Jewish federation in the Near East, the Jewish commonwealth shall join such a federation.

B. The War Platform

1. The Jewish people regards itself as involved in England's and her allies' war for freedom and shall assist the fighting democracy to the fullest possible degree.

2. The Jewish people shall take part in this war in a Jewish army, as an ally of the English army, under the same conditions that obtain for all allied armies.

3. Functions of the Jewish army:
  i. the defense of Palestine
  ii. the defense of English positions in the Near East
  iii. participation on all fronts of the world war
4. The Jewish army shall be drafted by the Jewish Agency:
  i. from the Jews of Palestine
  ii. from the Jews of the British empire
  iii. from Jewish refugees
  iv. from Jewish citizens of all countries, in accordance with the laws of those countries
5. The Jewish army has a Zionist flag; its anthem — HaTikvah, its command — Hebrew; the language of command — Hebrew. Strategically it shall be under the British High Command. In all other matters it shall be under the jurisdiction of the Jewish Agency.

C. The War and the White Paper

1. The White Paper regime in Palestine does not diminish the complete and unqualified identification of the Jewish people with the English people in its war against Hitler.

2. The Jews of America tender all requisite moral support to England and, as American citizens, support to the full the American administration in its efforts to provide England with military aid.

3. Nonetheless, the Jewish people's opposition to the White Paper ceases not for a moment, and American Jewry shall rise up against any attempt on the part of the Mandatory administration to enforce the White Paper during the war and deny the rights of the Jewish people in their homeland, for any such attempt to enforce the White Paper
  i. undermines the moral basis of England's war against Hitler
  ii. jeopardizes the future of the Jewish people

4. The war against the enforcement of the White Paper shall be conducted publicly, with the mobilization of maximal help of American public opinion.

5. In this war, Zionism shall dissociate itself from all who would attempt to exploit the White Paper to discredit England in America; but will also dissociate itself from those who, under the guise of false friendship with England or misguided American patriotism, would turn their backs on the rights, honor, and future of the Hebrew people in its homeland.

D. The Zionist Emergency Committee

The functions of the Emergency Committee:

i. To place before the Jewish people and the American people the Jewish question, in all its urgency and tragic dimensions, as one of the central and global questions of democracy, peace and justice.

   To unmask the lie of the so-called "territorial" schemes produced from time [to time] by Zion-haters, from Malcolm MacDonald to Jewish Communists and their friends in the assimilationist Jewish plutocracy.

   To explain to American public opinion, to the heads of the church, leaders of literature and the press, leaders in the Congress and the Senate, governors and American federal officials — that the post-war straits of millions of Jews can be remedied only by a vast settlement effort, conducted on a governmental, territorial scale, and that this can take place only in Palestine — as the history of Jewish settlement in Palestine and other countries has demonstrated.

ii. In order to enable the transfer of millions and their entrenchment on the land and in the economy, it is essential to designate Palestine as a Jewish commonwealth and enable the Jewish people itself to handle its own rescue.

iii. The Emergency Committee will render all requisite aid in America to the efforts of the Zionist Executive in London and Jerusalem to the establishment of a Jewish army; and when it shall be established, help raise its manpower.

iv. The Emergency Committee shall mobilize American Jewish aid for the bolstering of our economic bases in Palestine, for the continuation of absorption of *aliyah,* for the expansion of the settlement effort by setting up new points, *and the strengthening of Jewish security forces in Palestine.*

v. The Emergency Committee shall nurture the pioneer movement in America and shall aid in the readying of pioneer youth for the fulfilment of *roles in the upbuilding and defense* of the country during the war and thereafter. To this end it will aid in the training of Jewish youth in air and on sea, in technical upgrading and in sports programs.

vi. The Emergency Committee shall strengthen the inner unity of the Zionist movement in America and shall draw to its efforts all Jewish circles *who agree with the political agenda* for the course of the war and thereafter.

I assume that you have by now seen [Dov] Joseph and have heard of the situation in Palestine.

Two things worry me:

1. The economic situation in Palestine, necessitating greater and swifter aid.

2. The MacMichael regime, which is not far removed from a Nazi regime, and which calls for a vigorous response in America.

I have written to S. Goldman, as you requested, and have also written to Hadassah. I have sent a copy of my letter to Hadassah to [Arthur] Lourie; you can read it there. I do not have copies of the other letters.

> Be strong and of good courage —
> Yours, D. B. G.

Source: ZAL, Emanuel Neumann Collection, David Ben-Gurion File.

FIRST AMERICAN ZIONIST CALL
FOR A JEWISH COMMONWEALTH

RESOLUTIONS (SELECTED), UNITED PALESTINE APPEAL NATIONAL
CONFERENCE, WASHINGTON, D.C., JANUARY, 25–26, 1941

Jewish Defense of Palestine

The Conference expresses its gratification at the splendid contribution of the Jews of Palestine by providing nearly 8,000 volunteers for service in the British Army, partly in distinct Jewish units, and by mobilizing its agricultural, technical and industrial resources for the war effort, and expresses the hope that Great Britain will soon avail itself to a fuller extent of the readiness of the Jewish people to make its maximum contribution to the struggle against Nazism and for the defense of Palestine by the establishment of a suitable Jewish military force for service in that struggle and in the defense of Palestine.

Council of Federations and Welfare Funds

The National Conference of the United Palestine Appeal gathered at Washington, D.C., on January 26, 1941, reaffirms its devotion to and faith in democratic processes in American Jewish communal life. We therefore condemn as a threat to democratic procedure the proposal to establish a national budgeting service for American Jewish communities and we register our determination to resist conversion of an instrument hitherto useful as an agency for the dissemination of information into a dictatorial body which will presume to apportion the support which Jews may give to causes which they hold dear.

We declare our intention not to recognize any action by the Council of Jewish Federations and Welfare Funds whose effect will be to substitute such dictatorship for democratic control and the autonomy of American Jewish communities.

The White Paper

The Conference expresses its profound regret that notwithstanding the change in government and policy in the United Kingdom with the advent of Mr. Winston Churchill as Prime Minister, the White Paper Policy, with its restriction on Jewish immigration and land purchase, is still being adhered to by the Palestine Administration. The Conference appeals to His Majesty's Government to end this injustice to the Jewish people, and to open the gates of Palestine to those Jewish refugees who turn to Palestine as their only hope of salvation; and to remove the discrimination against Jews entailed in the land transfer regulations, so that Jewish colonization may proceed unimpeded as contemplated in the mandate for Palestine.

The Conference declares its belief that in the conditions which will prevail in postwar Europe Jewry will be faced with the task of finding a home for large masses of Jews from Central and Eastern Europe and that it is their deep conviction, proved by past experience, that only by large-scale colonization of these Jews in Palestine, with the aim of its reconstitution as a Jewish Commonwealth, can the Jewish problem be permanently solved.

Aid to Great Britain

This Conference gives its unqualified endorsement and complete support to the policy established and pursued by the Government of the United States of extending maximum aid to Great Britain and its Allies in their struggle to insure the survival of democracy, freedom and justice throughout the world.

The Conference expresses the hope that the victory of the Allied cause will vindicate and permanently establish the principles of individual and national freedom, equality and independence, and, accordingly, that termination of the war will result in: (a) equal individual and group rights for Jews in all countries where they reside, and the eradication of all racial, religious and national discrimination in any form; (b) the establishment of Palestine as a Jewish Commonwealth.

Source: *New Palestine* 31, no. 16 (January 31, 1941): 22.

BEN-GURION'S "GUIDLINES FOR ZIONIST POLICY"

SUBMITTED TO THE JEWISH AGENCY EXECUTIVE MEETING,
JERUSALEM, MARCH 23, 1941

A. The Goal

Zionism's primary task at this juncture is the full mobilization of the Yishuv and the Jewish people to ensure a maximally *Zionist solution* to the two central questions awaiting resolution at the war's end:

1. that of the regime in Palestine and
2. that of the destroyed Jewries of Europe (and other lands).

It is the task of Zionist policy to prevent *separate* solutions to these two questions, inasmuch as there can be no solution to the Jewish calamity outside of Palestine; and no solution to the question of Palestine may impinge upon, or deny, the Hebrew people's right to its homeland.

3. Concerning the regime in Palestine: firstly, the Yishuv and the Jewish people must, with all the means at their disposal, prevent Palestine's conversion into an Arab (or Christian) state or the continuance of the White Paper regime. We have three means to effect this goal: (a) the potency of the Yishuv, (b) the potency of *aliyah*, and (c) public political education [*hasbarah*].

4. Concerning the destroyed Jewries of the world: within world Jewry and before the bar of world public opinion Zionism must combat, ideologically and politically, injurious and fraudulent solutions — assimilation, philanthropic schemes, emigration (yet an additional dispersal), and territorial programs outside of Palestine.

5. Zionism's political goal at this juncture is to create such conditions as will allow, at the war's end, the establishment in Palestine of a regime geared to facilitate government-sponsored *aliyah* and settlement of

masses of Jews; and to ensure that the representative body of the Jewish people (the Jewish Agency or a Jewish government) will be given the authority and the means to effect the rapid transfer of millions of Jews and settle them in Palestine as a self-governing nation.

B. A Jewish Palestine and the Arabs

1. A massive *aliyah* and settlement program that will soon make the country overwhelmingly Jewish need not compromise — as it has not thus far — the genuine interests of the Arab (and other non-Jewish) residents of the country, nor impinge upon the legitimate aspirations of the Arab nation in Arab lands.

2. In the event that Arab permission for the free transit of the Arab population to neighboring countries is denied, Arab interests in Palestine should be guaranteed in one of the following ways:

a. In the event that Palestine shall become a separate and sovereign Jewish state, a regime shall be established therein that shall guarantee Arabs not only fully equal civil, political and national rights, but will strive as well to ensure that the Arabs' standard of living — economic, cultural and social — will be the equal of the Jews'.

A pact of friendship and mutual aid shall be contracted between the Jewish state and neighboring states.

b. In the event that Jewish Palestine shall be accepted as a dominion within the British (or British-American) Commonwealth of Nations, a regime shall be established in Palestine similar to that obtaining in Canada as regards [the equal rights of] the English and the French.

c. In the event that a federation or alliance with Near Eastern states shall arise and the Arab peoples shall agree to the establishment of a Hebrew Palestine as a member of such a federation, Jewish Palestine shall join this federation as an independent state with full autonomy in all internal affairs (immigration, settlement, economic and labor laws, security, and the like), along the lines of a dominion of the British Commonwealth.

d. In the event that a world federal regime shall be established after the war, abolishing separate state sovereignties for the good of an efficient commonwealth of nations, this highest authority shall supervise the safeguarding of the rights and interests of the Arabs, as in all other states containing national minorities.

3. Zionist policy toward the Arabs is based upon the following four assumptions:

    a.   The Arabs living in Palestine are natural citizens. If they do not wish to move their domicile to a neighboring Arab state, they deserve all the rights — civil, political, and national — of the country's residents.

    b.   There is no "Arab question" in the same way that there is a Jewish question. Whereas the Jewish people is a minority everywhere and Palestine is their sole homeland, Palestine comprises a homeland for but a small segment of the Arab nation, who have at their disposal an abundance of large and unsettled tracts of land.

    c.   The actual Jewish population of Palestine is but a small portion of the potential numbers that could live here given the full exploitation of agricultural and industrial potential on land and sea. Over two-thirds of Palestinian land is neither cultivated nor settled.

    d.   The Zionist enterprise in Palestine, limited until now to (approximately) one-twentieth of western Palestine alone, has proven, in effect, that the rapid expansion of Jewish settlement does not adversely affect the interests of the local residents; to the contrary, it improves their situation.

C. Vehicles of Zionist Policy

The vehicles for the realization of a Zionist solution to the problem of the nation and Palestine are as follows:

1. A sweeping campaign of public political education in England, America, and the British Dominions (and in other countries, to the degree possible).

2. The rendering of aid, by the Jewish people, to Britain and her allies in the fight against Hitler and in the establishment of a Jewish army in Palestine and in the Diaspora.

3. Readying the Organization [Haganah] and Jewish youth for offensive and defensive roles.

4. Readying all the resources and strength of the Jewish people for a massive *aliyah* to Palestine at the war's end.

5. A constant effort for the establishment of new settlements in Palestine during the war and thereafter.

6. Constant opposition to the White Paper policy.

7. Mobilization of the Yishuv and the Jewish people, and preparation, through research and organizational action, for mass *aliyah* and settlement and for a change of the political regime in Palestine.

D. Public Political Education

1. With Hitler's defeat, the Anglo-Saxon nations, upon the war's conclusion, will be the primary effectors of political decisions; hence Zionist public political education must be aimed primarily at said countries.

2. Our public political educative effort in these countries must be aimed at winning over public opinion; i.e., convincing the Anglo-Saxon peoples — and through them, their governments — to accept the Zionist solution to the question of the Jewish people and Palestine. We must not limit ourselves to official negotiations, but must concern ourselves as well with the press, the labor movement, churches, and parliamentary and intellectual circles.

3. The public political educative effort must be based on the following givens: (a) Jewish suffering as a concomitant of Diasopra life; (b) an historic link between the Jewish people and Palestine; (c) the success of the Zionist settlement effort and the failure of all other attempts at settlement; (d) the absorptive capacity of Palestine; (e) the refusal of the Yishuv to capitulate to the White Paper regime; (f) the necessity of *aliyah* and [a belief in] its capacity to burst all artificial constraints; (g) the right of the Hebrew nation, like all nations, to political independence in its homeland; (h) the need to transfer destroyed Jewries to Palestine swiftly and, to that end, to bestow governmental authority upon the Jewish Agency; and (i) avoidance of injuring Arab interests through Jewish settlement.

4. The vehicles for the Zionist political education of the public in the Anglo-Saxon countries are the Jewries of England, America and the British Dominions. Hence all Zionist energies must be directed to ready the Jewries of these lands for this political task, through missions to the

youth and the people; the creation of appropriate literature; and the bolstering of the ethical influence of Zionist Palestine.

E. Concerning the War

1. Zionism now mobilizes the support of the Jewish people — moral as well as political and military — for Britain's and her allies' war against Hitler, as one of Britain's allies.

2. In Palestine, we continue to provide all possible aid to the British army, foster friendly relations with the military authorities and encourage [Jewish] military service in Palestine and in neighboring countries.

3. In rendering military aid, Zionism aspires to the creation of a Jewish army in Palestine and abroad for first-line defense of the country. Jewish units from abroad will be available for service at other fronts if the need should arise.

4. Even prior to the establishment of such a Jewish army the Zionist authorities will continue to mobilize Jewish units in Palestine.

F. "The Organization" [HaHaganah]

1. Zionism regards the Organization as the backbone of the Yishuv, the vehicle for militant Zionism, and the motive force for the ever-growing settlement effort.

2. The Organization's role at this juncture is not solely the guaranteeing of the Yishuv's security, but, first and foremost, defending the Jewish people's rights and seeing to the settling of the homeland.

3. In order to prepare the Organization for state roles when the destiny of Palestine will be determined, and roles in effecting land settlement, all Jewish youth must be drawn to the Organization: we must train and equip it more effectively and enhance its Zionist discipline and awareness.

4. The Organization's functions necessitate [the imposition of] *strict Zionist authority*. Yishuv institutions must be co-opted into running the Organization. Supreme authority, however, and [specifically] Zionist education and political direction, must remain in the hands of the executive.

G. Concerning the White Paper

1. The Yishuv and the Jewish people remain firm in their active

opposition to the White Paper, and react vigorously, appropriately and effectively to any new impingement upon the people's rights and the Yishuv's interests; and oppose the civil regime in the country so long as that regime continues to exhibit hostility towards, and wanton disregard of, the Yishuv and Zionism.

2. Opposition to the White Paper regime shall not detract from the Jewish people's complete identification with the war of the English people nor in any way reduce the help extended the British army.

3. Zionism shall dissociate itself both from those who would sully the name of the British people and denigrate their war by excoriating the White Paper and the machinations of the Mandatary; as well as from those who would pass over the injury and insults of the White Paper out of empathy with the war of the British people.

H. Internal Policy

A Zionist policy cannot be effectuated unless Zionists in Palestine and in the Diaspora act with vigor and resolve. The Yishuv must stand up to the [British] authorities. Zionist discipline must be imposed in all external relations, bringing all Zionist parties together — all circles, all elements in Palestine — for united action; and intensifying mutual aid within the Yishuv. There must be: enlistment of youth in Palestine and abroad for the Zionist cause, and preparation of said youth for defense roles, enlistment for military duty and the founding of settlements; political Zionist education for weaker elements in the Yishuv (refugees and various ethnic communities); a strengthening of the link between the executive and all segments of the movement, whether in Palestine or in the Diaspora; a mustering of energies, solely through cultural-educational ventures, to combat any signs of weakness, capitulation, or defeatism in the Yishuv and among the Jewish people; and a launching, with ideological fervor, of a greater Zionism in Palestine and in the Diaspora.

I. Laying The Groundwork for Research and Logistics

In order to lay the groundwork for public political education; for official negotiations; and for broad planning of the country's development during the war, at its conclusion and thereafter — the executive shall establish committees and groups of experts to collate and publish, as the need arises, all materials relating to the country's absorptive and economic capacity, governmental norms and procedures, and desired neighborly relations in Jewish Palestine. Similarly these groups shall raise suggestions and propose programs — fiscal and technical — for setting up a rural, urban, and maritime economy that will absorb the post-war massive *aliyah*.

Source: Minutes of the meeting, BGIA.

THE OPPOSITION IN MAPAI: FIRST TREATISE

FACTION B: GUIDELINES (THE "ZIONIST POLICY" SECTION), PUBLISHED TOWARD MAPAI CONFERENCE, APRIL 1941

The dilemma of *Zionist actualization* lies at the heart of the movement's outlook and policy. As we face the destruction of Jewish communities, as we face millions of Jewish refugees and the loss of other [non-Zionist] options and possibilities — there rise in all their starkness the questions of the role, scope, and tempo of Zionist action at this time: *great and sweeping Zionism* — the rescue of masses of Jews by means of unceasing, large-scale *aliyah*; aggressive, massive land settlement; the crystallization of an independent Jewish force in Palestine; and optimal mobilization of the resources of Diaspora Jewry.

British policy in Palestine is one long, unfolding history of the regime's clash with the basic right of the Jewish people to return to its land. Jewish power in Palestine has been engendered through Jewish suffering, and through constant, tremendous struggle.

Britain's anti-Jewish and anti-Zionist policy, one of bald betrayal, has found its most naked expression in the White Paper. In the thick of the war the *White Paper regime* entrenches itself yet further in Palestine — this regime that strangles Jewish *aliyah* and land settlement, that brutally undermines the Zionist effort; this petty-minded, arbitrary and hostile regime, *a regime of the Atlantic's pogromists*.

The political struggle of a vital and practical Zionism must be based solely upon *an independent Jewish policy*, one held up to the light of Jewish interests and the needs of a greater Zionism. These needs and interests will dictate the movement's mode of relating to the Mandatory government and the content of that relationship; these will engender a Zionist policy that presupposes neither loyalty to, nor any partnership with [Britain], that puts no trust in others' kindness and does not mold itself to foreign interests, but is borne forward by a Jewish cadre of fighters and builders *independent of any [foreign] rule or law.*

It is practical Zionism that necessitates an *active fight* to break the White Paper regime through incessant and unbridled illegal immigration, the conquests of land settlement, and a self-defense force. This must be accomplished through guiding the community to readiness for popular warfare; and through the political leadership of the working class in independent, pioneering initiatives.

The enlistment of the Yishuv's and Zionist energies for Zionist readiness and active fight is among the primary political tasks of the workers' movement. The discovery of this strength has been inhibited by a perversion of the concept of the unity of the Yishuv and the Jewish people; by accommodation to class interests and the threats of autocrats of sorts; by bourgeois groveling before the authorities; by the fear of struggle and the conclusions to be derived from that struggle; by conservation of the status quo; by an abhorrence of decisive action, of imposing the will of the Yishuv; by refraining from using the full strength and weight of the Yishuv's working class. Only through daring fight and *independent initiatives of the working class* can the Yishuv become a fighting political bloc, with the masses and the faithful Zionists centering on the working class.

Zionist action and our political struggle *need not come to a halt, despite the reality of the world war.* Indeed, this war to smash the anti-Jewish, Nazi juggernaut highlights the need for an urgent solution to the plight of the Jewish masses, and sets this need at the very heart of our enterprise, of our immediate actions.

This war and our participation in the military anti-Nazi effort need not and cannot prevent our *unflinching struggle* against a discriminatory and oppressive regime, against decrees and attacks upon our rights and our honor, against limitations upon the means of *aliyah,* land settlement, and defense.

Our participation in the general war effort is *contingent* upon the assurance and strengthening of that *self-constituted* Jewish force that looks to our own interests; and in the establishment of a national *Jewish* fighting force on an equal footing [with other national units] to defend the country and participate in the war.

The movement must combat *any blurring or narrowing* of Zionist aspirations, and any politics of *self-abasement and self-negation* that accepts complete dependence upon law-and-order; that shrinks from the war for *aliyah* and illegal immigration, and the conquest of ever more territory for land settlement and self-defense; *that submits, in effect*, to the White Paper regime.

These tendencies have surfaced within our camp of late in a series of internal struggles wherein we have probed and debated the encouragement and defense of illegal immigration, and considered modes of massive public fight against the White Paper, against the land decrees, and against the regulations stifling *aliyah*; [these tendencies appear] in debates over setting up new settlements without permits, on confronting the dangers of Mandatory confiscations of arms, on the question of public battle for the freeing of Haganah prisoners, on the issue of making political statements without censorship, on arguments over Jewish military units as a condition for enlistment, on an active fight to prevent the expulsion of illegal immigrants arrived in Palestine (the *Patria* affair, the *Atlantic* affair, and now the *Dorian*), and in the many debates over Zionist policy during the war.

The refusal to take decisions, to determine our political path practically speaking, paralyzes the necessary political campaign and vitiates our movement's capacity and its influence on the people, Zionism, and our youth.

The current need is such that the Palestine Workers' Party [Mapai] and the Zionist movement are impelled *to choose a clear-cut path* of action, to wage a political war unclouded by generalizations and ambiguous phraseology likely to serve as a cloak for inaction.

The movement must *put at the disposal* of the practical Zionist effort and the political war *the entire Hebrew working class*, the social and settlement cells, and all the wealth and instruments it [the working class] has created, to be *the bearer and vanguard* in Zionism's political fight.

Our movement, the Yishuv, and the Zionist movement must make the following steps central to our endeavor:

- An active fight against the White Paper regime, against discriminatory edicts and acts of cruelty, and against infringements of the rights of the people and of Zionism, through the enlistment and activation of masses who are ready to serve.
- The encouragement and organization of constant *aliyah*, and illegal immigration by all means, and fight to defend it, mounting a public battle for the freeing of the illegal immigrants prisoned in camps in

Palestine, that we might add them to the ranks of our builders and defenders.

- The settlement of new areas, and this in disregard of the strangulation of the land decrees and the partition policy.
- The formation of new centers of settlement on the borders, in the Negev, the north and in the mountains, to buttress the Yishuv's security and create political facts; the conquest of Palestine's untilled lands.
- A wholly independent Hebrew defense force standing at the disposal of, and under the authority of, the Zionist movement, for its struggles and new tasks; increasing the strength, capability, and efficacy of this force and enlarging its scope through defense training of youth, involvement of women, and a general enlistment of the workers' community and the Yishuv as a whole for defense tasks; enlistment in Jewish units for the defense of Palestine.
- The raising of funds in the Yishuv and solicitation of contributions from the Jewish people for the purposes of Zionist actualization; shouldering the well-to-do in the Yishuv with the financial yoke of defense, unemployment, and Zionist action; fighting, with all the means at our disposal, to impose the will of the Yishuv on shirkers and defectors.
- Marshalling the political force of the Diaspora, readying their Jewish masses for bold and open warfare on behalf of the rights of Zionism and the Jewish people; education of the Diaspora Jewry to a greater Zionism; education of the Jewish youth in the Diaspora to attain to pioneering self-fulfillment in Palestine.

The Zionist movement and the workers' movement must engage in careful and unceasing political education and in *the forging of national neighborly relations, and a proletarian compact, with the Arabs*; and foster neighborly relations, meetings, and social contacts in all towns or villages contiguous, or close to, one another.

The efforts and political programs of greater Zionism are not opposed to the preservation of the personal, national, and socialist liberties of the Arab masses in Palestine; or to the currents of national liberation and independence in Arab lands.

Given the world upheavals, and looking to anticipated changes in the world order and in international relations, Zionism and the Hebrew workers' movement must step up *public political education* on all fronts to present the Jewish problem in all its breadth and severity; and demand *international assistance* for the transfer of millions of Jews to Palestine, to settle the entire country and forge independent Jewish political frameworks and [administration of] the upbuilding effort of Zionism in action.

The workers' movement must encourage and expand the political self-education of the world workers' movement, to the inclusion of all its sectors; and labor unceasingly and resolutely — involving the entire Zionist movement in this process — to break down the barriers of estrangement and resistance to the socialist-Zionist endeavor among the forces of progress and the future, who will determine the fate of the world.

Source: UKMA, section 13, container 4.

GLOSSARY

Aliyah (ascent, immigration) Successive waves of Jewish immigration to Palestine, beginning in 1882.

Berit Shalom (The Covenant of Peace) An association of Jewish intellectuals, mainly Central Europeans, aimed at bringing about Jewish-Arab accord. It favored constituting Palestine as a binational state. Founded in 1925, the association survived until the eve of World War II.

Betar (an acronym of, in Hebrew, Joseph Trumpeldor Alliance) Revisionist youth movement, founded in 1923.

Binationalism A political idea, aimed at bringing about understanding between Jews and Arabs by forming the whole of Palestine as a state based on the "absolute political equality of two culturally autonomous peoples."

General Zionism Liberal Zionist world movement, established in 1931. While group A supported Weizmann, group B advocated a firm policy vis-à-vis Britain and a struggle for the Jewish State as laid down in the Biltmore program. After the outbreak of World War II General Zionists B drew their strength mainly from the ZOA, and from Palestine, especially after the ZOA's leadership passed to Abba Hillel Silver.

Haganah (Defense) A Zionist clandestine defense organization, set up in 1920, from which the Israel Defense Force was founded in May 1948.

HeHalutz (The Pioneer) A nonpartisan Zionist association of pioneers preparing for *aliyah*, affiliated to the Palestinian labor movement via the Histadrut.

Histadrut (General Federation of Jewish Labor in Palestine) Founded in December 1920, it encompassed almost all Jewish workers in Palestine and a large cooperative sector. (Changed in 1965 to General Federation of Labor in Israel.)

Ihud (Unity) Founded in 1942 by Judah L. Magnes and other Jewish intellectuals, mostly of Central European origin. Intended to win support from Arabs and Jews, it favored binationalism. With the outbreak of the Arab-Israeli War and the death of Magnes in 1948, its activities declined drastically.

260

Irgun Zvai Leumi (IZL) The Revisionists' national military organization, formed in 1931.

Jewish Agency Recognized under the British Mandate as representative of Jewish and Zionist interests in Palestine. Expanded in 1929 to include non-Zionists interested in the development of the Yishuv.

Jewish Agency Executive On the expansion of the Jewish Agency (JA) in 1929 it was intended that half of the members of the JA Executive should be members of the Zionist Executive and the other half non-Zionists. In actuality, the Executive soon became based on the coalition of the principal Zionist parties. When the last non-Zionist member of the JA Executive resigned in 1947, the executives of the JA and the WZO became in fact identical.

Jewish National Fund Established by the World Zionist Organization in 1901 as a financial institution for the purchase of land for Jewish settlement in Palestine.

HaKibbutz haMeuḥad (United Kibbutz Movement) A Kibbutz movement. Founded in 1927, it soon encompassed more settlements and people than any other in Palestine. It was headed by Yitzḥak Tabenkin.

League for Jewish-Arab Understanding A society of leading politicians, mainly of the Left Poalei Zion and HaShomer haTza'ir, founded on the eve of World War II. The League disintegrated when, in 1945, a militant struggle against the Mandatory government began.

Mapai (An acronym, in Hebrew, for Palestine Workers' Party) Founded in 1930. It was the dominant party in the Yishuv and, from 1933, in the World Zionist Organization; and it was the pivotal party in Israel until 1977.

Mizrachi Religious Zionist world movement founded in 1902. Mizrachi of America was founded in 1911.

New Zionist Organization (NZO) A body led by the Revisionists that seceded from the World Zionist Organization. It was formally established in 1935. In 1946 the NZO decided to rejoin the WZO.

Poalei Zion (Workers of Zion) A world union of Marxist-Zionist parties, originally established in Russia in 1906. Its branches in Palestine and the United States rapidly amended the Marxist element in their ideology.

Revisionist party Founded in 1925 by Ze'ev (Vladimir) Jabotinsky. Of right-wing tendencies, the party demanded a nationalistic revision of Zionist policy. Its aim was the establishment of a Jewish state "on both sides of the Jordan."

HaShomer haTza'ir (The Young Watchman) Zionist youth movement established in

Central and Eastern Europe toward the end of World War I. Its members immigrated to Palestine from 1919 on and set up a kibbutz movement left of Mapai.

HaTenu'ah leAḥdut haAvodah (the Movement for Labor Unity) Originated in the opposition Faction B formed within Mapai in the late 1930s and early 1940s. It was composed of the majority of HaKibbutz haMeuḥad and a minority of militant trade unions in the cities. In May 1944 the faction established the new party, which existed from 1946 (under a somewhat different name) to 1948 and later from 1954 to 1968.

World Zionist Organization (WZO) World wide organization of Zionists, founded on the initiative of Theodor Herzl in 1897. Originally called the Zionist Organization, it came to be known as the WZO, a name it officially adopted in 1960.

Yishuv (settled community) The Jewish community in Palestine, primarily Zionist, before the establishment of the State of Israel in 1948.

Zionist Congress Parliament of the Zionist movement (WZO). Originally it met every year, then every second year; following World War II it met at irregular intervals

Zionist Executive (also known as the Zionist Inner Actions Committee) The executive organ of the World Zionist Organization, charged with implementing resolutions of the Congress and of the General Council. It transacts the current business of the WZO.

Zionist General Council (also known as the Zionist Greater Actions Committee) The supreme organ of the World Zionist Organization in the intervals between sessions of the Congress, it has legislative functions, decides general policy, and controls the Zionist Executive. It represents local Zionist organizations and parties.

BIBLIOGRAPHY

PRIMARY SOURCES

Archives

American Jewish Committee Archives (AJCA), New York, N.Y., USA.
American Jewish Historical Society Archives (AJHSA), Waltham, Mass., USA.
Ben-Gurion Institute Archives (BGIA), Sede Boqer Campus, Israel. Minutes of the meetings are located in the archives by divisions according to organizations (Jewish Agency, Mapai, etc.)
Central Zionist Archives (CZA), Jerusalem, Israel.
Hadassah Archives (HA), New York, N.Y., USA.
Haganah History Archives (HHA), Tel Aviv, Israel.
Histadrut Executive Committee Archives (HECA), Tel Aviv, Israel.
Israel Goldstein Archives, now part of CZA (IGA), Jerusalem, Israel.
Israel Labor Party Archives (ILPA), Beit Berl, Kfar Sabba, Israel.
Labor Archives, including the U.S. Poalei Zion Archives (LA), Tel Aviv, Israel.
National Archives of the United States (NAUS), Washington, D.C., USA.
Public Records Office (PRO), London, England.
The Temple Archive (TA), Cleveland, Ohio, USA.
United Kibbutz Movement Archives (UKMA), Tabenkin Institute, Ramat Efa'al, Israel.
Weizmann Archives (WA), Rehovot, Israel.
Yad Izhak Ben-Zvi Archives (YIBZA), Jerusalem, Israel.
Zionist Archives and Library, Archives now part of CZA (ZAL), New York, N.Y., USA.

Newspapers and Periodicals

Canadian Zionist, Montreal, Canada
Congress Bulletin, New York, N.Y.
Davar, Tel Aviv (Hebrew)
Hadassah Newsletter, New York, N.Y.
HaPoel haTza'ir, Tel Aviv (Hebrew)
Jewish Frontier, New York, N.Y.
New Palestine, Washington, D.C.
New York Times, New York, N.Y.
Opinion: A Journal of Life and Letters, New York, N.Y.

Palestine and the Middle East, Tel Aviv
Yidisher Kemfer, New York, N.Y. (Yiddish)

Books, Organization Documents, and Pamphlets*

Altman, Sima et al., eds. *Pioneers from America: 75 years of Hehalutz, 1905–1980*. Tel Aviv: 1981.

Ben-Gurion, David. *The Letters of David Ben-Gurion* [Igrot David Ben-Gurion], 3 vols. Edited by Yehuda Erez. Vols. 2, 3. Tel Aviv: 1972, 1974.

Begin, Menahem. *The Revolt: Memoirs of the Commander of the Irgun Zvai Leumi in Palestine* [Hamered: Zikhronotav shel Mefaked ha'Irgun haTzevai haLeumi be'Eretz Yisrael]. Tel Aviv: 1974.

Berlin, Isaiah. *Zionist Politics in Wartime Washington: A Fragment of Personal Reminiscence* — The Yaacov Herzog Memorial Lecture, delivered at the Hebrew University, Jerusalem, October 2, 1972.

Brandeis, Louis D. *Letters of Louis D. Brandeis*. 5 vols. Edited by Melvin I. Urofsky and David W. Levy. Vols. 4, 5. Albany, N.Y.: 1975, 1978.

Breslau, David, ed. *Arise and Build: The Story of American Habonim*. New York: 1961.

Dugdale, Blanche. *Baffy: The Diaries of Blanche Dugdale, 1936–1947*. Edited by N. A. Rose. London: 1973.

Elath, Eliahu. *The Struggle for Statehood* [HaMa'avak al haMedinah]. 3 vols. Tel Aviv: 1979–1982.

Feuer, Leon I. *Why a Jewish State*. New York: 1942.

Goldmann, Nahum. *The Autobiography of Nahum Goldmann: Sixty Years of Jewish Life*. New York: 1969.

Grossman, Vladimir, ed. *Canadian Jewish Year Book*. Montreal: 1940–1941.

Haber, Julius. *The Odyssey of an American Zionist: Fifty Years of Zionist History*. New York: 1956.

Jabotinsky, Vladimir (Ze'ev). *The Jewish War Front*. London: 1940.

————. *Letters* [Mikhtavim]. Tel Aviv: [1958].

Katz, Shmuel. *Days of Fire*. [Yom haEsh]. Tel Aviv: 1966.

Kenen, I[saiah] L. *Israel's Defense Line: Her Friends and Foes in Washington*. Buffalo, N.Y.: 1981.

Lipsky, Louis. *Memoirs in Profile*. Philadelphia: 1975.

Neumann, Emanuel. *In the Arena: An Autobiographical Memoir*. New York: 1976.

Sharett, Moshe. *Political Diary* [Yoman Medini]. 5 vols. Vols. 3, 4, 5. Tel Aviv: 1979.

Tabenkin, Yitzḥak. *Collected Speeches* [Devarim]. 7 vols. Vols. 2, 3. Tel Aviv: 1972.

U. S. Department of State. *Foreign Relations of the United States: Diplomatic Papers, 1939*. Vol. 4. Washington, D.C.: 1955.

Weisgal, Meyer W. *...So Far: An Autobiography*. New York: 1971.

Weizmann, Chaim. *The Letters and Papers of Chaim Weizmann*, 23 vols. Vol. 18, edited by

---

* Many articles by Ben-Gurion and others appear with full details in the Notes but are not included in the Bibliography.

Aaron Klieman; vol. 19, edited by Norman A. Rose; vol. 20, edited by Michael J. Cohen: vol. 21, edited by Michael J. Cohen. Jerusalem: 1979.

———. *Trial and Error: The Autobiography of Chaim Weizmann.* New York: 1966.

Wise, Stephen. *Challenging Years.* New York: 1949.

World Zionist Organization. *The Twenty-First Zionist Congress* [HaKongres haTzioni haEsrim veAḥad], Geneva, August 16–25, 1939. Stenographic report. Jerusalem.

Yizre'eli, Yosef. *On a Security Mission* [BiShliḥut Bit'ḥonit]. Tel Aviv: 1972.

Zuckerman, Baruch. *Memoirs* [Zikhroynes]. 2 vols. Vol. 2. New York: 1963.

Persons Interviewed

Akzin, Benjamin, with the New Zionist Organization until 1940; head of the Legal Department of the Library of Congress, Washington, D.C., 1941–1944.

Berlin, Isaiah, with the British Ministry of Information, New York, 1941–1942, and the British Embassy, Washington, D.C., 1942–1946.

Boukstein, Maurice (Moshe), member of ZOA Administrative Committee, 1940–1945.

Cohen, Armand, Conservative rabbi, Park Synagogue, Cleveland, Ohio, since 1935.

Cohen-Taub, Miriam, David Ben-Gurion's secretary on his visits to the United States.

Cruso, Phillip (Pinḥas), veteran of Poalei Zion–Zeirei Zion of America.

Elath, Eliahu, head of the Near East section of the Political Department of the Jewish Agency Executive, 1934–1945; director of the Political Department of the Jewish Agency Executive in Washington, D.C., 1945–1948.

Epstein, Judith, Hadassah president, 1937–1939; member of the Zionist General Council, WZO, 1940–1968.

Feuer, Leon I., rabbi, Cleveland, Ohio; close associate of Abba Hillel Silver.

Goldstein, Israel, president of the Jewish National Fund of America, 1933–1943; vice president of the ZOA, 1934–1943, president of the ZOA, 1943–1945.

Halprin, Rose, Hadassah president, 1932–1934. 1947–1952; member of Zionist General Council, WZO, 1939–1946.

Hexter, Maurice B., non-Zionist member of the executive of the Jewish Agency for Palestine, 1929–1938; with the Federation of Jewish Philanthropies of New York since 1938.

Justman, Yehoshua, associated with Palcor, 1934–1939.

Kenen, Isaiah L., editorial writer, *Cleveland News*, 1926–1943; chairman, Public Relations Committee, Cleveland Jewish Welfare Federation, 1933–1943; president, Cleveland Zionist District, 1940–1943.

Kook, Hillel (Peter Bergson), Irgun Zvai Leumi emissary in the United States, June 1940–May 1948.

Livneh (Livenstein), Eliezer, a founder of the Haganah's Internal Political Information Department and editor of its publication, *Eshnav*.

Merom (Mereminski), May, wife of Israel Merom, Histadrut representative in the United States, 1939–1945.

Miller, Irving, member of the National Executive Committee of ZOA since 1936.

Montor, Henry, with United Palestine Appeal since 1930, and its executive vice president, 1939–1950.

Pool, Tamar de Sola, Hadassah president, 1939–1943.

Silver, Daniel Jeremy, son of Abba Hillel Silver, rabbi, Temple of Cleveland since 1956.

Szold, Robert, helped found the Emergency Committee for Zionist Affairs, serving on its presidium from 1940 on; close associate of Louis D. Brandeis.

SECONDARY SOURCES

Adler, Selig. *The Isolationist Impulse: Its Twentieth-Century Reaction.* New York: 1957.

Akzin, Benjamin. "Jabotinsky's Foreign Policy" [Mediniut haḤutz shel Jabotinsky]. In idem, ed., *Questions in Law and Statesmanship* [Sugiot beMishpat uviMedina'ut], pp. 83–105. Jerusalem: 1966.

Avineri, Shlomo. *The Making of Modern Zionism: Intellectual Origins of the Jewish State.* New York: 1981.

Baram, Phillip J. *The Department of State in the Middle East, 1919–1945.* Philadelphia: 1978.

Barness, Joseph. *Willkie: The Events He Was Part of, the Ideas He Fought For.* New York: 1952.

Bauer, Yehuda. *From Diplomacy to Resistance: A History of Jewish Palestine, 1939–1945.* Philadelphia: 1970.

Bauer, Yehudah; Moshe Davis and Israel Kolatt, (eds.) *Studies in the History of Zionism* [Pirkei Meḥkar beToldot haTziyonut]. Jerusalem: 1976.

Bellush, Bernard. *He Walked Alone: A Biography of John Gilbert Winant.* The Hague and Paris: 1968.

Bemis, Samuel F. *A Diplomatic History of the United States.* New York: 1965.

Berlin, Isaiah, *Chaim Weizmann.* New York: 1974.

Chandler, Lester V. *America's Greatest Depression, 1929–1941.* New York: 1970.

Cohen, Gavriel. *The British Cabinet and the Question of Palestine, April–July 1943* [HaKabinet haBriti uShe'elat Eretz Yisrael, April–Yuli 1943]. Tel Aviv: 1976.

———. *Churchill and Palestine, 1939–1942* [Churchill uShe'elat Eretz Yisrael biTeḥilat Milḥemet haOlam haShniyah, 1939–1942]. Jerusalem: 1976.

Cohen, Michael J. *Palestine: Retreat from the Mandate — The Making of British Policy, 1936–1945.* London: 1978.

Cohen, Naomi W. *Not Free to Desist: The American Jewish Committee 1906–1966.* Philadelphia: 1972.

Dallek, Robert. *Franklin D. Roosevelt and American Foreign Policy, 1932–1945.* New York: 1979.

Dothan, Shmuel. *The Partition of Eretz Yisrael in the Mandatory Period: The Jewish Controversy* [Pulmus haḤalukah biTekufat haMandat]. Jerusalem: 1979.

Feingold, Henry L. *The Politics of Rescue: The Roosevelt Administration and the Holocaust, 1938–1945.* New Brunswick, N.J.: 1970.

Fuchs, Lawrence H. *The Political Behavior of American Jews.* Glencoe, Ill.: 1956.

Gal, Allon. *Brandeis of Boston.* Cambridge, Mass.: 1980.

———. "Brandeis' Social-Zionism," *Studies in Zionism:* 8 (Autumn 1987): 191–209.

Ganin, Zvi. *Truman, American Jewry, and Israel, 1945–1948.* New York: 1979.

Gelber, Yoav. *Jewish Palestinian Volunteering in the British Army during the Second World*

War: Volunteering and Its Role in Zionist Policy [Toldot haHitnadvut: HaHitnadvut uMekomah baMediniyut haTziyonit vehaYishuvit, 1939–1942]. 4 vols. Vol. 1. Jerusalem: 1979.

Gorni, Yosef. *Partnership and Conflict: Chaim Weizmann and the Jewish Labor Movement in Palestine* [Shutafut uMa'avak: Chaim Weizmann uTenu'at haPoalim be'Eretz Yisrael]. Tel Aviv: 1976.

Halperin, Samuel. *The Political World of American Zionism.* Detroit: 1961.

Halpern, Ben. *The Idea of the Jewish State.* Cambridge, Mass.: 1969.

Hattis, Susan L. *The Bi-National Idea in Palestine during Mandatory Times.* Tel Aviv: 1970.

Heckelman, A. Joseph. *American Volunteers and Israel's War of Independence.* New York: 1974.

Herberg, Will. "The Jewish Labor Movement in the United States." In *American Jewish Yearbook*, vol. 53. Philadelphia: 1952, pp. 3–74.

Hertzberg, Arthur. "Introduction." In idem *The Zionist Idea: A Historical Analysis and Reader.* New York: 1986, pp. 15–100.

Hilberg, Raul. *The Destruction of the European Jews.* New York: 1973.

Horowitz, Dan, and Moshe Lissak, *The Origins of Israel Polity: Palestine under the Mandate.* Chicago: 1978.

Ilan, Amitzur. *America, Britain and Palestine: The Origin and Development of America's Intervention in Britain's Palestine Policy, 1938–1947* [Amerikah, Britaniah veEretz Yisrael: Reshitah veHitpat'hutah shel Me'oravut Artzot haBrit baMediniyut haBritit beEretz Yisrael, 1938–1947]. Jerusalem: 1979.

———. "The Political and National Struggle over Palestine, 1917–1947" [HaMa'avak haMedini vehaLeumi al Eretz Yisrael, 1917–1947]. In Yehoshua Porath and Yaakov Shavit, eds., *The History of Eretz Israel* [haHistoria shel Eretz Yisrael], 10 vols. Vol. 9, pp. 20–85. Jerusalem: 1982.

Ishai, Yael. *Factionalism in the Labor Movement: Faction B in Mapai* [Si'atiut biTenu'at haAvodah: Si'ah Bet beMapai]. Tel Aviv: 1978.

Jonas, Manfred. *Isolationism in America, 1935–1941.* Ithaca, N.Y.: 1961.

Katzburg, Nathaniel. *The Palestine Problem in British Policy, 1940–1945* [Mediniyut beMavokh: Mediniyut Britaniah beEretz Yisrael, 1940–1945]. Jerusalem: 1977.

———. *From Partition to the White Paper: British Policy in Palestine, 1936–1940* [MeHalukah laSefer haLavan: Mediniyut Britaniah beEretz Yisrael, 1936–1940]. Jerusalem: 1974.

Kaufman, Menahem. *An Ambiguous Partnership: Zionists and Non-Zionists in America 1939–1948.* Jerusalem: 1991.

Kedem, Menahem. *Chaim Weizmann during World War II: Weizmann and Zionist Policy during the Years 1939–1945* [Chaim Weizmann beMilhemet haOlam haShniyah: Weizmann vehaMediniyut haTzionit baShanim 1939–1945]. Jerusalem: 1983.

Klausner, Yosef, *Menahem Ussishkin: His Life and Life's Work* [Menahem Ussishkin: Toldotav uMifa'al Hayyav]. Jerusalem: 1943.

[Kubowitzki, Leon A.]. *Unity in Dispersion: A History of the World Jewish Congress.* New York: 1948.

Langer, William L., and S. Everett Gleason, *Challenge to Isolation: The World Crisis of 1937–1940 and American Foreign Policy.* New York: 1952.

————. and S. Everett Gleason, *The Undeclared War, 1940–1941*. New York: 1953.

Lash, Joseph P. *Roosevelt and Churchill, 1939–1941: The Partnership that Saved the West*. New York: 1976.

Lerner, Natan. "World Jewish Congress." In *Encyclopedia Judaica*, vol. 16. Jerusalem: 1972, pp. 637–638.

Lubell, Samuel. *The Future of American Politics*. New York: 1965.

Manor, Alexander. *Life and Work of Israel Merom (Mereminski)* [BeMa'agalei haPe'ilut haYotzeret: Darko uFo'alo shel Yisrael Merom (Mereminski)]. Tel Aviv: 1978.

Manuel, Frank E. *The Realities of American-Palestine Relations*. Westport, Conn.: 1949.

Moore, Deborah D. *B'nai B'rith and the Challenge of Ethnic Leadership*. Albany, N.Y.: 1981.

Neustadt-Noy, Isaac. "The Unending Task: Efforts to Unite American Jewry from the American Congress to the American Jewish Conference." Ph.D. diss., Brandeis University, Waltham, Mass.: 1976.

Orren, Elhannan. *Settlement amid Struggles: The Pre-State Strategy of Settlement 1936–1947* [Hityashvut biShnot Ma'avak: Istrategia Yishuvit beTerem Medinah, 1936–1947]. Jerusalem: 1978.

Patterson, James T. *Mr. Republican: A Biography of Robert A. Taft*. Boston: 1972.

Penkower, Monty N. "Ben-Gurion, Silver and the 1941 UPA National Conference for Palestine: A Turning Point in American Zionist History, *American Jewish History*. 69, no. 1 (September 1979): 66–78.

Raphael, Marc L. *Abba Hillel Silver: A Profile in American Judaism*. New York: 1989.

————. *A history of the United Jewish Appeal, 1939–1982*. Missoula, Mont.: 1982.

Safran, Nadav. *Israel: The Embattled Ally*. Cambridge, Mass.: 1981.

Schechtman, Joseph B. *The Vladimir Jabotinsky Story*. 2 vols. New York: 1956–1961.

————. "Zionist Revisionists." In *Encyclopedia Judaica*. Vol. 14. Jerusalem: 1971, pp. 128–132.

————. "The Statesman" [HaMedinai]. *Ha'umah* 18, nos. 3–4 (September 1980): 359–367.

Shapira, Anita. *Berl: The Biography of a Socialist Zionist — Berl Katznelson, 1887–1944*. Cambridge: 1984.

Shapiro, Yonathan. *Leadership of the American Zionist Organization, 1897–1930*. Urbana, Ill.: 1971.

Shavit, Yaakov. "Fire and Water: Ze'ev Jabotinsky and the Revisionist Movement." *Studies in Zionism*: 4 (Autumn 1981): 219–236.

Shpiro, David H. "The Political Reaction of American Zionists to the White Paper during the Years 1938–1939" [HaTeguvah haMedinit shel Tzionei Artzot haBrit al haSefer haLavan baShanim 1938–1939]. In Yehuda Bauer, Moshe Davis, and Israel Kolatt, eds., *Studies in the History of Zionism* [Pirkei Meḥkar beToldot haTzionut], pp. 96–160. Jerusalem: 1976.

————. "The Role of the Emergency Committee for Zionist Affairs as the Political Arm of American Zionism, 1938–1944" [Tahalikhei Binyanah shel Moe'etzet haḤerum haTzionit..., 1938–1944]. Ph.D. diss., Hebrew University, Jerusalem: 1979.

Slutsky, Yehudah. *The Book of Haganah History* [Sefer Toldot haHaganah]. 3 vols. Vols. 2. and 3. Tel Aviv: 1963, 1972.

Stein, Leonard. *Weizmann and England*. London: 1964.

Stember, Charles H., et al. *Jews in the Mind of America*. New York: 1966.

Strong, Donald S. *Organized Anti-Semitism in America: The Rise of Group Prejudice during the Decade 1930–1940*. Washington, D.C.: 1941.

Teveth, Shabtai. *David's Zeal: The Life of David Ben-Gurion* [Kina'at David: Ḥayyei David Ben-Gurion]. 3 vols. Vols. 1, 2. Jerusalem and Tel Aviv: 1976, 1987.

———. *Ben-Gurion: The Burning Ground, 1886–1948*. Boston: 1987.

Urofsky, Melvin I. *American Zionism from Herzl to the Holocaust*. Garden City, N.Y.: 1975.

———. *A Voice That Spoke for Justice: The Life and Times of Stephen S. Wise*. Albany, N.Y.: 1982.

———. *We Are One!: American Jewry and Israel*. Garden City, N.Y.: 1978.

Wecter, Dixon. *The Age of the Great Depression, 1929–1941*. New York: 1948.

Weinstein, Jacob J. *Solomon Goldman: A Rabbi's Rabbi*. New York: 1973.

White, William S. *The Taft Story*. New York: 1954.

Zweig, Ronald W. *Britain and Palestine During the Second World War*. London: 1986.

INDEX

* Refers to footnotes.